Rowan Simons

Bamboo Goalposts

*One Man's Quest to Teach
the People's Republic of China
to Love Football*

PAN BOOKS

First published 2008 by Macmillan

First published in paperback 2009 by Pan Books
an imprint of Pan Macmillan Ltd
Pan Macmillan, 20 New Wharf Road, London N1 9RR
Basingstoke and Oxford
Associated companies throughout the world
www.panmacmillan.com

ISBN 978-0-330-50672-4

Printed and bound in Great Britain by CPI Mackays, Chatham ME5 8TD

Visit www.panmacmillan.com to read more about all our books
and to buy them. You will also find features, author interviews and
news of any author events, and you can sign up for e-newsletters
so that you're always first to hear about our new releases.

To Wendy, Helena and Rafferty

Contents

Acknowledgements

Football is a family, and without mine I would never have been able to go to China in the first place and certainly not to persevere with football after that. When the price of failure is returning to a wonderful home, it is much easier to take risks, and, even at the darkest moments, knowing you are there still sweeps away my doubts. Thanks to my parents, Tom and Wendy, my brother Shaun and his wife, Audra, and Nick, Dudley, Jenny, Joanna, Gina, Vin, Shirley, Sue, Nigel and Angie, Adrian (and family), Harry (and family), Krissie, Gwen, Sally (and family), David, Jan and Mark (and family).

As for friends inside and outside the game, with my memory for names any list runs the risk of offending more people than it acknowledges. Anyhow here goes: Adam, Akane, Alex (both sexes), Alfie, Alice, Ally, Amy, Andy (yes, you), Annie, Astra, Barbara, Barry, Bettina, Beth, Carla, Cat, Catherine, Charlie, Chol, Chris, Daisy, Dalida, Daniel, David, Denise, Diane, Dimitri, Dom, Ed, Emma, Etienne, Finn, Floris, Gabe, Gaby, Gary, Glen, Graeme, Guo, Henry, Hongyu, Ingrid, Islay, James, Jamie, Jan, Jane, Jason, Jean, Ji, Jianhua, Jo, Joanna, John (all sizes and spellings), Josh (at least three of you), Juanita, Judy, Julia, Lee, Leslie, Lorien, Louisa, Louise, Luca, Katherine, Katie, Keith, Ken, Kevin, Kim, Malcolm, Mandi, Marcelo, Marion, Mark, Martin, Matt, Meryl, Michael, Mimi, Napoleon, Neil, Nick, Nicki, Nina, Pablo, Pad, Pat, Paul, Penny, Peter, Philip (and foreign versions of), Rachel, Rafferty, Richard, Rik, Rob, Robin, Rodrik, Ruth, Sally, Sara, Sarah, Sean, Schlong, Simon, Simone, Sophie, Stefan, Steve, Tal, Thelma, Thierry, Tim, Tony, Trev, Tuva, Vicki, Wanda, Xiong, Yasmin, Yennie, Yun.

At the same time, I have been very fortunate to work with many partners, colleagues and clients who would be in the above list if it were not also for your support in helping me make money to spend on football or providing me with the platforms to shout about the game. Thanks first and foremost to my partners, Keith and Dave, at ClubFootball; Anke, Kristian and Tammy at CMM-I; Jeff at Chinalive; Andy at OMI; all my ex-colleagues at Beijing TV; and Anil, Anna, Antje, Arjan, Arnaud, Bangjie, Beisheng, Ben, Bin, Calum, Cedric, Changbo, Changshui, Chaojun, Chi, Chris, Chunli, Chunmei, Debbie, Diyi, Dongzhi, Fei, Florian, George, Gilbert, Guhua, Jonathan, Haihong, Heng, Horst, Hu, Hua, Hui, Ian, Janine, Jian, Jiang, Jiansheng, Jianxiang, Jianying, Jitian, Jochen, John (US and English), Julian, Jun, Kai, Katie, Keith, Leland, Li, Lily, Liang, Ling, Louis, Lu, Marcel, Mark, Mei, Michelle, Ming, Nan, Neil, Nick, Oliver, Paul, Pierre, Rod, Qi, Qiang, Qingquan, Rogan, Rui, Runsheng, Shani, Simon, Shu, Stephen, Sudong, Tao, Tiky, Tina, Tingting, Tyra, Vanessa, Wei, Weidong, Wenbing, Wendi, Wenlan, Xiangdong, Xiaodong, Xiaomeng, Xinmin, Xiongxiong, Xumin, Yang, Yi, Yin, Ying, Yong, Yonggang, Yu, Zhifeng, Zhiping and Zhiyi.

It is customary to thank agents, editors and publishers and in my case for very good reason. I would never have started writing about myself if it was not for Laura at the Susijn Agency, and you are in all the lists above and below. Thanks to my editor, Richard, for giving me the licence to explore life in football through China, still a bizarre concept to many. Macmillan have also shown great faith and I would like to thank Helen in particular for giving this book the best possible chance as the world goes China crazy. Thanks also to Luciana at Record in Brasil: yours is the ultimate market for any football writer.

Finally, thanks to the bone fide stars who first inspired me and who have kept popping up to lend a helping hand, most without knowing it. My two grandfathers, heroes both; Bob Marley, Joe

Strummer and Deng Xiaoping for shining lights; Sir Bobby Charlton and Pelé for saving me in Brasil; Trevor Brooking for inspiring me to study reasonably hard at school; and Ian Rush for being the first star to stand up for little ClubFootball in front of the Chinese nation.

Notes on Chinese

Chinese words   These are written in the *pinyin* system, which magically turns Chinese characters into the Latin alphabet. However, not all *pinyin* letters are pronounced as they are in English or other alphabet-based languages, so I have sometimes included English pronunciation in brackets.

People's names   I have great difficulty remembering names. For Chinese names, I try to link the general sound with characters that I know. The problem is that every sound in Chinese has four tones that totally change the meaning. I am a fairly successful cheat, but things can become muddled. For example, Li (Lee) is a very, very common name, and there are many characters pronounced *Li* in common use, including one that means 'plum'. So in my mind, Mr Li might become Mr Plum or, more affectionately, Big Plum or Little Plum.

Conversations   Since most of my conversations with Chinese people have happened in Chinese, I have recalled conversations as close to how they occurred as possible. While this might not scan as well as a polished version, it much better reflects China people how use China language talk words.

Prologue: Spirit of the Game

Before I started studying Chinese in 1986, I had already discovered South America, and it was in that fanatical continent that
I became truly inspired by the power of football. On leaving
for Brasil on a six-month teen adventure, I was given a piece of
advice that I have followed ever since. Noting recent news about
military juntas, kidnapping and armed robberies, a respected
friend of my father told me, 'It's dangerous out there; you'd better
pack a . . . football.'

He got a nervous laugh from my mother, but he was serious,
and I took him literally. The several footballs I ended up carrying
on that trip helped me turn suspicions into smiles from northern
Brasil to southern Chile. Despite some very occasional encounters,
I had always been an 'enterprising' Sunday league left winger, so
playing football in various places had always generated more
friendships than fights. It only took that trip to South America in
a World Cup year to prove to me beyond all reasonable doubt that
football could save the world.

It started in Rio, where I was told in the most carnival fashion
that Brasil was spelled with an *s*. One day, still recovering from
sunburn, I turned up in my shorts on Copacabana beach with
my football and, on strict advice, nothing else. Within minutes,
I was captain of the 'International Tourists XI' that went on to
beat the 'Beach Pickpockets XI' in a closely fought match on the
sand. Football passion was everywhere. Emboldened, I decided to

set off on my own adventures up the Brasilian coast and promptly lost everything I owned.

On the very first day of my journey, a little way up the coast from Rio in Buzios, I emerged from the coach to find my rucksack, cash and all, had not travelled with me. That same day, I borrowed some money and returned to my family friends in Rio to start the process of cancelling my passport, credit card and all the other things that come with losing your possessions. I thought about forgetting my trip and returning to England. Then, two days later, came an unexpected call. It was the Rio Long Distance Bus Office. They had found a rucksack with a football in it. In the top pocket, alongside some cash and traveller's cheques, the duty officer also found a small address book. He had searched through it until coming to a number he recognized as being in Rio. He called that number and was finally referred by friends to my number.

When I went along to the station, it was all there, my cash and passport included. Intensely proud of their service, the whole office greeted me, and I was so grateful I gave them all the cash and the football. My rich friends in Rio said they had never heard of such a thing as money being returned. It was something of a miracle they said, so I decided to stay.

The very next day I got another life-changing call. It was a family friend called Barrie Gill, one of the pioneers of sports sponsorship and a respected figure in world motorsport. He was coming to Rio for the Brasilian Grand Prix and needed a driver. Unbeknown to me, Birmingham was bidding to host the 1992 Olympics, and had decided to hold a motor race in the city centre as a promotional event. Naturally, Barrie thought it would be a good idea if the local council visited Brasil to learn about hosting a Grand Prix. The VIPs, led by Sir Reginald Eyre MP and Denis Howell MP, needed ferrying around, and I was to drive them.

There can be fewer contrasts in world sport as big as that between a kick around on the beach with people from a *favela*, or shanty town, and F1, the greatest sports circus in the world. Instead of the public beach, I found myself visiting the opulent Sheraton Hotel, which has its own private beach and sits just opposite the mountainside tin homes to which I had been invited after playing football.

For me, the only visual attractions of a Formula 1 jamboree in Brasil were the unfeasible numbers of beautiful young women wearing what I would have to describe as 'T-shorts'. At the 1986 race, several hundred promotion girls were lining the route to the circuit, with giggling groups clustered outside the sugar cane filling stations. They wore Marlboro red and white and really wanted me to try some of their free cigarettes. With exclusive rights inside the circuit, the next groups of lovely young women were clad minimally in JPS black. Their cigarettes were free as well, but they really *really* wanted me to try them and were not shy of stroking various parts of my body to arouse my interest.

But then, as fast as it had come, it was over. I would see Barrie Gill again in China, but the Formula 1 circus disappeared, along with its tons of equipment, to the other side of the world. Which just left me in Brasil with the girls and the football.

As a bonus for not killing the Birmingham delegation, I was presented with a small sugar-fuelled white Fiat rental for another month to explore Brasil. I bought a couple more footballs and set back off up the coast. So confident in the power of my football did I become that, when I stupidly ran my car off the road back in Buzios, I set off happily armed with my football and a pocket phrase book in search of help. After a couple of worryingly thirsty hours, I came across a small shack selling drinks and about thirty Brasilian workers, resting in the shade. I handed the ball to the man who had stood up first and started explaining that my car was broken. *My carrho is qebrada!*

Before long, the leader of the group – he called himself Benevenuto – understood my predicament and called up a truck. The whole gang jumped on board. Sitting in the cockpit with him and the driver, we set off in the direction of my car with all the men singing in the back. A massive cheer went up as we came to the top of a slope and could see my small white box car stranded on the side of the road with two wheels in a big crevice. Everyone disembarked, and I was instructed to sit in the car. Then, surrounding it, the leader shouted for them to lift, and suddenly I was up and moving sideways.

Back on the road, Benevenuto joined me in the car, and we headed back to the shack with even more singing on the truck behind us. Back at the base, I took out the fifty dollars or so I had in cruzeiros and invited everyone to cold drinks and snacks. It was a party. Then Benevenuto asked if he could have a go driving the car. Despite all his hospitality, I was convinced this was the moment when I would lose everything again, this time including a car. Anyway, there was nothing I could do and I was wrong. We set off around town just so he could drive past all his friends' houses in a small Fiat and we finally ended up at his own shack in the countryside. Behind it was a small patch of marijuana, and we shared a relaxed evening until I headed back to my hotel.

Further up the Trans-Amazonian highway, the atmosphere changed, and, when I pulled in at a remote service station one night, a group of what looked like vagabonds with machetes descended on me. Protected by my sheer naivety, I wasn't scared at all and knew exactly what to do. I simply smiled and walked around to the boot. Reaching inside, I pulled out a trusty size 5. Presenting it to the crowd on my left, I shouted, 'Brasil! Pelé!' and to those on the right I shouted, 'Eng-er-land! Bobby

Charlton!' There was silence, but interest as they looked at each other.

Still confident, I threw the ball in the air and, as it came down, I jumped up, closed my eyes as usual and headed it over the heads of the 'Brasil' team, before shouting one of my few Portuguese words – 'Goooooooooooooolllllllll!' – and chasing after it. Within seconds, the machetes were piled to one side, and trucks were carefully moved to provide floodlights so we could have a barefoot replay of that famous game in the car park. Several bottles of *cachaca* later, I was waved off by my new friends minus the football, which seemed like the opposite of a price to pay. Back out on the road, I understood what it felt like to be a Rio taxi driver during Carnival, so I turned up the music and weaved on down the road.

The 'England/Bobby Charlton' routine worked everywhere, except in Argentina. But even there, football was about to help solve the problem in front of my eyes. When I passed through as fast as possible on my way to Chile, the country was still smarting from the Falklands War. If there were any other British tourists, they weren't wearing Union Jack T-shirts. When I applied for a visa in São Paulo, the consulate official seemed strangely unfriendly, but the guard at the border crossing just laughed in my face. 'Welcome to Argentina,' he said, '*loco* – you crazy,' and pointed in the direction of his country. When I emerged from the building, the first thing I saw was a huge sign that read 'Las Malvinas Son Argentinas'.

It seemed best to keep my head down, but the whole continent was more gripped by Mexican World Cup fever than that war, and it was frustrating not to take part in the build-up. As it was, my ChileBus schedule did not allow stops, and it was with considerable relief that I reached the Chilean border in the middle of the Andes.

On my arrival in UK-friendly Chile, I was arrested. OK, that's exaggerating a bit. I was briefly detained for carrying a bag of oranges, in flagrant violation of the law on fruit imports. Apparently, the frigid Andes are nature's barrier to flies and other fruit pests and diseases. Good work. The discovery of a football in my luggage again elicited broad smiles, and the guards were delighted to tell me that England had lost 1-0 to Portugal in their opening game of the World Cup.

While I was in Chile, two things shook me. First, there was a small earthquake. Second, there was a series of anti-Pinochet marches in Santiago, each organized by, and consisting of, different groups from the community. One day, I happened across a march organized by the mothers of disappeared children and I ran with them down the street as police with tear gas and water cannon followed. It was the first time I had witnessed such distressing scenes, and it left me feeling numb.

Too soon, it was time for me to face Argentina again. This time, World Cup fever was pandemic, and there was no choice but to ask how England was doing, to see if Lineker was living up to his potential. But, with English the only language I could use, every time I even mentioned the World Cup, 'You English?' would come back at me in angry and threatening overtones. If truth be told, while praying for an England win, I was simply not prepared to get beaten up or even court controversy because of it, so I went under-cover. Was that wrong? It was anything to avoid death at the hands of blue and white pampas cowboys.

Finally, I settled on Australia. Not only did they speak a simple form of English, they were not in the competition so, if the conversation developed, I could justify at least asking about England, even empathize with the sweet sensation Argentina might feel at seeing them lose in the World Cup. As it was, Maradona's Argentina team was among the favourites, and England seemed lucky to have found their stride. This meant both teams made it through to the quarter-finals, the stage on which Maradona treated the world to the infamous Hand of God and then the best individual goal of all time as he skipped past the entire English nation.

Argentina went on to lift the trophy, but beating England in that way wiped away some of the bitterness left from the Falklands War on the street. Overnight the attitude in the country changed perceptibly. As many Argentinians saw it, in the great game of life, the score was now 1-1. I warmly accepted that result without Mrs Thatcher's permission, and we all moved on with our lives. Back in Brasil, the girls were still lovely, and I nearly decided to stay on the beach for ever.

When I did finally return to the UK in the summer of 1986, I looked like Socrates. I carried my football like a bible, but also a universal translator, a character reference, a community credit coupon, a valued gift and a get out of jail free card all rolled into one. Surely a football is man's best friend.

It was with this naive, but unshakable, faith in the power of the people's game to bring the world's already lovely people together that, after a year of intensive Chinese language study at Leeds University, I passed my compulsory AIDS test and headed off in completely the opposite direction: to spend a full year exploring the totally unknown quantity that was the People's Republic of China.

Part One

1

Learning to Forget the Rules

Even in the 1980s, China was still a largely grey place in which virtually all urban populations were employed in state-owned work units. Under the Communist system, the work unit was responsible for all aspects of life, from food to the blue or green uniform code to the allocation of Flying Pigeon bicycles to marriage and imposition of the single-child law.

The Beijing Foreign Languages Institute, known as Beiwai (bay why), was such a work unit, with its own school, hospital and security force, all happily guided in the right political direction through the Communist cadre system. As its name suggests, the college specialized in foreign languages, and many of its graduates disappeared into the fast-growing Ministry of Foreign Affairs after graduation. I have since met many of them at Chinese embassies around the world. However, as a result of China's opening to the outside world, Beiwai's responsibilities had been extended to include teaching primary-school Chinese to foreign university students.

Although much had been done to improve conditions for the soft foreign guests, when I arrived with the Chinese Studies group from Leeds University in September 1987, our first impression was that we had been sent to prison. We had swapped what now seemed like luxury student bedsits for tiny concrete cells with iron beds, wooden bookshelves and rickety tables and chairs. Even the full-grant socialists were horrified. There was no hot water in the building, and so our personal supplies had to be carried in red flasks that could be filled only from a small boiler room across the yard. The separate shower block was only open a couple of hours a day for group sessions.

Our introduction to the student canteen or *shitang* (sh tang) (widely known among foreign students as the *shit*-ang) revealed that Chinese students didn't have sandwiches, all day fry-ups and cheap curries. Instead, they queued (way too early) for breakfast, lunch and dinner, receiving for their trouble selections of intestine and strangely mixed chunks of gristle, bony fish, rice gruel and pickled vegetables slopped from massive pots by angry small people in white hats. At least the hats were usually whiter than the soggy rice which came with everything and often included nice crunchy bits of pebble from the roads on which it had been dried. In winter, the cabbages suddenly appeared. They were everywhere, including the kitchens, and they did not leave for months.

We didn't know much about China when we arrived, but I did know from students who had already had their exchange year that, under the Communist work unit system, sports grounds were shared communal areas used for all types of physical exercise and for large political gatherings. On inspection, the games that had their own areas in our university were table tennis, volleyball and basketball. Hook up a net and it seemed badminton could be played anywhere there was space. The rows of outdoor table tennis tables were very popular. They were made of concrete and had bricks for nets, so they lasted considerably longer than the balls. Just listening to the sound of thousands of 'clicks' as the balls pinged back and forth, you could understand why the Chinese were the best in the world. It was a sporting import that had become the people's culture.

Since all sports activities were also controlled by the work unit, specialist sports facilities like a grass football pitch or all-weather tennis court could only happen to the detriment of the general population, and that was not allowed, unless one of the leaders fancied a game of tennis. As it turned out, the leaders at our academic institution quite liked tennis and went on to build a new court for themselves, just opposite our dormitory.

My first quick tour of the campus did reveal a single unevenly baked mud area that was disguised as a football pitch by putting goalposts at each end. It looked like what it was, a poorly maintained parade ground. Four young men were playing a kick-around at one end, but on other bits there were people practising sword play, and it was littered with pebbles, rocks and glass.

Back at our prison block, we were introduced to our Chinese roommates. Hand-picked for the strength of their political beliefs and (as far as their handlers knew) accordingly steeled to resist the lure of the western decadence to which they were about to be exposed, China's model students arrived in our little cells with very different stories to tell. My roommate, Mike, came from a province in central China and had won his place in Beijing through national exams that involved millions of students. His family did not have many special connections or much money, so his achievement was a source of immense pride in his community back home.

Over the year, we both learned a lot about our respective countries, mostly stark realizations of how similar we all are as individuals and how different we are as citizens of our various nations. If there was one main personal difference, it was that, while I saw a tertiary education as something of a right, Mike saw it as a huge honour for which he was grateful every single day. On the first day we met, Mike told me that what I viewed as a prison was, for him, a luxury hotel. In the Chinese student dormitories, there were six people sleeping in triple bunks in a room the same size as ours. The foreign students' *shitang* was considered the best in the school.

As I settled in and got to know the rules, all considerably loosened for the foreign students, it became clear that I had not come to a prison or to a university – I had been sent to a Chinese Communist boarding school. The freedom to study and play we had enjoyed in Europe was replaced with set lesson schedules every morning, six times a week, and our freedom to move was restricted by guards at the gates and guardians in the lobbies of each dormitory block. The gates closed earlier than an English pub, and only repeated banging on doors could raise someone to unlock the student buildings at night.

Locking people into the building didn't seem very sensible but, after a while, we discovered so many ways to get in and out after hours that we didn't worry about that too much. As I slowly became used to the conditions and small frustrations, such as having to book phone calls home between three and eight hours before connection, the rooms slowly seemed to become less claustrophobic. Some of my new *tongxue* (tong sway), or classmates, liked eating a lot and quickly introduced me to local restaurants to avoid the *shitang*, including one inside the campus. They offered a much better variety of tasty Chinese dishes, including steamed dumplings, known as *jiaozi* (jow ze) and *baozi* (bao ze), and lots of cheap beer. Silly-priced beer.

Of course, the Leeds students from the UK were not the only bunch of 'foreigners' at the school, and most of our outside knowledge was gleaned from those who had already spent a year or more in Beijing. The real China hands, some of them born in China, were yet to deign us as valid company. At that time, China was the melting pot of the world, and its universities were like a hippy United Nations. With its staunch Communist ideology, China was rebuilding friendships with most of the Soviet bloc, bringing

Russians, Bulgarians, Poles, Yugoslavs, Mongolians and Cubans into town to study under government-sponsored programmes.

But China was also in a period of 'opening up and reform', instituted by paramount leader Deng Xiaoping, and had very quickly become friends with everybody else, including much of Africa and the western 'democracies'. And so it happened that in a small number of brick blocks scattered across western Beijing and other cities, the flowering youth of the Democratic People's Republic of Korea, the Union of Soviet Socialist Republics and the People's Republic of China came face-to-face with the bizarre cultural selection of young Americans, Italians, Germans, Australians, Spanish, French, Japanese, Brasilian and British who had (by and large) chosen their own educational path to China.

The small garden between the foreign student blocks became party central, with power and music supplied out of the rooms of the English and American ringleaders and large quantities of beer handed out by Russians in bottles they opened with their teeth. As the Cold War rushed towards its end outside, it didn't take us long to realize that the Iron Curtain shouldn't have been drawn at all. The fact that we had all chosen Chinese, supposedly the hardest language of them all, as our common tongue rather than English just meant that group debates could be joined by everyone, even the French.

This same tongue-in-cheek multicultural spirit of friendship applied to the football team that naturally forms when enough people who play all live together in one place. In line with the stereotypical Chinese description of westerners as *da bizi* (da bee ze), or big noses, my first season in China was spent playing for Big Nose FC, in a team whose starting line-up presented formidable opposition and included noses of all shapes and sizes.

In goal was Tim, a giant American martial arts student, who

had never played soccer but who could pluck the ball out of the air with a single hand, roll over and launch the ball to the half-way line like a killing spear in a single deadly movement. He had also learned a technique from his Master that he believed enabled him to leap like a salmon and that he adapted for corners.

He was protected by a back four from the western Soviet Union, as wide as they were deep. They formed a brick wall of Communist satellite states trained for total denial of unauthorized entry by enemy personnel. For this back four, pre-match small talk inevitably turned to war, and I learned that, to be a real man, you had to be able to 'assemble, disassemble and reassemble a Kalashnikov rifle'. Their philosophy about the Soviet Union was summed up by their favourite joke, told in the same deadpan way after every game and at every party. 'Rowan,' they would say, 'have you heard about the latest Russian micro-computer? It is the largest of its kind in the world.'

To my right in central midfield was Pavel the Pole, once a contender for the national basketball team and a natural ball player. With the outside positions filled by a hard-running Kiwi and an Englishman, Robert, the whole team was geared to getting the ball to the front two, Ulli, our traditional German centre-forward, and, out wide on the right, a North Korean called Kim. Kim came on a temporary transfer from the North Korean group of students, whose own team I dubbed Hermit FC. Temporary, because the North Koreans were not officially allowed to take part in the foreigners' football activities as we had an imperialist American goalkeeper and occasionally invited Japanese subs.

With the team more practised in playing on a Chinese baked-mud pitch and learning to deal with the deep grit-filled flesh wounds to the hands, elbows and knees that were part of the game, all we needed was suitable opposition. It was during my search for a team to play that I found out that not only were there no amateur football clubs in our area, there were none in the whole city. In fact, various Chinese friends expressed complete bewilderment when I explained and asked if anyone wanted to join one.

Mike was not a sports fan, but he thought it had no chance of success since running anything was not allowed without specific permission from the authorities. He thought they would be as likely to agree to let me to start a football club as establish my own political party. According to the rules, all meetings involving groups of ten or more people had to be submitted for approval so, in theory, even a five-a-side match with a referee was banned from happening spontaneously. A full eleven-a-side game with five on the bench, game officials and possibly a few spectators was out of the question.

In short, the rules dictated that you couldn't play organized games unless you were in a team inside the elite sports system or part of a work unit team. What the hell was going on? In direct opposition to FIFA regulations regarding government interference in sport (more on that later), the Chinese government had effectively managed to include the most basic unit of football – the game of – in its technical ban on social group meetings. It was outrageous – a situation not common in Britain since the Middle Ages. As I would come to learn fast, absolutely everything comes from the top down in China, and that usually spells death for any movement that attempts to build from the grassroots up, just ask the *falungong*, which started out as a registered sports organization.

On Mike's advice, I went to the Foreign Students Office, or the *waiban* (why ban), universally feared as the international Gestapo arm of the foreign student command and control apparatus. As I entered the office, the man said no officially without looking up and then enquired privately what it was that I wanted. 'We want kick football,' I said.

'How many persons?' he asked suspiciously, but also hinting there might be an outside chance. 'A few foreign friends,' I continued vaguely. 'Exercise body, play-play, kick-kick, organize small competition.' Bad move.

'Organize competition,' he repeated, raising his eyebrows, 'organize what competition?' Obviously, organizing a competition wasn't a good idea, so I tried to back-track. 'Sorry, not have competition, have small play-play, Chinese speak not good.'

He didn't fall for it and, jumping up and pointing his finger as if he had just extracted a confession after days of torture, thundered back, 'Organize competition! Organize competition! Foreign students not allowed organize every activity, first must have *waiban* agree!' Having won his own argument, he settled down at his desk again and lit a cigarette. Mike was right.

'Teacher,' I said, deciding to abandon sophisticated argument and play the foreigner's trump card when faced with petty officialdom, 'if we still want play football, we possibly give our embassy write letter, good (or) not good?' Of course we could write letters to our embassies, and he knew he didn't want to be the reason for causing an international incident. 'Football exercise body,' I continued, giving him a reason to agree, 'help many countries' people each other know.'

Since getting things done in China is often comprised of a wonderful series of mini-barters, people tend to get over the disappointment of losing an argument very quickly (hence the relative absence of road rage amidst today's intolerable traffic conditions), but one always tries to extract some face during the retreat.

'You not allowed organize competition,' he said, 'only play-play. Not allowed with Chinese students play, I tell you, little lad, not with Chinese students play!'

So, by agreeing to play only with other foreigners and never 'organize competition', I gained some sort of unwritten approval for our nefarious activities. I also learned that, in China's bizarre reverse apartheid, the domestic majority had voluntarily decided to give the foreign minority elite status. What a strange but intriguing place.

Living in the multicultural foreign student world of the late 1980s, surrounded by warm and welcoming Beijingers who were always ready with a smile, it was hard for me to imagine that China had only recently emerged from the Cultural Revolution and that society was still rebuilding social bridges burned by relatives and friends who had betrayed each other in a desperate effort to survive. Having always enjoyed a healthy disregard for authority without serious consequence, I found it equally hard to comprehend how anyone could convince me to join in a paranoid frenzy of destruction of all that had value. And yet, that was the experience of the students who had walked my campus a generation earlier.

The Cultural Revolution is not a subject for me, but the absurdity of its objectives and the haunting reality of its impact were brought home every day as I watched an intriguing, but nameless, worker who shuffled uncomfortably around our campus. According to Chinese student legend, he had been a scholar at the university back in the 1960s. Indeed, he was regarded as one of the cleverest students in China. A fine artist, calligrapher and even a strong middle-distance runner, he was widely tipped to achieve great things in the career that would be chosen for him at graduation.

When Mao released the forces of the Cultural Revolution, first the dean and the senior faculty were sent to the countryside to be re-educated, and the administration of the university was turned over to people described as 'illiterate peasants'. In order to show their revolutionary zeal and love for Chairman Mao, the new administration decreed that all students must stick a portrait of the Great Helmsman on their desks in the classroom. Like everyone else, our student did not want to draw attention to himself and went along with the order.

However, as the weeks passed, his intellectual anger at the ridiculous policies introduced by the idiot farmers grew, so he started thinking of ways to challenge their assertions, ways to make everybody see the contradictions of Mao's personality cult. One day, so the legend goes, he raised his hand in class and told the peasant teacher that he was grappling with a problem and needed guidance.

'Teacher,' he said, 'because we all love Mao Chairman, we all place his picture on our desks.' Told by his superiors to beware of intellectual trickery, the teacher paused for a moment and then nodded his agreement. 'Because already pass several weeks,' the student continued, 'picture already scratched. Teacher, scratched picture is (or) not is disrespectful to Mao Chairman?'

After thinking for a while, the teacher replied. 'Of course, disrespectful! Definitely must change pictures!'

'Teacher,' he went on, 'if I try try Mao Chairman picture take off, destroy picture. Destroyed picture is (or) not is disrespectful to Mao Chairman?'

Again, the farmer-teacher thought about it. 'Of course, disrespectful! Definitely not allowed destroy pictures!'

'But, teacher, if I place new picture on old picture, (it) covers Mao Chairman's face. Teacher, covering Mao Chairman's face is (or) not is disrespectful to Mao Chairman?'

'Of course, disrespectful! Definitely not cover Mao Chairman's face!'

'Teacher', he then concluded, 'leave not respectful, take off not respectful and put on not respectful. How best respect Mao Chairman, not disrespect him?'

What a hero. To me, it was a piece of brilliant, simple and damning logic and, naturally, the teacher was totally stumped for an answer. Worried that he was going to be in trouble whatever happened, he is said to have run straight to the office of the Party secretary. Explaining the student's questions, he awaited the answer and his instructions.

'Very interesting,' the Party secretary replied. 'You see see, intellectuals able use every method make you confused. Student asks what do? I tell you, we what do! This student today expel (from) school, go countryside, go learn how really respect Mao Chairman!'

According to the stories, the student's flippancy earned him several years in the countryside before he was finally rehabilitated and could return to the school. Broken intellectually and physically by the ordeal, he was given the same low-level jobs that I was now watching him perform each day. Thinking about his quiet rebellion, I realized that he was but one from a generation of ambitious youths who had had their minds and then their lives snatched away. How could people think about organizing a football team when you couldn't even talk to your friends?

The younger generation could not personally remember those times, but the residues of that paranoia still more than lingered, along with deep government suspicion of foreigners and the Chinese who mixed with them. There were restrictions on several aspects of normal life and keeping quiet about forming a football team was just one small example.

With every leap in my understanding of where I was and who I was living with came the realization that I was, first of all, the alien I was labelled. I was living in a world where the local authorities had an incredible ability to turn a blind eye to just about anything, but only as long as it occurred in alien languages or among alien communities. Given that I shared a room with a Chinese student, most of these restrictions seemed ridiculous.

Most bizarre of all was that Chinese and foreigners were not allowed to dance together. This became apparent when, out cycling one evening, our group came past a lively little building with a massive 'WELCOME' sign in English and several young men and women milling around. We deduced that, as the sign was in English, we would be 'welcome', but our entrance was blocked by the uniformed guards on the grounds we were foreigners and this was a Chinese-only establishment. 'Why use English write "welcome"?' I asked.

'Don't know. Go away,' they replied in unison, crossing their arms.

None of the school freedoms afforded to foreigners was extended to Chinese students, and, like the ban on communal dancing, there were still several even more fundamental direct barriers to interaction that didn't make sense. To me, if something didn't make sense at school, it deserved challenging.

Perhaps not surprisingly, when China started its cautious opening up to the West, one of the first things that worried the government was how to deal with foreign money. Not sure how to handle exchanges of the national *renminbi* currency, the leaders decided it might be safer to create a new currency especially for foreigners to use. Known as Foreign Exchange Certificates, or FEC, the notes were printed with English on them in case anyone got confused. FEC was the only type of money that could be legally changed back into hard currencies. It was like having two types of pound: one for locals to use and another one for aliens.

Foreigners, along with unfortunate compatriots from the 'yet to return to the motherland' territories of Hong Kong, Macao and Taiwan, were meant to use FEC for everything. Foreign-invested ventures like the Shangrila Hotel only accepted FEC from people like us, though bizarrely they welcomed normal *renminbi* from local Chinese people. The currency you used was decided by your passport. Since nobody else in the whole of China used FEC, each time I shopped at a local store or ate in a local restaurant, the change I received was inevitably in local *renminbi* and could never be changed back. And so it was that China started building its foreign exchange reserves. In 2006, they reached a trillion US dollars.

FEC represented the only way locals could get their hands on dollars, so a well-organized black market emerged to help foreigners who didn't like getting ripped off and Chinese who wanted hard currency. These 'change-a-money' markets appeared all over China. For each FEC you could get nearly two *renminbi*. Very simply, the process was as follows. Take a US$100 bill and change it in a bank or a hotel into 1,000 FEC. Then, take a short bike ride to the nearest clothes market and swap the FEC with a nice man for RMB 2,000. After a while, most foreign residents bypassed the FEC altogether, changing dollars directly into *renminbi* in the same little stalls.

Having established the FEC, the leadership became aware that there were some problems. Apart from western foreigners with 'loads of money', there were also some Communist foreigners without very much money and lots of foreigners who had been invited to contribute to China's modernization drive that China had to pay. Since Chinese organizations had no FEC and were not allowed dollars, they couldn't pay their new foreign employees. Foreigners were not allowed to use local *renminbi* in foreign-invested enterprises and they didn't know what to do. Indeed, the special 'Friendship Stores', which stocked strange things only foreigners wanted, like milk and cheese, only admitted foreigners, which, in itself, was a contradiction in terms and very unfriendly.

In such a situation, it might have been an idea to consider

scrapping the FEC altogether and letting everybody use the same money, but the Chinese government decided to take another route. It created a special card, the *youdaizheng* (yo die jung), known as the White Card, which allowed selected foreigners to totally ignore the nationality-based FEC regulations and openly spend *renminbi* everywhere they went. Before I had fully understood the implications of all this, each of the students in the Leeds group was given a White Card, which was yellow, with his or her name and photo on it.

While Mrs Thatcher was doing her best, the UK still had a student grant system in 1986 and we were manoeuvred into the category of 'government-sponsored' exchange students along with the Soviets. Since it is more expensive to live in the UK than in China, the student exchange agreements between Leeds and Beiwai included a provision for the Chinese side to pay a monthly *renminbi* stipend to each British student in China.

The yellow-coloured White Card gave each of us the official power to abuse the special foreigners monetary system, and we all made best possible use of that freedom, changing our pounds directly into *renminbi* on the black market and spending it in the expensive 'foreigners' places that normally would only accept the dreaded FEC.

Armed with White Cards, the highlight of the student week was Sunday brunch at the Shangrila Hotel, a massive western buffet that cost 33 FEC (about three quid). With the help of the black market and the White Card, that price dropped to RMB 33 (about one quid fifty). If you didn't eat at all on Saturdays and woke up in time, you could spend from 6 a.m. to after midday in there for that price. When we started inviting lots of other friends to breakfast and whipped out White Cards to pay for everybody, the Shangrila started getting angry about the loss of FEC business. Finally, it instituted a policy of each waiter asking 'One cheque or separate cheques' before the order, a policy that remained well after the abolition of the FEC.

Like the school rules, I approached the FEC and many of China's other strange regulations as challenges and sought to exploit the weaknesses mainly on principle. As it was too expensive for the People's Bank of China to manufacture special FEC coins as well as notes, both currencies shared the same coins. The smallest, one *fen*, is worth about 0.0007 p. That was also sneaky foreign exchange business for China, but it did mean the coins were technically valid for use in the Shangrila even without a White Card. So, at the end of the year, all the students collected up their entire collections of *fen*, and a representative team went for a last buffet. When it was time to pay, a massive bag of *fen* was lifted onto the counter while further slices of cake were consumed.

Our White Cards had a limit of just RMB 2,700, exactly equal to the ten months of monthly stipends we received from the university, but the last and possibly juiciest fault of the White Card was that it was printed on very poor-quality paper. Since the whole idea of two currencies and monopoly foreign money was a joke, I felt little guilt in 'redefining' my credit limit from time to time.

Despite the many advantages of this system, like all other foreigners who fought daily in small ways to end these silly barriers, I was among those celebrating when the FEC was finally abolished . . . in 1995. My only regret is that there was no time to launch the anti-FEC T-shirt campaign I always dreamed of. It simply said in massive black letters, 'FEC OFF'.

2

'The Ball Is Round,
the Pitch Is Rectangular'

Given the effective ban on groups of ten people or more and the suspicion about any type of spontaneous group activity, it was also much clearer why there was an unnatural absence of local opposition for our new football team. But, I still had a lot of questions. To start with, and possibly most important of all, the Big Nose XI needed to test its strength against another team or it would have no meaning at all, the name 'football team' reduced to a cheap and ironic joke from the girls' end of the corridor.

Not allowed to play football with the Chinese student body, my only option was to badger the small group of Chinese lads who also played on the college pitch once in a while. They were the off-spring of families who lived on campus but were not enrolled at the university. The first and only match I could get together was against their rag-bag group which I often joined for a kick-around in the evenings, and I affectionately dubbed them Idle Sons FC for the occasion.

Not surprisingly, since most of us foreigners came from countries where we had played organized football since an early age, we were the only 'team' that turned up, and there was not much of a game. In fact, the highlight was Idle Sons' captain, Little Flat, who howled in protest at the rugged performance of our Soviet back four in open play; they took no prisoners even at 7-0.

Little Flat himself was a good player and he sportingly promised a rematch once he could get a better team together. At least Big Nose FC had played a game. We were a team of strength, skill and speed, deadly on the counter-attack and impossible to beat from dead-ball situations in all recorded competitions.

We then found out that the North Korean Hermit FC, having refused to play us, had agreed to have a game with Idle Sons. I sneaked along to take a look, and it was more or less the same as our game; Kim Il Sung's men were superior technically and physically. In terms of self-reliance, there was no contest between them. In fact, Idle Sons collapsed into a bickering mess early in the second half, and the match was abandoned as poor Little Flat lost control of his less-talented teammates and they launched into each other.

We always used to bump into the North Korean players around the campus and finally, after very diplomatic negotiations over cheap *erguotou* (er guo toe), the local firewater, German Ulli issued a formal challenge to the coach of Hermit FC, who was also their political cadre. As the only other undefeated team in the school, we appealed to their sense of honour and they rose to the challenge despite the political implications.

They knew they would only get into trouble if they lost, so they trained like soldiers to make sure that didn't happen. Turned out in crisp white uniforms, they thrashed us 3-0. It was a farce that included me missing an easy header that I can still see today with my eyes closed. Our back four might have been solid, but half of them couldn't move. The other problem was that our kung fu goalie Tim had never played competitive football before. It was OK if you smacked it from range, but if you dummied it or got a flick, he went flying the wrong way because he was concentrating on the striker's solar plexus, just as his Master had taught him.

All three Hermit goals were conjured by a single North Korean wizard called Kim, and we knew we had been loaned the wrong one. As I walked off the pitch, Little Flat cheekily appeared from nowhere to offer his condolences. At dinner in the *shitang* later, the coach of Hermit FC led his team in forming a group smile. It was the smile reserved for superior political systems. Once that was done, then they smiled again as individuals and invited us for drinks. North Korean after-match drinks involved them knocking back unfeasible quantities of the purest spirit available and then strumming with awkward guitars and singing loud revolutionary songs. When they were too drunk to walk properly, they showed off their *taikwando* skills. Having identified various objects higher than their heads, each of them jumped, span round and fell over flat on his arse, missing the objects and eliciting laughter from everyone else.

A couple of weeks later, Little Flat wandered over to our campus to say that he was now ready for another go, and we started preparing for action again. I didn't know it then, but he wasn't any more confident of beating us for size, speed or skill, so he had devised a fail-safe back-up plan.

I knew it wouldn't be a normal match when the smiling groundsman arrived carrying a watering can full of white paint that was spilling over the edges. With the can in one hand, he set off running at middle-distance pace across the centre of the pitch, pouring as he went. About two-thirds of the way across, he stopped to get his bearings, creating a large pool of paint. Swinging the can to his other hand, he was off again, now at sprinting pace.

The final result was inevitable. None of the lines were parallel. One penalty area was a large square and the other a small trapezium. In some places, the line was thick and smudged, while in others, it hardly existed or was splattered in small blobs with occasional splashes. As he finished the final stretch at walking pace, he gave a cheerful wave and emptied the rest of the can where he stood. For the first time in my life, I realized that painting touchlines was not necessarily a scientific pursuit. It could also be art. After all, rules were abstract to start with and if the teams changed ends at half-time it would still be fair.

He approached his job with such wild abandon that I came to admire him more and more each time I saw him perform. Instead of repeating the same old, same old, he created different spaces for you each time you played. He couldn't remember foreigners' names, so he brilliantly dubbed me Xihongshi (see hong sh), which means 'Tomato'.

Rather like a traditional Chinese landscape artist, his mission was to hint at the truth, but never to define it. Not surprisingly, his favourite job was marking out the tennis court, where all line calls are potential matters of life and death. Thanks to my understanding of his special sense of space, I had an unfair advantage when the 1987 Beijing Universities and Colleges Tennis Championships was later played at our campus. To his great pleasure, Tomato took the title.

As a proper international football match had never been seen before, quite a crowd had assembled before we finally got underway. The wiggly touchlines succeeding in blurring the definition of 'in' and 'out' and, as nobody had kit either (the big noses played in skins) there was no clear way to know who was playing and who was watching.

Confident, we started the game with a series of passing moves that showed our superiority, quickly making a number of openings that Ulli, the striker, missed, much as expected, since Idle Sons had demanded his glasses be removed. Although our passing was good, the chances started drying up as the Chinese team buckled down to chasing and started getting to loose balls first.

As they upped the pressure further, I looked round to check

Kim's position and saw that he was closely marked by two players. Ulli was also marked by two and there were two spare men at the back as well. Counting the remaining players, I realized there were thirteen of them on the pitch. I stopped the game, and it took some time before Little Flat could find two players who would agree to go off. Back to even teams, we started again. About five minutes later, I did a quick number count and now there were fifteen. Again they were removed. As the game continued, I realized what they were doing. As we all followed the ball, behind our backs they were simply rolling on players from the crowd. Perhaps we should have let the extra players stay: perhaps they needed this kind of dispensation or they would just give up. But if we did change the rules, wouldn't it defeat the whole purpose of the game?

As I contemplated another hollow victory later, it struck me that on the football pitch there should be no place for face. Little Flat knew how to kick a football, but he didn't understand how to play the game. He had placed too great an importance on 'face'. While winning it he would have considered worthy of gleeful celebration, losing it was an entirely different matter that he believed must be avoided at all costs.

Whereas Big Nose FC reacted to our embarrassing defeat to Hermit FC by challenging them again (and losing again), Idle Sons FC only knew how to give up. Given the circumstances, I could not blame him. I should have supported him as he tried to encourage his friends to get into the game, but I was young and saw only that he had tried to cheat to save face. And yet, this was not always so.

The idea that the spirit of fair play and impartial refereeing in football provides good training in terms of promoting social harmony and justice was actually well understood in ancient China. As the Confucian scholar Liu Xin (ca. 50 BC to AD 23) noted (among his seven teachings), 'football (strengthens) the fighting power of soldiers'. It wasn't much different from the rest of the world, where countless generations of youth have been dispatched full of that essential ingredient for successful warring – team spirit.

There were a lot of wars in ancient China, and passion for football was well documented. According to one such story, during the Warring States, a man from the state of Qi called Xiangchu was mad about playing the game. When he fell terribly ill, the famous doctor Canggong diagnosed a period of complete rest, instructing him to avoid all strenuous activity. But Xiangchu loved football so much that he couldn't stop playing and dropped stone dead after a game.

One of the great joys of living in China is being surrounded by a culture spanning five millennia, and hidden within this incredible legacy are several ancient football paintings and documents that still survive today. They reveal fascinating details about how football was used to overcome the human urge to cheat, even emerging as a popular sport in civil society. Amazingly for any era in history, it was a game played by both men and women of all ages. One story tells of a young girl who single-handedly defeated a team of soldiers, while prized pottery often featured images of children playing with their footballs.

One particular form of football became popular during the Han Dynasty (206 BC to AD 220). While Jesus was struggling to find a twelfth man he could trust, the Han Emperors loved nothing more than to visit the local stadium to watch a game of *cuju*, or 'kick ball', complete with teams, rules and competitions. The Han didn't mess around with bundles of old cloth, but created exquisite silk brocade spheres, the value of which is still recognized in the modern character for ball, *qiu* (chew) which includes the character for 'king'.

One of the earliest images of a football player is found on a monument at the bottom of the holy Song Shan (Song Mountain) in Henan province. The bottom of Song Shan is better known as the site of Shaolin Temple, one of the centres of Chinese martial arts. Inscribed nearly 2,000 years ago, it shows two spectators. They are watching an unnamed player in a long silk gown complete a move described by FIFA's historian as 'firing a rasping left-footed shot on the turn'. One-nil.

In 2004, FIFA went further, allowing China to secure its historic claim over football with Sepp Blatter's acknowledgement that China is the birthplace of the game and that *cuju* is the true origin of the sport. To be more specific, the Linzi district in the city of Zibo in Shandong province has been confirmed by football authorities as the place it all got started.

The ancient Chinese mostly played six-a-side, which may well be the best format for the country to adopt if they ever decide to bring back the game. The number of players, and the requirement for fair play, was laid out by the Han writer Li You (ca. 55–135 AD), and in terms we can all understand. Next time you take part in a six-a-side competition, insist on playing according to the Rules of Li. They state (in the official FIFA translation):

> The ball is round, the pitch is rectangular,
> A symbolic image of (the universal elemental forces) yin and yang.
> Using the (twelve) moons (months) as a guide (for the number
>   of players), they lay siege to one another.
> With six (members) each, (the teams) are balanced.
> A head (referee) is named and an assistant appointed.
> Their interpretations of the rules must be constant.
> Unprejudiced (they must be towards team members) near or far.
> There shall be no currying favour or high-handedness.
> With an honest heart and balanced thoughts,
> No one can find fault with wrong decisions.
> (If) football is regulated correctly like this,
> How much this must mean for daily life.

An incredible seven centuries later, Chinese football was still going strong, but then branched off into two different directions. The first form continued the game's traditions as a competitive team sport with defined rules, special arenas, standard goals, corner flags, bamboo goalposts and various other markings. Towards the end of the Tang Dynasty (618–906), this competitive form of the game got a huge boost in attendance when an enterprising man filled his silk ball with an inflated bladder. The extra bounce offered by his new balls required players to develop new techniques and tactics that the spectators loved even more. Unlike in the UK, when some members of football's congregation left because they couldn't keep their hands off the ball, in China, the second form of the game was created by splittists more interested in playing 'keepy uppy' with the silk embroidered size 2s. It was altogether much easier in their long robes and, of course, easier to sneak in a quick game when the Emperor wasn't looking.

Cuju was also popular during the Song Dynasty. In the famous story *The Water Margin*, the Emperor was won over by the *cuju* skills of a treacherous court official called Gao Qiu. The story tells that he was so good that he could make the ball stick to his body, which is still something that the best players can do. Two kinds of professional *cuju* troupes emerged to meet demand for what was a well-established brand of entertainment during the Song period. One type of footballer was attached to the royal court, while the other was a journeyman freelancer.

Large cities even set up a *cuju* organization known as the Qi Yun She, or Yuan She. This is widely considered the earliest professional *cuju* club, and its participants included amateur lovers of the game and ex-pros. To guarantee and protect the profession, amateur players were required to formally acknowledge one of the professionals as their teacher and had to pay for the privilege of becoming a member.

Some time after that, the practice of football as a sport through which one could test one's sense of honour and discipline disappeared in China and was replaced by Genghis Khan's version of the Olympics, and it has never been seen since.

3

To Get Rich Is a Glorious Goal

With an entire city of wide and carless streets to explore by Flying Pigeon bicycle and regular small games of football with the rest of my leagueless team, student life in the late 1980s in Beijing was full of learning experiences and a great laugh, especially as my level of spoken Chinese improved. It took me one year of quite intensive study in the UK and four or five months in China before I felt I had reached the top of the first big language mountain and could see the hills far away. If you study in China from the start, most people could probably get there in a year. It's a great view – in both directions.

As with many foreign students with a decent range of memorized characters locked away (we had drilled over 1,000 during the first year), my Chinese lessons spontaneously started taking place outside the classroom in completely unstructured and natural ways. For a start, most Chinese teachers liked to make sure the whole class proceeded at the speed of the slowest student.

We spent what seemed like many weeks repeating the character *ren*, which means 'person', until every student could say it properly. Outside, my spoken Chinese improved immeasurably, as did my understanding about how people actually use their language to communicate in real situations. However, it is true there was a downside to self-prescribed lesson plans – I had already failed to achieve the year's minimum 80 per cent attendance rate less than half-way through. This ruled me out of contention for 'model student' status. After that, there just seemed no point.

Along with other academic miscreants approached by worried teachers who had never come across the concept of truancy (at least for non-political reasons), and certainly not as a rational educational choice, I was questioned compassionately about my abysmal record. Were there medical reasons, they wondered? It was while facing Teacher Jin's simple question: 'You why not attend class?', that I first found myself adopting Middle Kingdom logic in a negotiation. It was an intellectual, linguistic and cultural breakthrough and for me unlocked one of the secrets to succeeding in China. The ability to *jiang daoli* (jeeang dao lee) or 'speak (with) reason'.

'Classroom out,' I told her, 'have ten hundred million Chinese-language teachers, but only have one student, he is me. Classroom in,' I continued, 'have one Chinese teacher, but have exceed twenty students. Have some students, how to say, study very slow. Impact my progress.'

I finished with one of the small rhyming slogans that had also started popping into my head at about that time and I raised my fist to illustrate the point.

Jiaoshi Wai, Xue de Kuai
Jiaoshi Nei, Xue de Lei

In English, it would be something like, 'Outside the class, study is fast; inside the class, study's a farce.'

As long as I did my homework, there wasn't much pressure in the end. Just as at school in England, my teachers realized I was politically a lost cause and re-education through hard labour was no longer an option for petty offences, especially for the rest of the world's errors.

Indeed, the lack of seriousness with which China approached foreigners' study and many foreigners approached Chinese study

methods was later confirmed when we peeked at our own graduation certificates as they were carried along the corridor before we
took the final exams. Of course, there were honest and conscientious students with genuine academic ambition among our group
who struggled on in classes with diminishing numbers of students
around them. Ironically, by the end they were nearly getting the
one-to-one tuition needed. To avoid embarrassment, both shall
remain nameless here.

Because having fun was included in the list of things Chinese
students were not allowed to do, our entrepreneurial minds soon
grasped the central tenets of Deng Xiaoping's opening and reform
policies. In short, we started trying to make some money doing
things we liked. In this respect, China was a fantastic place to be,
a placed where tried and tested business models were regarded as
radical innovations.

Of course, football clubs are not the only places that active
young people like to spend time. Given that Chinese and foreigners couldn't dance together in regular discos, it was clear lots of
help was needed on that front. So I joined my mate Josh in starting to test the ban on mixed dancing by organizing 'underground'
parties. Educated, like me, at a British public school, he had also
adapted well to the system in China and was a willing collabora-
tor in the 'sixth-form rebellion' at our university.

We started by moving the party beyond the reach of the
Foreign Students Office. It wasn't hard because their legendary
powers of search and detention of non-accredited intruders
ended at the school gates. Like a dog on a firm leash, they could
bark but they couldn't bite us. As our local partners assured us,
'They not care us, we not care them.'

As most Chinese restaurants were closed by 8 p.m., we took
over big dining halls and ran DIY events. They may have looked

like country village discos, but they were revolutionary at the time. The parties were attended mainly by foreign students and long-term inmates of the giant Friendship Hotel, but they also attracted the more rebellious Chinese youth, including China's emerging rockers. They were led by Old Brittle, China's Bob Dylan, John Lennon and Bob Marley all rolled into one.

Old Brittle was a keen footballer and one of the few calm members of the outrageous Rock Stars FC, among the most 'passionate' of the amateur teams that started to emerge in Beijing towards the end of the 1980s. Along with his crowd, there were a lot of then impoverished young artists (now enjoying record prices at art galleries near you) and growing numbers of angry urban punks.

The punks' anger reflected the challenging speed set for the transition from Communist to secular truth. China's rapid opening revealed the world outside, releasing an incredible encyclopedia of combined human knowledge about every subject you can imagine, and hundreds that could not be conceived. Just think about music alone. For young Chinese musicians searching for inspiration to help articulate their conflicted emotions the entire experience of modern popular music was suddenly accessible from foreign student bookshelves. Where would you like to start your education? Elvis perhaps, or shall we go straight to the Sex Pistols?

In this way, China's 'opening' provoked a re-evaluation of everything that young people knew to be true but in no particular order, while 'reform' promised only a tantalizing glimpse of how they could shape their own futures. The revelations came thick and fast and included the realization that they had been tricked in many ways. It was too late for our Chinese roommates, but they too learned that engaging in sexual relations before the marrying age of twenty-two for men and twenty for women was not necessarily hazardous for health, though appropriate care should always be taken. Slowly, the educated young urban generation in the peaceful China of the late 1980s became bitter. Their anger was the natural growing pain that resulted from the radical departure from the path of centrally planned economics that their grandparents had chosen after the end of the terrible Cultural Revolution.

With the deeply personal sentiments of the younger generation bubbling underneath, and ordinary workers voicing concerns about trade union rights, the smallest thing could spark a public outbreak, including the performance of the national football team. One of the earlier incidences of trouble spilling out onto the streets had come when the Chinese national side did the unthinkable in the spring of 1985. After negotiations with Britain over the reclamation of Hong Kong had been completed, it lost, at home in Beijing, to the tiny British colony and crashed out of the World Cup. So humiliated were the fans who rioted after the match that the ugly affair was even given its own status as the 'May 19th Incident'. In fact, when I arrived a couple of years later in the autumn of 1987, Chinese fans told me they had never had much to get enthusiastic about when it came to football. It was, then, with some surprise, that the China Olympic team beat Japan in a pre-qualifier just a few weeks after we landed in Beijing. In fact, it was one of the best days in Chinese football history.

Although I missed the expedition, a few *tongxue* cycled down to Tiananmen Square to get a flavour of China's passion for their national team. When they arrived there was nobody there and it was eerily silent. But, as they circled the square on their bikes, small pockets of people slowly started emerging out of the dark, and suddenly there were large groups happily waving Chinese flags. One of the Leeds students, Napoleon, fell in line with a small group of cheering young fans, and soon one approached to ask if he knew any good football songs they could sing. Since they were singing already, it seemed like a good idea.

Although you might think that Napoleon made him French,

the French do not tend to call their children that name, and he spent much time explaining how he came by this imperial moniker. His mother was Irish and his father English. His maternal grandfather was so upset that his daughter had married a Protestant Englishman that he named his grandson after the man he thought would most annoy the English family. This Irish blood gave Napoleon a streak of wild adventure, and he was always up for meeting new people. He was not a hardcore football fan, preferring dancing to sports, but he came up with 'Oggi, oggi, oggi, oi, oi, oi!', which was an excellent choice, and soon the chant was taken up by the growing crowd of cyclists around him. Before long, another young fan waving a hastily made national flag offered it to him to wave. Once he had the flag in hand, other friendly cyclists gently encouraged him to move up to the front so everyone could hear the chant better. Almost by intuition, those ahead of him started falling in behind. Without really thinking about it, he had changed from being an interested observer into the celebrity foreign ringleader of a mob of amazingly well-organized football fans on push-bikes in the centre of Beijing, shouting strange alien slogans, possibly anti-government rhetoric, although nobody understood what 'oggi' or 'oi' could mean.

Elsewhere, sections of the crowd had crossed the line and started shouting 'Beat Down Japan' ('Down with Japan'), and as his happy group turned the next corner of the square, Napoleon looked ahead and saw a wall of police cars and policemen a few hundred yards ahead. With his smile fast receding, he realized he was riding towards them holding a home-made Chinese flag. He looked round to his fellow riders for support, but they were all gone, vanished into the myriad *hutongs* or small alleyways of Qianmen.

With the instinct to disappear overwhelming, he careered off down a side road and swung left into a small alley. Chucking the bike to one side, he threw away the pole, stuffed the flag up his jumper and hid in a dark corner. As he waited with heart pounding, a Chinese police jeep pulled up nearby and a policeman sauntered up to him, shining a torch. At this point, what should you do? Napoleon did the best thing for a foreigner to do, he pleaded the fifth, or rather he feigned ignorance. Ignorance of the Chinese language, ignorance of the Chinese flag stuffed up his jumper, ignorance of his entire predicament. Emerging from the shadows, he offered a friendly and upbeat 'Hello', and started repeating just two words: 'Tourist, Shangrila'. Other policemen who couldn't speak English soon appeared, and they were followed by inquisitive onlookers drawn to the flashing lights. As Napoleon continued to repeat his tourist mantra, he saw that the group of football fans who had encouraged him to start chanting had now reappeared to watch him being arrested. Thanks a lot.

Finally, the police understood what he was trying to say and proudly told him, 'You live at Fragrant Shape Inside Pull Hotel!' Then, with great courtesy, they drove him back to the Shangrila safe and sound and with his bike sticking out the back. The policemen were never once threatening or angry, but then again he was only guilty of celebrating the victory over Japan.

A little bit earlier, two other classmates who were in the middle of the crowd in the square had been intrigued to hear Chinese fans shouting 'Oggi, oggi, oggi' in the distance. As they too became surrounded by ecstatic fans doubly happy to celebrate with foreigners, they slowly became separated. In an effort to find his friend, Liverpool fan Henry shouted for him by name, and the chant 'Lobby, Lobby' was taken up by the Chinese fans all around. Robert, who was surrounded by his own group of fans not far away, was surprised when his Chinglish name floated across the Square, but he responded in kind, setting off an alternative chant of 'Hen-li, Hen-li'. In the end, their efforts to encourage synchronized chants of 'Add Fuel China' ('Come On China'), rather than 'Down with Japan', excited the crowds around them so much that they too were escorted from the scene by the cheery police, in their cases being politely led into the closed Forbidden City for their own 'safety'.

Surely, I thought, as they told their tales back at the university, if Chinese fans could be so passionate about their national team, they could turn out some decent teams on a Sunday. But it is all too easy to mistake nationalist fervour with sporting passion, and it was the former that lay at the heart of the excitement in the square. As I was starting to find out, few of those celebrating a famous victory over the auld enemy would be aiming to re-create that winning goal themselves the following weekend.

4

Mouthpiece of the Party

At the same time as Chinese football fans were learning how to jump hysterically in the air when they beat Japan and with violence when they lost to Hong Kong, the opening and reform policies instituted by Deng Xiaoping were allowing the TV industry to commercialize, but only within rigid and absolute Party editorial controls. This liberalization delivered the technology and the advertising revenues for China to start acquiring the broadcast rights to international TV content that they had previously genuinely believed to be free. Quite naturally, sport was the most obvious genre to start with. Only indirectly political, TV sports could provide Chinese TV stations with an incredible volume of never-ending original soap drama, complete with stars (who rise to prominence and are killed off regularly), goodies and baddies and a coterie of fringe actors all involved in the quest for the ultimate treasure – Holy Trophies.

In this tele-dramatic way, state TV revealed to China's population the superteams and superstars at the top of the world football pyramid. There was a new and widespread admiration for the great European teams of the decade, such as Juventus, Hamburg, Steaua Bucharest, AC Milan and Liverpool. Liverpool even played in China's favourite colour and had a Welsh dragon playing up front.

This early and exciting introduction firmly established football as a TV entertainment product in China, and the Italian and

English leagues and the FA Cup quickly became part of the sports schedules at China Central TV (CCTV) and the regional stations led by Beijing TV, Shanghai TV and Guangdong TV. In an internal deal between CCTV and the regional broadcasters, over which it enjoys 'big brother' status, Italian and later German football was broadcast extensively on the national network, while English football went to the regional network based in the more affluent provinces and cities. Despite attempts by various English, Italian and German league rights holders to excite competition for their products over the years, this broadcast division remained broadly in place until pay-TV claimed the FA Premier League in time for the 2007–8 season.

Naturally, the emerging Chinese TV stations and print media discussed only the top European clubs. The huge audiences in 1980s China learned nothing about the wide participation and organization at lower levels that preceded it, that made it possible and that still sustains it today. As a result, the introduction of European top-level football on TV had little effect on the millions of young people in China it should have been encouraging to get out and play. Even if they wanted to, they couldn't join a local club because they didn't exist. With junior football efforts focused on packaging elite athletes, and no political scope for the independent community-based initiatives that had sparked the growth of football elsewhere, the introduction of the TV game created only a generation of football couch potatoes. Highly knowledgeable and enthusiastic about football where I come from, they were disappointed and frustrated by their own country's performance and ignorant about football as a community participation sport.

Consequently, football quickly became the favourite ice-breaker when foreigners met Chinese in various social situations – everywhere except the football pitch. Every day it was the same. People often liked to begin conversations with foreign friends by asking where they came from. In China, the answer, 'I am British person,' would elicit the following positive response: 'Aaahh, Hero Kingdom,' the enquirer would say knowingly, thinking about the Opium Wars, Hong Kong and other humiliations inflicted on China. 'Hero Kingdom football very good. Liverpool, very good!' Well, they were very good, although the good times were ending.

European football's popularity as a TV sport fascinated me, and as I had a general interest in the media, it seemed logical to try and get closer to the TV stations in China to find out what was going on there. I didn't have any contacts, but, out of the blue, our group was contacted by the amazing Ms Touch, a producer and compère working at China Central TV, which has more viewers than any other TV station on earth.

Born in India to Chinese parents, Ms Touch had arrived in the UK as a young girl and had grown up in Liverpool before returning to China in the 1970s. She was one of the first 'overseas Chinese' to commit their prodigious energies to helping the PRC media reform and she became an inspiration to millions learning English. Tasked with developing CCTV's fledgling English Service, Ms Touch was looking for students to take part in her CCTV Christmas Gala. The Christian-based consumerfest was a solar calendar event finally gaining official tolerance as the opening policies started to take effect, and we met her need for Christmas crackers perfectly.

The show was to be filmed over two nights at the Sheraton Great Wall Hotel, one of the best hotels in town, so it meant we would get to eat there and become famous on Chinese TV at the same time. To ensure as many people as possible could get the free lunch, a group of us came up with an appalling sketch called 'Don't Follow Me', a parody on the popular English-learning TV series *Follow Me*. Our sketch was based around illustrating a series of proverbs like 'Don't look a gift horse in the mouth' and 'Too many cooks spoil the broth'. Cheap, tacky and crassly amateur, it was all they could afford and all we could offer.

And so, at Christmas 1987, I found myself the willing victim of the 'look at the foreigner' fascination of the Chinese state media. It would be another two months before China got a look at the greatest exponent of them all, Da Shan, a Canadian who became famous in China because he could speak Chinese.

In our Christmas show, I played a dumb waiter, a much-coveted role involving very few lines and special trips deep into the bowels of the hotel to be dressed in a Sheraton waiter's outfit. This meant having the run of the hotel dressed in an employee uniform, a little adventure into the world beyond normal foreigner experience. While we were waiting around, I went down to the bar and took orders from the guests. The guests and the staff enjoyed it much more than the management, and I was quickly escorted back to the ballroom. Back on the set, I realized that, while we were students having a laugh, all the other acts were bona fide Chinese stars, ranging from great singers to China's famous acrobat twins and the great mime artist Wang Deshun, whose funky chicken routine is hilarious and whose performance of life and death is spellbinding.

Once again, I found that being a foreigner in China made you different: not only did many of the social rules not apply, but everybody got celebrity status – no talent required. It has taken western TV many years to catch up with such base and cheap ways of generating prime-time content. The British ambassador turned up for one of the two performances, and when it was finally broadcast, I noticed a cut-away of him laughing during our sketch. As he had not laughed at all during our performance and wasn't even present on the version they actually broadcast, I also woke up to the obvious truth that TV people really do distort reality without even blinking.

•

Our often repeated show brought wide street recognition in the days following the broadcast, and a number of us grabbed Ms Touch's offer of an opportunity to teach English to the presenters at CCTV English Service. Here, through a series of English role-playing games, I discovered that Chinese journalists are quite different from western ones, and that it was nearly impossible for even well-educated young Chinese people to break away from their 'comraderie' backgrounds.

A simple example is the game where the first person says, 'I went to the market and bought an apple,' and the next person adds another fruit or vegetable beginning with B and so on. It's a fairly simple game where I grew up, but it proved impossible to play with a group of young Chinese journalists. As soon as one of the team started to struggle, the others would be so overcome with pity for their comrade's discomfort that one of them would blurt out the answer. When it was explained that anyone shouting the answer out of turn would also be out of the game, they tried whispering. With whispering, notes and hand signals all outlawed, I didn't see any way they could spoil it. But as soon as one of them stumbled on the letter G, they all looked at each other with increasing anxiety. Just as I was going to call that person out, they all shouted 'grapefruit' together. If one was out, they all were.

That do-or-die team spirit is exactly what you need in football, but you can't extend that principle of mutual support to sports clubs without leadership of some kind, and that wasn't being taught. In fact, it was clear that China's new generation of journalists had little idea of the investigative principles behind the profession in nations with even a moderately free press. Having journalistic pretensions myself, I was shocked by this, but understanding the guiding principle that the media is the mouthpiece of the Party would stand me (and them) in good stead in our future work at the heart of China's propaganda machine. At least the

Chinese Communist Party does not try to hide its manipulation of the media, it glorifies it, and so you know exactly where you stand.

In one mock press conference set up by Ms Touch, I played the role of a key but uncooperative company official whose answers were always blunt and offered minimal information. Rather than grilling or even gently probing me, the Chinese journalists simply turned their attention to the 'PR representative', who was primed to talk a lot about what they wanted to hear. Of course, the government has very good reasons for training people who don't even look like journalists to me, and they do an excellent job reporting the government's news.

If you watch Chinese TV or attend Chinese press conferences, you will notice that most reporters are young women and men, recently graduated from government colleges to report for the government press. When the news is always good, they are the perfect mediums to convey Party messages on line and on cue. In China, for the most part, the only combative veteran hacks still working are foreign.

By the late 1980s, China's economic progress was starting to become an international media story, and, inflated with cigarette money, a number of international sports federations and entertainment companies started running global PR stunts and landmark events in Beijing and Shanghai. In that respect, the bizarre Wham! concert that rocked everywhere except the Beijing Workers Gymnasium in 1985 was an excellent example.

As China didn't yet have professional football or basketball leagues, there was room for everybody to have a go, including sports such as snooker, with its very slow-burn impact. In the spring of 1988, Josh and I had helped a young British reporter called Sebastian Scott with a series on Chinese youth culture for

Channel 4, and it was his cameraman who introduced us to the subterranean world of snooker. Booked to follow the foreign players participating in the 1988 Kent Snooker Cup, led by the irrepressible Alex 'Hurricane' Higgins, the cameraman tasked us with helping him look after them, on and off camera. It proved to be an education in the media, in athlete management and in colourful celebrity excess.

The first thing we realized was that Higgins hated the rest of the Framework snooker stable of which he was a member, and they all hated him. Racked along with such stars as Joe Johnston, a friendly young John Parrott and Tony Knowles, Higgins was the first to break from the pack. He took us on a wild journey. Each morning we listened outside his room as he shouted and screamed about being woken up and then started his day by washing his pills down and dancing on his bed to Madonna. I guess that alcohol accounts for at least half the reason foreign football teams lose to Chinese teams in summer tours, and Higgins drank like a football team. During the tournament, his 'orange juice' was frequently replenished with triple vodkas by one of the huge bodyguards travelling with the team. In fact, he was the only star player who looked like losing to a Chinese player in the first round.

In snooker, like football, China was a backwater. But, unlike football, the antics of Higgins and other characters being covered by an increasingly hungry sports media encouraged millions in China to fashion their kung-fu fighting staffs into snooker and pool cues. Twenty years later we are starting to see the results at world level with the emergence of Ding Junhui and others coming behind him.

When Higgins finished the match, he had no stomach for waiting around for his team and wandered up to where I was sitting in the stand. The stadium wasn't full, and we were soon approached by a middle-aged Chinese woman who announced herself as a journalist from the *People's Liberation Army Daily*, an important national newspaper. She asked me if she might have a brief interview with the famous world champion on this, his first visit to China, and I translated the request. Higgins seemed open, and we began with classic Chinese questions such as 'Do you like China?' It started OK, but I could see that he was quickly getting bored. When the journalist asked him, 'You like (or) not like Chinese food?' he pointed at her notepad as if he wanted to check it. She handed it over, and he promptly ripped out the page, stuffed it into his mouth and started chewing it. Stunned, it took her a couple of seconds to comprehend what had happened and then she was on her feet, screaming and shouting blue murder. The whole stadium stopped as I jumped up to try and calm her down, but she continued shouting at the top of her voice, 'This is what kind behaviour? How can like this towards *Liberation Daily* reporter? You are what kind of world champion?'

By now, the entire arena had turned to see what was happening. What they saw was me and the journalist engaged in a heated argument; Higgins had quickly jumped a few rows down and was now sitting quietly, looking at us like the rest of the crowd, shaking his head at the interruption to the snooker. Bastard.

Following his expulsion from the venue, it was Josh's job to make sure Higgins got back to the hotel. As there were no taxis on the street (they were queuing for FEC outside the big hotels), the team bus was the only choice. On the way back, Higgins insisted on stopping to offer lifts to various pedestrians and cyclists. Having collected a selection of grateful commuters, he returned to the hotel and instructed Josh to tell the driver to return to the venue only after delivering his new friends to their homes. The rest of the team was stuck for hours.

Over the course of the week, he carried out a number of little scams, most of which I had to admire for their creativity. One was 'five-pound poker', which involved the code numbers on five-pound notes. Higgins always won because he always read the codes on all five-pound notes that he handled and kept the one with the best numbers. He also regaled us with stories of how he had tricked various people. Always cheeky, but never too serious, when he was finished with his story-telling, he charged our much-appreciated drinks to Tony Knowles' room.

He told us that, although he had a reputation for binge drinking, smoking marijuana and snorting cocaine, he never mixed the three. He was in a drinking phase at that time, but he told us a story from when cannabis was his favourite muscle relaxant. Given his fame and notoriety, he told us, he couldn't go round with fat Jamaican spliffs, so he had cannabis rolled inside his cigarettes and kept them in a normal packet.

Once, he was playing an exhibition match in London that was being refereed by a former top official who was retired, but still invited to participate in non-ranking events. As Higgins was down to play in the second match, he told us he headed down to the pub with the referee and his opponent for a quick pint. When the referee asked for a cigarette, he said nothing, but opened up his special pack and watched as the old ref chuffed away. Back at the venue, in the first frame of the match, both players were involved in an early exchange of safety shots with the pack of reds largely intact. When his opponent made a breakthrough and followed his first red with the pink, the unsteady ref stepped forward. Wiping the pink as he moved to replace it, he let it slip from his hand and crash into the pack below, scattering reds all over the place. Instead of reacting calmly, he tried to stop the balls, grabbing wildly in different directions. After considerable embarrassment and a rerack, Higgins said the referee came across to where he was sitting silently. Whispering out of the side of his mouth, the elderly official said to him, 'That's the first time

I have dropped a ball in thirty years of refereeing. What was in that beer?'

With several shopping trips included during their days off from the tournament, all the snooker players wanted to spend their money on the best that China had to offer, starting with 'er, china'. Higgins, however, had bought a massive silk carpet for 'his blonde' in a televised sequence at the Friendship Store and so faced a real problem getting it back to the UK on the same flight. So, he gathered the TV crew, and we all set off for the Beijing office of British Airways. Without warning, Alex Higgins and film crew burst into the office to discuss the issue of his carpet with the bemused representative. Stunned by the lights and the presence of a well-known sporting figure, the official quickly agreed to arrange for the carpet and Higgins' other purchases to be transported on the same plane home.

To give him some credit, he shared the good news with the rest of the team and instructed everyone to buy, buy, buy. Buy they did, and when the team set off for the airport there was a second bus to take all their new stuff. Or was it just his carpet that was exempt, and the others all got hit with excess baggage claims? That would have been like him too.

One day I was out shopping with Higgins in Qianmen when he suddenly said he had a great idea. He asked me to take him to a Chinese alcohol shop and there he told me to buy two bottles of the cheapest possible liquor, ones with big Chinese characters. Each bottle cost RMB 1 (less than 10p), so I told him it was my gift to him. Then, he asked me to introduce a fine Chinese liquor and bought two bottles with his own money for RMB 400.

When we got back to the hotel, Higgins spotted a man he called the most gullible player in snooker and shouted for him to come across. He told him that I had taken him to a special alcohol shop and helped him buy two bottles of the finest drink in China.

Higgins said that because he liked him so much he was prepared to sell one bottle at the same price he had paid for it. The other player was delighted and immediately asked Higgins how much it had cost him. 'To you,' he said, '400 *renminbi*.' Happy to have a special gift to take back home, the player pulled the money from his wallet and went happily on his way with one of the 1-*renminbi* bottles I had bought. Higgins was giggling like a schoolboy and gave me one of the expensive bottles he was still carrying. He had one bottle of each for himself, and it had cost him nothing. That was Alex Higgins.

But Higgins was not all fun and games, and, while he took us under his wing, we also saw the ugly side. Along with the rest of the players, after the tournament finished we headed off to Juliana's disco at the Lido Hotel, one of the very few proper discos in town, which had ten-pin bowling lanes next door. Higgins was already drunk when we arrived there and became particularly abusive to the cameraman. Using his 'concerns' that Josh and I would not be paid as an excuse, he pulled at his jacket and spat out insults, introducing me to the phrase 'fucking four by two'. He was always angling to be the mouthpiece of the party.

Once he was bored of this, he went into the disco to annoy other people, accompanied, as always, by two of the massive body-guards. Picking on a young blonde woman dancing with her boyfriend, he sidled up and started trying to flirt with her. The American boyfriend was polite at the start, figuring correctly that he had nothing to fear from what he saw as an unknown skinny old midget. But Higgins wanted a reaction and started to become more aggressive, pushing the boyfriend away and acting sugges-tively to the shocked woman. Finally, the American had had enough and stepped in to push him away. Immediately, Higgins lashed back against the bigger man, but it was only a feint, and he quickly darted behind the advancing bodyguards who now blocked the way. Cowering behind them, he revealed the other side of the people's champion, a pathetic, cowardly drunk, so bored that he had to revert to provoking fights in a disco that he knew he wouldn't have to prosecute.

Higgins could be ugly, but he was never boring, like most of the other players. When all the team, except Higgins, visited the Summer Palace and stood to admire the view across the lake, one of the players was unable to use his own 'point and shoot' camera. Another had the arrogance to say he had a better view from his own house and did not even bother to take a picture at all.

Throughout the week, Higgins had been trying to convince me to offer him a cool trilby hat given to me by my friend Big John in Shanghai and to which I had attached a small panda motif. He offered several bribes, but I wasn't interested. As he was packing, he begged me again, claiming he needed suitable headware for the media when he arrived back in London. Pulling out a suit from the wardrobe, he offered a swap. It was, he showed me, a hand-tailored silk number from Louis Copeland and Sons in Dublin, the top tailors in Ireland. Apart from its quality, he told me it included a special inside pocket made for him to hold his beta-blockers and, sure enough, there were four small pills inside it. Reluctantly, since I was considerably taller than him and couldn't possibly wear it, I accepted and returned to the university with this strange trophy. The suit was later worn by my mate Barry when the president of Ireland visited Beijing, so he could say he was wearing a suit from the same tailors.

Throughout my student year in China, apart from taking time off to look after snooker stars and enjoying western and Chinese public holidays, there were any number of spurious religious or national obligations that could be cited as a valid reason to disappear from class to explore the rest of the country. The Queen's birthday in the Netherlands, St George's Day, St Patrick's Day, the Hajj, the opening of parliament, the bullfighting season – it didn't really matter if they were legitimate or not; all of them could work as a reason for leaving the college, which was meant to require special permission. Once again, the freedom enjoyed by foreign students was not shared with our Chinese friends.

Given this special flexibility, I decided it would be a great idea if my parents and my brother came to visit me during the Chinese Spring Festival, the largest annual away day on earth, when hundreds of millions travel back home to share the traditional celebrations with their families.

5

Freedom to Travel

Chinese people are often described by westerners as 'inscrutable', but I quickly discovered that most of this reticence was based on the fear of not being able to communicate. As a Chinese speaker, I found that almost all my encounters with local people were positive affairs, and so my brilliant plan for my first Spring Festival in China involved maximum amounts of travelling on overland and over-water public transport. From Beijing, I would take a winding route down to Hong Kong with flag-wielding Napoleon and then I would take another winding route back up to Beijing with my family.

We started off from Beijing by heading into central China, destination Shaolin Temple. As kids we had learned about Shaolin from the TV series *Kung Fu*: it was the place where heroic Grasshopper, played by actor David Carradine, had honed his amazing fighting skills, and we both wanted to take a look.

To get to there we had to take the train to Zhengzhou, a major rail hub and the capital of Henan province. Once the train set off, we settled into our 'hard-sleeper' carriage with its triple bunk beds and started getting to be known by the incredibly friendly people in the surrounding bunks. Each was armed with a personal jam jar to hold his or her tea and everyone had enough snacks to last a week, which they shared with fellow travellers. It all made for a wonderful atmosphere and, consequently, was quite unlike any train journey I ever took in Britain.

The same could not be said of the toilets, which featured a couple of bricks straddling a hole. On the wall opposite the hole was a piece of Chinese graffiti. As I read it, I became happier and happier. I knew all the characters. Reading it back again, it slowly dawned on me that it was a filthy rhyming poem about sex. I had never seen anything like it in China, so I read it a few more times to make sure. It read, 'Person on (top of) person, meat inside meat, up down slippery movement, happiness without limit.'

After a few hours, news about the two Chinese-speaking foreigners in carriage eight had reached the other end of the train, and we were visited by several delegations, each bringing their own snacks and requests for information about us, our country and, above all, our language. It was like holding an English out-patient clinic and was a great way to meet people and speak Chinese.

Just as we were helping a manager from Wuhan translate his company's name into English, the train suddenly screeched to a halt in the middle of nowhere, and we all looked at each other with a shared sense of passenger shock. Seconds later, the guard came running up the carriage with news that we had decapitated an old peasant woman walking along the track, and the train could not leave until her head was recovered for identification purposes. If the passengers wanted to get away quickly, he said, we had better all move to the windows and help look for it.

Although Shaolin Temple had been around for a while (people were playing football there 2,000 years ago after all), those living in and around it were only just starting to realize its commercial potential as a tourist and training centre. In a dusty square next to the long-distance bus stop, cheaply painted signs declared the buildings in the distance to be the offices of various private martial arts schools. Quickly noting us as travellers and not potential students, we were handed over to the care of roving hotel agents, each with a selection of the 'best' low-cost accommodation available. The choice was very limited, and we ended up in a *zhaodaisuo* (jow die suo), a simple hostel, without any heating and with 'mattresses' made from wooden planks.

The next day, we headed towards the temple and came across the construction site for the Shaolin International Martial Arts School, already mostly finished. The smiling manager took us on a tour and told us it would be used to welcome students from all over the world. The walk to the temple itself and the forest of stupas nearby offered a real chance to contemplate the symbolism of Shaolin, though it would be many years before I understood even a little about the natural laws of the martial arts.

Inside the temple, we happened across a small gathering of people receiving wisdom from an old man with a long white beard. He wasn't blind but, apart from that, he could have been the Master from *Kung Fu*. He was sitting behind a small table with some soft drinks on it. 'He is ninety-seven years (old),' whispered one of his awed disciples.

The Master was taking questions, and when he was asked the secret of his longevity, we craned our ears to hear his response. For a few moments, he just sat there musing and then he leaned forward and poured himself a drink. Raising the glass in his hand, he revealed his secret to long life: 'Coca-Cola,' he said, with a broad grin and then a wry smile at the pair of us.

The feeling of quiet but pervasive energy was even stronger standing at the top of holy Song Mountain and looking across the valley with the temple nestled below. As we picked our way back down from the summit in the evening, small martial artists in blue tracksuits raced each other to the top. It was awesome commitment and discipline in action, and they reminded me of top junior footballers back at home.

After Shaolin, we travelled on to Luoyang to view the famous

Longmen Grottoes, the site of thousands of Buddhist carvings. It is an inspiring sight, serene figures of all sizes quietly staring out beyond you towards the river from their fragile cliffside homes.

If there were 10,000 Buddhas looking at us at Longmen, it seemed as if there were 10 million people staring at us in the nearby town. When Napoleon stopped to have his shoes shined on the street, we quickly became surrounded by inquisitive locals. Within minutes, the crowd had swelled to 200. Just standing there silently, they stared at him having his boots shined. In no way was it threatening, it was more like having joined a novelty show by accident; the whole road drawn like a magnet to the 'experience'.

As Napoleon came towards the end of his shoe-shine, I thought it would be a good idea to try a little experiment. 'If everybody is staring at us,' I said to him in English, 'and we stare at somebody else, will they start staring at him?' It sounded like a good idea and we scanned the crowd for a target. Soon, we both saw the same man. He was standing about five rows in and, apart from his toothy grin, was noticeable for two reasons. First, his hair was white and was sticking up in the air. Second, he had a huge wart on his cheek. No, that would be unfair. Finally, we settled on a nondescript man standing nearby and began staring at him instead, interrupting our gazes only to look at each other to make exaggerated expressions of surprise. Slowly, it started to work. More and more people in the crowd diverted their attention to look where we were looking, before glancing back at us again. It was like Wimbledon with all the eyes. At last, someone in the crowd twigged and started a tentative guffaw. Suddenly, we were all laughing at each other and ourselves. Once the hilarity subsided, I stood forward with my hand outstretched. It was time to call it a day.

'Thank you, thank you,' I said, 'we are Hero Kingdom Public Street Performance Troupe. Please give a little money here, thank-thank!'

Immediately, the crowd started melting away, and soon the street was back to normal. After finally accepting Napoleon's efforts to pay on the third attempt, the cheery shoe-shiner took a theatrical look into my empty hand and waved us off with a hearty laugh. This was the way to approach China and you didn't even need much Chinese. Just smile and make universal jokes, and 'old friends' could be instantly created.

The next section of our journey took us to the mountainous city of Chongqing, where we planned to join a cruise down the famous Three Gorges of the Yangtze River. Confident in our language ability, we decided to avoid the foreigners' tourist boats and join a local vessel that plied the route down to Wuhan. It was a big mistake and an even bigger mistake to go third class.

For two nights and three days I failed to eat, the combination of dog fat and gristle accompanied by lowest-grade rice husks turning my stomach each time I saw Napoleon tucking in. As it was, he was only able to eat it after being forced to drink white spirit by a young entrepreneur. He also tried to force me to drink, but the smell alone was enough to set me retching again, and after that his girlfriend stopped him from pushing me out of pity.

By the time we disembarked, I couldn't care less about the bloody Gorges, and my stomach had shrunk to a fraction of its normal size. Despite the fresh vegetables and fish available in Wuhan, I could only pick at my food, and my happy smiles to those around were weak. When we arrived in Guangzhou to meet up with other students, I was a stick insect. In fact, we stumbled across a lady on the side of the road selling the chance to use her weighing machine and found out I weighed less than one of the girls, which was worrying for both of us.

After just six months in mainland China, Hong Kong came as a huge relief I didn't know I needed. Arriving on the overnight ferry from Guangzhou, we were turned out into the city in the early morning. I headed straight to the nearest McDonald's. Not to eat, but to take a shit. Unfortunately, another recent arrival from China had got there before me. As I waited my turn, there seemed to be a lot of scuffling and bumping around in the cubicle. A few minutes later, the door opened to reveal a Chinese peasant who lowered his head and left at high speed without washing his hands. Behind him, he had left a dirty protest that need not be detailed here. As I fetched the attendant, I realized what had happened. He had never before used a sit-down toilet. Unlike me, he was used only to public toilets designed very sensibly so your buttocks never touch anything. Faced with this strange raised contraption, his quite logical instinct had been to balance on the toilet seat and aim for the water from there. It was obvious he had slipped more than once. Anyway, I couldn't wait for the clean-up, so I girded my loins and headed at top speed to the hotel reserved by my parents.

Mothers always worry about their children, but I was shocked to see mine burst out crying as soon as she saw me. It wasn't so much that she had missed me but more because, like any decent human being, she felt great pity for all those entering the latter stages of what looked very much like a hunger strike. Boosted by a few days of unhealthy western food and tender loving care, it was my turn to play parent as we set off back into mainland China. This time, I was accompanied by three other aliens who might have resembled me, but who couldn't even buy a ticket or order a meal.

The word 'China' evokes many images in the mind of outsiders, but even today very few of them have anything to do with tropical beaches and palm trees. However, China does have a tropical paradise on the island of Hainan; at least it did until, like so many sleepy seaside havens, it was changed for ever by the advent of mass crass tourism. Traditionally seen as a destination only for those banished from Beijing, it is the most southerly island in the

People's Republic except for the Nansha, or Spratley Islands, which are disputed by several countries. By the way, if you ever want to publish a map of China in China, make sure you include the Nansha or you will have to reprint it, as I once found out.

After becoming famous on TV the previous Christmas, some of my fellow stars and I had spent our first New Year's Eve in China on one of the beaches near the southern city of Sanya. Knowing my father's love of the sun, it seemed like the perfect place to start National Lampoons' China family holiday. We flew into the capital, Haikou, and spent a wonderful evening sampling the street markets and restaurants before retiring to our fancy new hotel, which wasn't quite finished.

Rather than take the hotel limo across the island, I thought it would be fun to travel like the locals. It was only a six-hour journey and it would be good for my dad to meet some friendly people. He needed to chill out, and I felt sure the huge Chinese respect for, and warmth towards, the 'family' would work wonders. Tickets in hand, we joined the other lively passengers making what, for most, was a regular journey across the island. Naturally, we were going to be the centre of attention, so I took the liberty of short-cutting a thousand questions by borrowing the bus intercom and introducing my family to the fellow travellers. Everyone was very happy to see them and started offering fruit and other snacks. This response was in stark contrast to what my family was used to in the UK, and, although my dad wasn't very happy squeezed into his seat, even he had to smile at the warmth of the reception from all around.

Half-way into the journey, we were all getting stiff and were pleased when the driver pulled into a clearing at the side of the road. Stretching our legs, we could see a few stalls selling fruit and soft drinks lining the edge of the undergrowth. To the right, several paths converged then disappeared as the ground fell away sharply into a wooded slope. We wandered across to the stalls, and I bought four coconuts, which were chopped open in front of us by a toothy man in a huge grass-weave hat.

'Forget the coconuts,' said my dad, 'where is the loo?'

'Toilet at where?' I repeated his question to the stall holder.

'Have two,' he replied, 'have one there, also have one over there at bottom, but best not want go that one, extreme dirty, have pigs, you not like use!'

As he had only nodded the direction of the first toilet, but pointed the direction of the second, my father was looking across at the slope. I realized in that instant that I had the chance to send him one of two ways in his life. To the foreign traveller-preferred water closet or down the slope to a place described by the locals as unusable and frequented by swine. In the end, he solved my dilemma by complaining loudly that he would never take another bus again and marching off in the direction of the toilet down the slope. I said nothing. Five minutes later, my father returned a changed man. Sheet-white and drawing heavily on a cigarette, he was shaking like he had seen a ghost. Waving away my brother's cheeky offer of a banana, he boarded the bus murmuring something about albino lizards and pigs and never being able to trust his son again.

Luckily, the beach and the restaurants at Sanya were much more to his liking, and we were soon able to relax and enjoy the sun and some great meals organized by David, a local businessman I had met on my last visit. Unfortunately, after just a few days, the sun went in, and my mum quietly suggested we leave before my dad got grumpy again. However, the change in the weather was also affecting the flights, and we could not leave, despite two wasted trips to the airport.

Finally, there was a break in the weather, and we took the chance to give it another go. With no time to organize a van, I commandeered four motorbikes with sidecars and told the drivers to step on it. We flew through the town and into the countryside, waving at the bemused local people watching our bizarre genetic procession – smiling young man, anxious mother, second smiling young man, grumpy father. Unexpectedly, the bikes veered off the road and into a tiny village. With horns blazing, we disturbed the peace and sent chickens scattering in all directions. Then we were into the undergrowth, racing along a sandy path. Suddenly, we broke through the bush and the whole landscape opened up. We were on the runway.

Battling with each other to take the lead, the cheering bike drivers sped across the concrete towards the small building in the far corner. As we crossed the main runway, I looked behind me, half expecting to see our plane landing on us, but the sky was mercifully blue. Pulling up outside the building on the runway side, the officials in the building came out to greet us. Helping us with our luggage, they walked us around the building to the front entrance and then walked us through the building again until we were back where we had started. I love Hainan.

At the end of our flight from Hainan, during which the pilot appeared in the cabin to share a cigarette with my dad, we found ourselves in Nanjing, the ancient capital that spans the Yangtze River. There, my mum became ill and my father quickly concurred with her that we should abandon the damp and dingy Nanjing Hotel for the joint-venture comfort of the Jinling Hotel. Neither my brother nor I complained about that.

To complete our journey, we had to catch a train from Nanjing to Beijing, and I decided that we should go 'soft-sleeper', the priciest option, but one that promised a private cabin with four beds, which would be better for my mother. Unfortunately, however much I tried, I couldn't get four soft-sleeper tickets. In the end, the station official took pity on my story of an ill mother and managed to find three tickets plus one for me in hard-sleeper. That was more than good enough, and we packed up to leave as soon as I returned to the hotel.

In Nanjing at that time, taxi rides were not widely calculated according to the meter, but through post-arrival negotiation. Before leaving the hotel, I had asked the concierge the price of the trip from the hotel to the railway station, so I knew it was RMB 20. When we arrived, the driver wanted 50 FEC, so I started negotiating as per normal practice. With my family standing in the station square surrounded by our luggage watching me, the debate became quite heated in a Chinese barter kind of way. I couldn't see that, to my uncomprehending relations, it looked like I was in a fierce argument that could turn violent at any moment. Indeed, after a very short time, the taxi driver and I were surrounded by a crowd of intrigued onlookers. I knew they were friendly, but my family didn't. I also knew I was right and, when it was my turn to explain to the crowd, I told them the simple truth. Everybody knew it was RMB 20 to the station and charging 50 FEC was cheating me, a government-funded student invited to study in China. Pointing at my family, I told the crowd I was here on holiday with my parents and my little brother, and this cheating was giving the city of Nanjing a very bad name. The crowd turned to look at my family, who returned blank smiles. Thankfully, the introduction of this physical exhibit combined with the actual truth led to the crowd agreeing with me. Resigned to the democratic result, the taxi driver finally accepted his payment in good cheer. When we finally got into the station, my dad asked, 'Why do we have to have an international incident every time we take a fucking taxi?'

'It's barter banter,' I responded happily, 'and you lot are helping me win every time.'

As originally planned, we finally made it to Beijing just before my twenty-first birthday. I am not usually big on my birthday, but along with a few classmates, including my roommate, Mike, my parents invited everyone to the Shangrila Hotel, where we started with a western meal and followed with cocktails in the lobby bar. Next on the agenda was some fun at the hi-tech basement night-club.

Just as the Chinese disco guards had told us months before, all our Chinese friends were blocked at the door, and we were told the only Chinese allowed into foreigners' discos were Chinese with passports. Passports meant they had probably already witnessed western decadence, so there was no point in trying to keep such places secret. What about the waiters, I asked, they haven't got passports. Rather embarrassed, Mike and his comrades went home, and the foreigners went dancing. I know we should have walked out too.

By the time my parents left China, my relationship with my father had changed for ever. For all his grumbles, several years after I first beat him at tennis, he had finally accepted there were situations in which I was the leader and he respected that. We had reached an understanding that never wavered from that point, no matter what I did.

As spring 1988 turned to summer in Beijing (which took about a week), there was a memorable day when lowly Wimbledon, the place I was born, was pitted against the mighty Liverpool in the final of the FA Cup. As the Beijing TV feed went live, it clicked again that my growing interest in working with the Chinese media should be directed towards football – it really was reality drama of the highest level.

Sitting in our student block, huddled around the communal TV set, we were just one of thousands of groups of fans across the country tuning in to what was billed by the TV stations as a spectacular football occasion, the final of the oldest cup competition in the world. When long-ball Wimbledon won the match it was icing on the cake for me, but it seemed strange that the millions discussing the huge upset the following day were only talking about the Hollywood drama of the TV coverage. It was a tournament that China, with no clubs at all, could not fully understand. For Chinese fans, Wimbledon FC was an abstract concept, as it ironically now is for the people of Wimbledon, following its controversial 'franchise' move to Milton Keynes.

As my dreamlike academic year in China came towards its conclusion in the summer, our professor visited to discuss options for the third and fourth year of studies back in Leeds that would lead towards our university degrees. Far from wanting to go back to Yorkshire, Josh and I had already moved on in several ways and we were both looking for ways to stay in Beijing. I loved the work at CCTV and felt that a career working inside the state media in a country where everything was very cheap, there were beautiful women and foreigners were treated like VIPs might not be a bad choice.

At the same time, I had not particularly enjoyed my time in Leeds, and the life of a student was much less appealing now. After a year sharing a room with a conscientious student who was grateful every single day for the educational opportunity he had been given, I started to question the 'poor me' ethic of most students in Britain. My life had already started in China, and I wanted it to continue.

I asked the professor what options for learning about the Chinese TV industry I would have back in Leeds. His response, that there were no professors in that subject, and few if any books on an industry that was commercially less than ten years old, was not encouraging, so I decided to drop out and pursue jobs that would keep me in Beijing. For many people this would be a difficult decision, but I found it easy; being stuck in rainy Leeds learning Tang poetry was much harder to contemplate.

There were some good leads, even the possibility of a permanent foreign expert position at CCTV, and I was confident of getting some work relating to the media or in sports sponsorship with Barrie Gill, who was starting to explore the Far East. From time to time, I would meet with him and attend business meetings relating to the Asian Games that was to be held in Beijing in 1990. This provided a further insight into the sponsorship business as well as revealing the advantages of speaking Chinese. A shrewd operator, Barrie suggested that I attend the meetings as a silent translator, not revealing I could speak Chinese, but keeping tabs on the Chinese side's interpretation.

The first meeting I attended was with a group that wanted to invite Liverpool to play in China the following year. When he asked about the hotel in which the team might stay, Barrie received the response that they would, of course, stay at the Sheraton Great Wall Hotel. It sounded fine in English, except that I had heard the head of the Chinese delegation say to the translator, 'Tell him Great Wall, we can put in Huadu.'

It was little tidbits like this, and my performance at official banquets, where I could engage the leaders directly with Chinese and a cigarette, which encouraged Barrie to see a role for me in the joint-venture his partners were thinking of establishing. But, the project was just starting and no company had yet been formed.

Separately, the cameraman from the Alex Higgins project had been in contact to say that he was representing the BBC in China and wanted Josh and me to work with him as sub-agents selling BBC programmes. I thought it was very strange that the BBC would agree to a couple of students representing its catalogue and I didn't really believe him. So I made direct contact with BBC Enterprises, the commercial arm of the UK's public broadcaster, and asked them if it was true. It wasn't, and, at the BBC's request, I asked the cameraman to send me a letter formally appointing me as his sub-agent for BBC sales in China. When I received exactly such a letter, I sent it to them and they quietly dealt with it.

Now that I had decided to stay in China, I contacted David Risner, the BBC's head of video, and asked if he wanted a market report anyway. As my report showed, VHS players were virtually non-existent, and it was subsequently an entire generation of retail technology ignored in China. Without much trouble, I researched myself out of a job. However, all these work leads were potential ways back to China, and still I felt that my decision to leave university without 'the piece of paper' was the easy one. I loved China and all the people I had met, so why leave for two years? Josh agreed.

Having made our decisions, we enjoyed the rest of the academic year, especially the visits of short-term summer students, including a crazy bunch of Danish girls. Soon after they left, I became involved with a young Chinese woman from a different college. Her name cannot be revealed for my own political protection, but let me just say she was always quite radical.

Following the issuing of our pre-stamped graduation certificates and the subsequent exams, a summer of travel beckoned for the Leeds group. With my girlfriend banned from seeing me and the football team disbanded, my own plans involved organizing backpacker tours to the Great Wall with Josh until my crazy friend Lucy arrived and we travelled across China.

Our tours were a great effort to make some money and have a good time, and so they only lasted until the authorities got wind of our activities. Simply by hiring a tourist bus, we created an informal tour company and we drove it down to the Qiaoyuan Hotel, the first choice for the brave independent backpackers exploring China in increasing numbers. The bus had a loudspeaker, and so we rolled up in front of the hotel with Bob Marley playing and introduced our tour. 'Overnight trips to the Great Wall, air-conditioned bus, beer and music, spend the night. Just thirty *renminbi* and optional buffet breakfast at the Shangrila Hotel on the way back.'

While we may have had a preference for inviting groups of female backpackers, we would always get a good crowd together and usually filled up the bus. We headed for Mutianyu, the better of the two restored sections close to Beijing, and set camp at the last roofed watchtower before the old wall began, a spot where the sunset and sunrise were spectacular. Loaded down with beer and tunes, nobody fell off, and wonderful evenings were spent. For me, one of the highlights was still the buffet breakfast at the Shangrila when I could use my special White Card to pay for everybody's breakfast.

For a while, everything went fine since we arrived after the tourist office closed in the evening and were gone before it opened in the morning. But one night the police found our driver asleep in the car park and were not pleased to hear there was a group of more than ten people who had gone up the wall without permission. Luckily, he didn't tell them we were foreigners and did tell them we would come back at nine in the morning, so we made a clean escape before they returned. Unfortunately, the driver got cold feet, and that was the end of that.

Without the tours to keep me busy, I was delighted when it was finally time for Lucy to arrive and I headed off to the airport to meet her. Although she had grown up to be a successful international model and was now working in Japan, I had known her first as a snotty-nosed little girl who liked rats, but not snails. She was more like a sister to me, and her outgoing personality made her a great travel companion.

Arriving early at the small and old-fashioned Beijing airport,

I had a quick word with the passport official on duty to see if I could go airside to meet my friend as she did not speak Chinese. I was quite surprised when he smiled, 'No problem, you go!' and gestured that I should go straight in and ask again at the immigration desk.

6

Same Father, Different Mother

With further kindly directions from assorted customs and immigration officials, I found myself going deeper and deeper into the arrivals section at Beijing airport, finally ending up at the gate where Lucy's plane from Japan was just about to unload. When she got over her surprise at seeing me there to greet her, we set off together to retrieve her luggage.

Lucy has one of the most beautifully genuine smiles in the world, and, as we walked up to the immigration desk, the same official who had let me in without a passport waved us both out again with a beaming grin. In fact, he was so happy to see Lucy, he didn't even look at her passport, but instead complimented me on her beauty. I would get tired of that.

The trip I had planned would take us along China's coast and, consequently, included cities in which various foreign powers had played shameful historical roles. From Qingdao, the former German port that now runs on beer, to Shanghai, the Paris of the East with the riverside that looks like Liverpool, and on to the former Portuguese enclave of Xiamen. From there, I planned to cut across to Guangzhou, the place foreigners first sold opium on the mainland. We would finish with a trip to the tropical beaches of Hainan, which, to my amazement, was never colonized, before exiting to Hong Kong and Macao, still operated from London and Lisbon respectively.

I had bought tickets for the 00.30 train to Qingdao on 8 August.

This suggested to me that our train would be leaving early in the morning of 8 August. Not in China. As we boarded, it became apparent that our seats were occupied by people with tickets for 7 August, so there was little I could do but ask the guard for clarification. He explained that, since the last trains to leave Beijing each day departed just after midnight, those last few trains were included in the previous day's schedule to avoid confusion. No matter how many times I protested by asking him to confirm that the date and time on my ticket was the same as that on his watch, he could not and would not remove the other passengers from their seats. The train was full, so we sat on the floor for the six-hour journey as the other passengers chuckled quietly and offered Lucy melon seeds. She didn't complain, but it was clear that this type of mistake on my part would not be tolerated again.

It was only on our arrival in Qingdao that we started to encounter problems with the rules in Chinese hotels that forbade men and women who are not married from sharing a room. Although these rules have all but disappeared today, and there is a massive industry built around nocturnal visits to hotel rooms, in 1988 the rules were still enforced with mini-registration desks on each floor. One needed creative explanations just to get somewhere to sleep.

Our light-hearted solution was to shock them into agreeing a twin room. This involved Lucy standing there with a big grin repeating simple Chinese phrases and me explaining quietly that we were *tong fu, yi mu* (same father, different mother). This was a relationship not explicitly covered in the hotel regulations and always seemed to work. The only downside from my point of view was that the revelation was always followed by close inquisition from curious reception staff, who wondered how Lucy could be so beautiful. It was, I told them, a question I deemed extremely rude to both me and my beautiful mother. Once she understood the routine, Lucy found it very amusing too.

Qingdao is the Chinese equivalent of Rio de Janeiro, a major city with beaches, and there the similarities end. In 1988 the sea had only recently been discovered as a destination, so beach fashion was decades behind. As Lucy pointed out, there was only one stripy type of elasticated material used both for the swimming trunks and the uni-fit one-piece women's wear. The overall effect was psychedelic when there were lots of people around.

Unlike most Chinese people, who avoid the sun whenever possible, Lucy was more interested in catching it to keep up her tan and she quickly found a quiet spot to listen to her Walkman while I wandered off to get some food. When I returned twenty minutes later, I couldn't find her. A bit further up the beach there was a large crowd of people gathered together, and I sauntered over, expecting to discover Lucy juggling. At the centre of the crowd she lay in her bikini, still dozing with her sunglasses and Walkman on. The crowd had formed silently around her in a well-organized ring, with those closest squatting, the row behind crouching forward, the row behind that standing and new arrivals craning their necks on tiptoes at the back. As more people arrived, they silently squeezed into one of the rings. Working my way through, I tapped Lucy on the shoulder. She woke up screaming, causing the crowd to scatter immediately.

As well as frightening the Qingdao locals, we also tasted first-hand how Deng Xiaoping's reforms were starting to affect the economy, particularly the restaurant trade. One evening, we went looking for a good seafood restaurant with a terrace overlooking the sea, but there weren't any, a lesson in itself. The Chinese appreciation of the 'outside' used to be very different from mine. For urban sophisticates, it was seen more like a transition, a place to have your picture taken before retiring indoors for a proper meal. In the only state-owned restaurant in the vicinity, we arrived at 7.30 p.m. to be told by rude staff that it was closed and, even if it wasn't, there was only one horrible dish left.

Over the road, private entrepreneurs had established a street market, and here the response could not have been more different. Welcomed with open arms and cold beers by all the restaurateurs, we chose a simple place that delivered the best seafood steaming hot and at bargain prices. As they waved us off, they gave us business cards to give all our friends.

As we continued our journey through Shanghai, these entrepreneurial changes became a little more evident, but it was still a largely grey city with little to recommend it to the traveller, especially the tired old Peace Hotel, with its stories of days long gone. Nevertheless, from Shanghai, we decided to travel back in time by heading for the port city of Xiamen in style: by magnificent, empty, cruise ship.

More accurately, we were persuaded we could travel in the presidential suite at very little extra cost by Lucy's Japanese standards, and so we enjoyed two nights sleeping on huge double beds with silk sheets, dining alone in a huge hall and retiring to our private sitting room at the bow of the boat. After running around the ship, Lucy came back with a group of new Chinese friends, but we found that only we were allowed inside our own apartment. Finally, by arguing that it would be rude not to let my half-sister's poorer relatives share the view, we were allowed to invite the ship's other foreign passengers to join us after dinner.

On arrival in Xiamen, we visited the famous pedestrian island of Gulangyu and met with students from Beijing who had moved to Xiamen University. One of the few seats of higher learning that backs onto its own beach, it is highly recommended.

Despite the wonderful setting, travelling together non-stop was starting to get to both of us. Lucy was increasingly upset that I was not providing running commentaries of all Chinese conversations, and I was tired of always providing them. It finally came to a head with an argument about nothing, and Lucy stormed off on her own. When I finally caught up with her, she was at the rooftop terrace of the Lujiang Hotel. Not only was she more than a little drunk, she was on stage in the karaoke hall. Worst of all, she was singing.

After morning hangovers, Lucy decided that we each deserved punishment for our roles in the argument and proposed the professional model's way of ending the matter. We would go to the huge clothes market in town and buy the ugliest clothes we could find for each other. These we would wear to the Lujiang Hotel that night, where Lucy's new fans would be waiting for a repeat performance of her variety act.

At the market, the stall holders gathered around us as I called them to attention. 'Today, we not want your beautiful clothes. Today, we only buy your most ugly clothes. We want most ugly clothes. My little sister choose men's clothes, I choose women's. Thank you.'

It took some time for the sellers to alter their pitches, but soon we were being led to what they believed to be the least suitable clothes in stock. In the end, I was overwhelmed with what they thought least suitable, simply because almost all of it was. I finally decided to go with a short brown polyester dress with light yellowy-browny flowers. It was disgusting and it made me laugh. Lucy was having just as much fun in another part of the market and picking up some nice items for herself.

That evening, we turned up giggling at the hotel, Lucy squeezed into my scratchy 'shit-coloured dress with bits of sick on it' with me sporting her selection of light-brown flared trousers with ill-fitting blue-yellow checked jacket. Nobody even blinked; we were aliens anyway.

From Xiamen, my plan was to take a bus all the way to Guangzhou and to pick up another boat to Hainan from there. It sounded easy, but before we set off I knew this was going to be another ordeal, and it was lucky Lucy and I had patched up our differences. For a start, instead of following a time schedule, the bus service operated according to an 'only when full' schedule. Although that in itself was not unusual, we had just missed a bus and had to wait some hours before all the seats were finally occupied. The wait gave me plenty of time to ponder on what would happen if the 15.30 from Zurich refused to leave until the bus was full.

As foreigners, we attracted a typically high level of interest from the other passengers, and, since Lucy was always up for a performance, I again avoided endless idle gossip by introducing ourselves. For this reason, the bus was in quite high spirits when we all set off from the bus depot. Less than 200 yards up the road, one of the back wheels fell off. Exiting the bus in a silent single file, we joined the other passengers walking back to the depot to await a solution in the shade. After an hour, it was announced by the fixit men that the bus was ruined. The good news was that, if they could just borrow the remaining tyres, they could equip the reserve bus, and we would be away in a few hours.

Rather faster than that, the exchange was made and we lined up to board again, exchanging pleasantries with the other passengers we had met before. Although nobody else complained, I was horrified to find that the bus was an old rust bucket with hard wood benches. Without any other option, we squeezed into our seats with my knees digging into the row in front whichever way I angled them. This was going to be fun, and Lucy's grimace told me that I was once again heading for the dog house. It was not long before the bus stopped again, but this time it was obvious the engine was playing up. As some of the passengers started rising for the walk back, the driver shouted to sit down as he coerced the spluttering bus back towards the depot with us all on board.

Again we waited, and Lucy gratefully accepted another passenger's kind offer of a Chinese hand fan to keep the humid air moving around her. Finally, somebody rustled up another wooden bus, and we set off again. Five or six hours into the journey, the comfort factor reached zero, and I was the only one moaning more than Lucy. It was pitch black outside when I heard the engine shouting in pain as well; it sounded like it was going to explode. The driver heard it too, but bravely managed to block out the sound for an unfeasible number of miles, until he finally pulled into the Chinese version of a motorway service station, and the passengers spilled out into the humid night.

Apart from two aching foreigners, the passenger list offered a broad section of Chinese overland travellers. Most notable were a businessman in glasses and a Buddhist monk, whose bright orange robes were matched only by his smile and sunny countenance despite the situation in which we found ourselves. With a replacement bus on its way, we waited around until morning, drinking tea and warm fizzy drinks.

As the sun rose, Lucy decided we should explore the surrounding area, and we headed into the nearby village. When the whole bustling market stopped to look at us, it struck me that it was highly unlikely that foreigners had visited before as the village was half a mile off a major trunk road. Telling Lucy to bow and wave, I explained to the crowd that we were from the Hero Kingdom and had travelled many thousands of miles to visit their market to try their famous snacks. We were quickly given the freedom of the town and wandered among the stalls being offered samples of exotic fruits and nuts. As always, the Chinese people proved their amazing ability to provide a warm welcome, multiplied when you can jump over the language gap and tell a good story.

We returned to the service station with fresh goodies to share and found the other passengers waiting it out without complaint in small groups at the restaurant tables. When the driver jumped up and headed out into the yard a couple of hours later, I figured the replacement bus was here. But, as we followed him outside, we saw it wasn't a bus at all, but a pick-up truck.

'Fuck, you said have new bus come!' said the businessman, surely echoing even the monk's sentiments.

'No, I say have people fix bus come,' said the driver.

'Rubbish words,' I interjected angrily. 'I asked you, have not have new bus come, you say new bus come! Cheat people!' Several of the other passengers agreed with me, and further shouting at the driver ensued. Finally, the monk stepped forward to add his insight. For a moment, nobody noticed him, but slowly everyone quieted down to listen.

'New bus not come,' he said, before stepping back again. As we waited for more words, I slowly realized that he was finished. It was a brilliant summing-up of our predicament and exposed the absurdity of the argument about what the driver had originally suggested. New bus not come.

Forced by the monk's words to wait it out until the engine was fixed, we headed back into the restaurant. At our table, the businessman was trying to console himself and cheered himself up by explaining that he felt most sorry for the two foreigners. Surely not, I argued, it was he who was unfortunate since he would not get to his meeting on time, while we were on holiday and pleased to meet them all. No, he insisted, the saddest people were Lucy and I, since we were the only ones who had the opportunity not to be there at all. 'You are foreigners. You choose use public bus, not go air machine. Luck very not good! Doesn't matter, dry (your) glasses!'

Twenty minutes later, the driver poked his sheepish head around the corner and called us together. We prepared for the worst. 'We fix,' he said unconvincingly, 'but fix not finish, bus broken. Not want anxiety, already made phone call, new bus already set out.'

'You already told us have new bus come,' I shouted, 'really have bus come or have other not able fix bus man come? You not want again with me say so many rubbish words!'

The driver realized this was the end game and gave up the truth. Lowering his head and his voice at the same time, he told us the facts, 'Fix bus team six hours, new bus fifteen hours.'

Amazingly, after a bit of grumbling, the other passengers were quite easily resigned to their fate and returned to their seats. He could have said three days for all they cared. The monk gave no hint of his position on the revised timetable, which seemed a bit suspicious to me. For Lucy, again frustrated at the lively exchanges she did not understand, another fifteen hours at the Crossroads Motel did not seem like a good option, and I suggested we could always hitchhike. Unsure of this option, Lucy suddenly brightened up and said, 'Let's ask the monk,' before heading across to the tree under which he sat fingering his beads. 'Teacher,' I said, 'we cannot wait new bus fifteen hours. Want today reach Guangzhou. You have (or) not have good suggestions?'

'Don't go,' he replied, 'stay here with group. Together wait!'

Shit! Now he had spoken, I wished we hadn't asked. If we did try our luck out on the road, it would be without the blessing of Lucy's monk. But the road it had to be, and we gathered up our bags. This created a lot of interest among the other passengers (all of whom agreed with the monk that it was safer to wait), and a large group walked with us as we headed down to the road. Taking up positions from where they could see, but still close enough to run back into the restaurant should we suddenly explode. Only the monk accompanied us to the side of the road to give his blessing. Although he wanted us to stay, as we had decided to go, he said he had no option but to wish us all the best.

Whatever the passing drivers thought of our strange group led by a foreign girl dancing wildly to a small ghetto blaster with her thumb out, we were obviously interesting, and it was not long before a huge old truck pulled over so the driver could see what was going on. Although he wasn't going to Guangzhou, he could get us to Shantou, from where we should be able to catch another bus. That was good enough, and we jumped into the cabin, leaving the waving monk behind at the side of the road.

Several bone-crunching hours later, we arrived in Shantou. As far as I could tell, it was closed, and we were forced to wait in one of China's first attempts at a coffee shop. Without proper coffee beans or machines, it consisted of Nescafé, to which milk powder and three tablespoons of sweetener were automatically added.

After waiting all day in a state of cheap caffeine despair, we finally got tickets for a night bus heading to Guangzhou. Again, it was an old wooden bus used by ordinary Chinese cross-country commuters, and again it did not take long before lack of comfort became pain as everyone squeezed into the narrow seats. When we set off, it was only to immediately pull up around the corner. We were just 50 yards from the bus station. Lucy and I laughed maniacally at each other. This time there was not any mechanical failure, it was worse. When the doors opened, I could see a long line of people. Not much room for them, I thought, as they started getting on. As each passed the driver, they slipped him a crumpled note and they kept coming until all the space that wasn't taken by seats with people in them was full as well. There was also a lot of activity on the roof.

When everyone had settled down, sitting next to me on the floor was a smiling fisherman travelling with his catch of live crabs. The crabs had rearranged themselves in their own hellish cage, and a few had managed to squeeze a single claw out and were grabbing for the only thing in range – my right leg.

In the middle of the night, my sleep-deprivation torture was interrupted when the bus was called to a halt by a large group of police and other officials from some type of inspection department. Everyone was instructed to leave the bus, to lay their bags out on the ground and to take out all of the items inside. Although the orders were not directed at us, I translated for Lucy, and we started unpacking our stuff onto the road.

'Hey, you not need do,' said the closest official, 'foreigners not need do!'

Slightly angry that they thought it impossible for Lucy to be smuggling whatever it was they were looking for, I hung around to watch the procedure. It wasn't polite. Just as we were presumed innocent, the other passengers were all considered guilty. In the face of loud and rough questioning, it took ages for each passenger to explain away each little trinket in their sacks.

When we finally arrived in Guangzhou the next morning, the happy passengers disembarked as they did every day. Finally, there were just two pathetic foreign backpackers lying close to death in one of the middle rows. At the last stop, we transferred to a taxi and made a beeline for the backpackers' hostel on Shamian Island.

Figuring that we had earned a holiday and deserved no more hard travel, I booked tickets on a passenger boat leaving for Hainan Island the next day. Then we slept for twenty-four hours, only leaving enough time for a quick visit to the famous Qingping wild animal market. When we came out, Lucy was a confirmed vegetarian, and I promised to pass on dog and cat meat in the future.

Whereas my last trip to China's holiday island had been with my parents and brother, this time I was accompanied by an international model, and my local friend, David, was mighty impressed when he saw us on the deck as the ship docked.

'Is your girlfriend?' he asked, looking at Lucy with wide eyes.

'Not is my girlfriend,' I replied, 'my younger sister.'

'Same father, different mother,' added Lucy, giving me a hug. As I saw him take in the news and then start to smile, I snapped, 'You not say anything, OK!'

Our days in Hainan were as they should be: lazy sunbathing, interrupted only by clear blue sea swimming and vast quantities of fresh seafood served with an amazing variety of Chinese flavours. The only interruption to the calm days was Lucy, or rather the locals' continued fascination with her in a bikini. On the beach, her presence caused confusion among the local fishermen, who were hauling nets, so I banished her to the balcony of our room. When I returned one afternoon, she was sunbathing topless, essential to avoid a tan line. As I announced my return, I spotted a man leaning out from the balcony above taking a good look at her exposed breasts. He was being held there by his friend, so I don't know how many had already taken a look or what he was charging them.

More and more students in China and backpackers on the Asian trail were hearing about Sanya and choosing it as a break from the rest of China, but it was still a small town, and it took us no time to meet with all the other foreign guests, including a couple of amorous German men who fancied Lucy and made me just a little bit jealous.

We also had my friend David, his car and its driver, which

meant we were not restricted to the beach but could explore along the coast and into the interior of the island with ease. China had finally made it to the Seoul Olympic Games football finals, and David and I joined hundreds around an outside TV set for their opening match against West Germany. China lost 3-0, but I enjoyed the group occasion, even if Lucy chose it as a chance to go off with the Germans.

David was an entrepreneur and quite interested in the English football that he watched on TV. On one of our trips along the coast, he asked me about Britain and how people managed to travel around. I didn't quite understand his question, so asked him to repeat it.

'You London person,' he said. 'If you want go Manchester, who gives you write introduction letter?'

'We not have introduction letter stuff,' I answered, 'if I want go Manchester, I drive car go Manchester!'

Neither David nor the driver seemed satisfied with this response, but they didn't reply. A few minutes later, the driver asked, 'If no introduction letter, Manchester hotel how can give you room? They how can know you are who?'

There it was again, right in the middle of my summer holiday, the reminder that I was an alien. Whereas I had the unfettered freedom to travel across China, buying my tickets at special ticket counters, using local money, my wonderful hosts couldn't even get a hotel room in another city without the right stamp of approval. I mean, how would the hotel know who had given them permission to be there?

I explained patiently that people didn't really belong to work units, so there was no Party head to write the letter and none to approve it. No hotels would ask you for such a letter.

'True freedom,' he said, shaking his head and considering the idea, 'whole country all can go.'

'Not only whole country,' I said, thinking about it, 'except a few countries, whole world all can go, not use introduction letter. One passport OK.'

The whole world was a little too much for him to take in at one time, and, as in any conversation that can change nothing, we contemplated the exchange of this knowledge in silence as the lazy palm trees sped by. In line with our agreement, I recounted our conversation to Lucy, who consoled David by agreeing that it was incredibly unfair.

Too soon, it was time for us to leave the enchanted isle, and we made our way back to Guangzhou and then on to Shenzhen for the crossing into Hong Kong. As we handed over our passports at the border, I remembered that the very first official Lucy had met, the kindly young man who had waved her through the airport in Beijing, had not stamped her passport. This gave the official in Shenzhen a problem. Even with her smile, how could he stamp her out of China if she hadn't been stamped into China?

I didn't know the answer and nor did he. We were stuck at the airport for hours. Finally, they decided to book a call to Beijing to check. Check what, I asked them. You can hardly ask if they had a record of someone they didn't record! They may well have dredged up the passenger lists, but equally they may have given up. Either way, we were finally allowed to leave and, once again, fall into a deep sleep, this time in the Hong Kong hell house known as Chungking Mansions.

My official year in China was over, but it was not nearly enough. I had only just started to feel at home, and the more I discovered, the more I wanted to know. However, having decided months earlier that I would stay in China, by the time I had said goodbye to Lucy and returned to the UK, my classmates were back in Leeds, starting their third year of Chinese study. Mike had returned to the east campus of our university and was now sharing a crowded dormitory for his final year.

While I was still hoping for a job in the media or sports in China, I had managed to find Josh a job moving things into and out of Beijing. On one of his visits to Beijing, Barrie Gill had introduced me to TNT Skypak, which was offering a job starting that autumn. I passed it to Josh, and he had now taken the lifeline and was well set up in Beijing. I wanted to be there too, but my immediate reality was different; I was a university drop-out back living at my parents' house in England.

7

The Biggest Crowd in the World

To get back to China, I wrote to, and met with, as many interesting companies as I could find. After six frustrating months with many rejections, I finally managed to agree a combination package of three different part-time positions that suited me perfectly and I arrived back in Beijing in early 1989.

First, sports sponsorship guru Barrie Gill was now fully engaged in China through a joint-venture with the *Observer* newspaper and a trading house called London Export Company. Their new company, China Sponsorship Limited (CSL), was being set up to market the 1990 Asian Games, the biggest sports event that China had ever attempted to organize. As the part-time Beijing manager, my job was to work closely with the Asian Games Organizing Committee (BAGOC) at their offices behind the Great Hall of the People in Tiananmen Square.

With top priority from the highest levels of the central government, the actual running of the project (like the 2008 Olympic Games) was mainly controlled by the Beijing municipal government. As an official marketing partner, CSL was responsible for selling sponsorships in certain categories, some of which were exclusive and some of which turned out not to be. It is often hard to establish the real people with power in a Chinese organization without inside information, and I knew that the non-Chinese-speaking senior managers who trooped into China to preach their solutions were at a major disadvantage relying on translators. At the same time, the inexperienced Chinese staff sometimes seemed unable to grasp what the foreigners were trying to achieve.

In the same relaxed way I had engaged with everyone I had met as a student, very quickly I was able to establish a good relationship with our non-English-speaking partners. Having broken down many of the social barriers that language is so effective at maintaining, I slowly gained acceptance among the BAGOC team – not the distant leaders, but the deputy directors and managers who actually ran things. As they felt more comfortable with me, the veneer of politeness often presented to foreign guests started to be replaced by direct discussion and, crucially, the rude, but friendly, joking that is reserved for close friends and colleagues.

There were, however, a number of working customs that were strange at the beginning. Among the most amusing was the practice of keeping beds in the office, so one could take a midday nap after lunch. Many were the times I arrived for a 2 p.m. meeting to find Mr Mile and his colleagues snoring in the corners. Pouring myself a cup of tea, I would wait as they roused themselves and put their shirts back on. When important people visited, it was all suits and formal meeting rooms, but at other times, it was great.

When I wasn't working on the Asian Games, I was developing sales leads in my second position as the first China consultant for BBC Enterprises. Following my report on home entertainment, this relationship had developed with the support of Keith Owen, sales director at the BBC's commercial arm. On the understanding that I would be employed by CSL, BBC Enterprises agreed to fund a one-year consultancy project. My brief was to look more deeply into the market and establish forward commercial relations ahead of Charles and Diana's scheduled visit to an expo in late 1989.

This meant setting my own meetings at CCTV and at state-owned audio-visual companies to explore what they might like to buy. As I had already reported to David Risner at BBC Home

Entertainment, nobody in China had VHS recorders, and the lack of a hi-fi market meant cassettes retailed for RMB 6–8 (40–60 p), leaving little room for profit when various costs and commissions were factored in. However, Keith could see the market had to grow and continued to back me as I presented the catalogue in Beijing. It was not too long before the director of the Import/Export Department at the China Record Corporation fell in love with an album by Enya. We started the process of licensing it with an initial run of 20,000 copies. At least it was a start.

Meanwhile, Keith Owen had also introduced me to the UK trade paper *Television Week*, and writing as a freelancer on Chinese media became my third part-time job. After early features on CCTV and an interview with Ms Touch were well received back in London, I sought an introduction to Beijing TV, the local government broadcaster that was fast emerging as commercial competition to the national network in the capital region. I interviewed the president, Mr Dragon, in his office and was impressed by his vision. Indeed, Mr Dragon would later become a very senior official in the Beijing government and then the director of the General Administration of Press and Publications, with responsibility for deciding how much of this or any other book can be published in China. Ever since that first interview, he has kept a watchful eye over me, and it is very unfortunate that he was removed from his post last year.

Apart from Mr Dragon and his international director, Mr Tiger, who both wanted to discuss business as well as do interviews, I still had many social friends back at our university, and a new year of Leeds students was already well installed and busy having their own adventures. On Chinese campuses, however, the disenchantment with the government's policies was making some of the students even more radical.

The Chinese rock scene was much more punk than in the previous year. In particular, Josh was still organizing parties and often invited a band called May Day. Their best-known song was 'My Life Is Rubbish Dump' and was written by their singer, called Drink.

This undercurrent of anger coming from the young generation had exploded a couple of years earlier with student protests, leading to the sacking of Party General Secretary Hu Yaobang, and it spilled soberly out into the streets again with his death and unofficial funeral in Tiananmen Square. Hu had taken a soft line on previous student demonstrations and had lost his position as a result. By chance, Josh and I were in the area at that time and we noticed that a black wall had been erected in the centre of the square. As we walked closer, the wall slowly melted into the edge of a mass of people. They were just silently standing there, looking towards the Monument to the People's Heroes. As we moved through the motionless crowd, Josh's beeper went off, shattering the calm. The crowd looked round at us and we scurried away, heads down.

By the seventieth anniversary of the 4 May student democracy movement, my travel to the Asian Games HQ was being disrupted by growing student-led demonstrations. Our meeting room had windows high up on the wall that looked onto the Avenue of Everlasting Peace, and I was distracted by all the banners as their carriers moved past into the square.

I had only been back in China a few months, but my regular meetings were soon suspended altogether, and I continued to travel to the Asian Games office just a couple of times a week to exchange documents. One day, thousands of soldiers appeared inside the compound on what is now the site of the French Egg, or Opera House. Nobody outside knew they were there. Something was about to explode, and there was no way I was going to get out of the way.

With the student demonstrations freeing me from my work with the government departments, I was able to spend the next weeks travelling between Tiananmen Square, my apartment in the Jimen Hotel and my former university in the west of town. The Jimen was the first peasant cooperative to run a hotel open to foreigners in Beijing and is located in the north of the city, on Xueyuan Lu (College Road). College Road was the main avenue used by most students to get into the centre of town.

Before long, it became impossible to take taxis and much easier to cycle or catch a lift on a truck loaded with students being taken into town for free. All I had to do was stand on the pavement and wave. Within seconds, a truck would stop, and I would be lifted aboard, the international support universally welcomed.

Down at the square, the atmosphere was very similar to that at the Glastonbury Festival. However, unlike Glastonbury, the beaming faces and guitar sing-a-longs at the camping sites were not aided by artificial chemicals, but deep emotions released by the massive public statement of support for an end to corruption, greater freedom of the press and recognition that the student movement was peaceful and patriotic in nature. Nobody who was there could possibly disagree with any of the above, and, on one amazing day, the Chinese state media actually reported the truth. The very next day normal service was resumed.

Although I lost a number of bicycles in the huge mass left at the Xidan (see dan) market so people could walk to the square, I have never seen a more peaceful or positive crowd. Amazingly, given the numbers of people involved, the whole procession into, around and back out of the square was coordinated solely by students holding pieces of string. There were no policemen to be seen and virtually no crime. Even the entrepreneurs who descended on central Beijing with their *sanlunche* (three-wheeled bikes) to sell ice lollies and cold drinks were encouraged by the crowd to keep their prices at the same level. On one day, I saw a seller offering cold drinks at triple the normal price which, from his point of view, was easily justifiable since there were millions of people with no drinks and he had cycled miles to get there. However, a thirsty crowd soon surrounded him and became animated when he kept to his new price.

'Bad egg!' they shouted at him. 'You how can use students make money? We all support students, you cheat students, cheat people. Shame you, shame you!'

The seller gave in to their demands with a smile in the end, but the political stalemate continued for weeks as the government became paralysed, one faction demanding that the open rebellion be ruthlessly put down and the other preaching caution, even recognition of the students' still reasonable demands.

The die was finally cast on 19 May, when one of the student 'leaders', called Wu Er Kai Xi, was given the unprecedented chance to discuss the students' case in a live TV debate with the prime minister, Li Peng. As I watched the incredible exchange, my heart sank as the young student interrupted the Premier and behaved in a childish and disrespectful manner. That was the students' best shot to win over the whole nation and they blew it because they were so young.

The following day, Saturday, 20 May 1989, everything changed. I remember it very clearly because it was the FA Cup final – Liverpool v. Everton. After watching the match to its thrilling Ian Rush inspired 3-2 conclusion in the early hours of the morning, I decided to head out to see what was happening in our own drama in Beijing. Without a bicycle and with no cars on the road, I started walking south. I soon came to a group of people standing at a junction, and there was fevered debate. I wandered over and was told that martial law had been announced and that a curfew was now in place. Everything seemed quiet, and so I carried on walking. As

I went, the scene was the same: at every intersection small groups gathered, whispering conspiratorially. I knew that I had to walk all the way to the square. As I walked down Changan Jie (Avenue of Everlasting Peace), more and more people were coming from their homes onto the pavement, some watching, but others joining the rest of us walking towards the square. An atmosphere of resistance was building.

When I finally arrived at the square, I picked my way through the students to the Monument to the People's Heroes, where they had set up their command. Sections to the north and west had been reserved for foreign journalists throughout the occupation, and my foreign face and the letters 'BBC' on my card were always enough for any student on duty.

The student leaders were carrying smart Hong Kong-bought walkie-talkies, and now that outside interests were supplying them with equipment and money the hardliners in the government finally won their argument, revealing that 'black hands' were manipulating the students. Now it was time to take action.

In a final effort to persuade the students to avoid their fate, Party Secretary Zhao Ziyang had come down to the square himself to tearfully urge them to return to their campuses, but, hearing that martial law had been declared, the students held a meeting and decided to stay. Now they were frantically organizing their defence, and spotters had been dispatched to the suburbs to report signs of army movement. I knew that there were thousands waiting just a few hundred metres away behind a wall.

As I stood in the foreign journalists' section, I saw that American network CBS was preparing for an on-the-spot report from its star presenter. His name was Dan and he was wearing a ridiculous safari suit, so I moved closer to listen in. Starting with the lie that it was nearly dawn in Tiananmen Square, he continued that the army had entered Beijing and that the scared students were expecting them to arrive at the square at any minute. When he was finished, he did it again, but this time continuing with the line that the army had entered Beijing, but was unlikely to try and enter the square that night, leaving the students anxious. Then he did it a third time, this time explaining to American viewers that, although there were rumours of the army being sent into Beijing, none had been seen yet, and everything was calm on the square. The lights snapped off, and he left the scene for the Shangrila Hotel, confident that the story was covered. So that's how it is done.

Soon after he had gone, it all started. A student leader ran across and shouted for two foreign journalists to accompany some trucks that were going to meet the army at several points where they had been spotted rolling towards the city. I was the only one who could understand in Chinese, and my hand shot up without permission. An American print journalist was standing close by, and, when I told him what had been said, we both headed across to where the trucks were being loaded up in the centre of the square. We were hauled on board by the students, and, when the truck was full, they lifted the tailgate. They were open trucks, and those at the edges were sitting on the rim. Revving their engines, the drivers roared off towards the Great Hall of the People.

Cheering crowds of students surrounded us; a road opened up in front of us, and the trucks picked up speed. Suddenly we were off the square and onto the road that surrounds it, where thousands more were cheering, flags and banners swirling around. Abruptly, we turned to go north, and I realized the driver was going far too fast. With no sides to keep us in, the human contents of the truck were catapulted out across the road. As the irresistible force reached me, I too flew out of the truck. But, by pure fortune alone, I was standing away from the side that spilled out first and I landed not on the road, but on the soft and unfortunate people now underneath me. Disoriented, but not hurt in any way, I rose to my feet, with the crowd yelling and flags still spinning all around. I could see other people who had fallen off being helped to their feet and climbing back on the truck. Without thinking, I followed them. As soon as the truck was full again, we started off. I looked back to see some of those who had fallen off were still lying on the ground. The American journalist was still with us. He looked at me and shook his head. He looked shaken.

The driver must have been shaken as well, because he slowed right down so we could make the next turn. Soon we were heading west, and he picked up speed again, catching up with the other trucks ahead. All along the street, the edges of the road were lined by enthusiastic crowds cheering us on to our unknown destination. The excitement was double on the truck, and I was totally caught up in the moment. The students and citizens of Beijing were heading for a peaceful showdown with the People's Liberation Army, and I was on board. Forget the thrill of a football match; this was the biggest crowd in the world.

As we headed west, the people on the streets slowly thinned out, until our progress was marked only by small clusters at the junctions similar to the ones I had seen on my way into town. As we passed, they shouted support and helpfully provided directions. Soon, the other trucks disappeared as they headed for other entries to the city to block the army's progress.

When we plunged into the darkness of Beijing's suburbs, the American journalist decided enough was enough and got off. Finally, we turned south and after a while came to a raised junction over an expressway. Taking the roundabout, we arrived at the top of the slip road for traffic coming from the west. The driver reversed the truck so it was side-on, blocking the road, and turned off the engine. There was silence.

We jumped off the truck, and conversations started up as a few locals emerged from their homes to find out what was going on. A couple of minutes later I saw them. Coming from the west was a line of PLA troop carriers. As the first ones came closer, the distance continued to fill with the headlights of more behind. There was no end that I could see. Finally, the first army truck reached the bottom of the access road we were protecting and started coming up the slope towards us. When it reached us, it stopped. It had to because our truck was in the way. The PLA driver just sat there, not knowing what to do. With the column coming to rest behind him, the people shouted for him to turn off his engine. Some of the people who had come with me on the truck ran round to the back and started shouting to the soldiers inside.

'People Love Liberation Army! Welcome come Beijing!'

I went over to the bridge to look at the army convoy as the troop carriers way back into the distance finally came to a halt, all caused by our truck at the front. It was amazing, and I was transfixed there with people shouting at the soldiers to my left. Behind that first army truck, the second and third now had a few of their own warm-hearted hecklers as the neighbourhood's residents turned out in support of the students. Without warning, the shouting around the first truck suddenly stopped. Slowly everybody started looking around until their eyes found me. Then the shouting started again, and I was pulled across to the truck. Guns had been spotted stacked at the back, and it was time to bring out the foreign 'reporter'. Lifting me up, they pushed me to the edge of the truck and started bouncing me up and down to the great surprise of the soldiers. 'Carrying guns! Carrying guns!' they shouted. 'Tell all world! Give all world report!'

Again, it was hard not to be caught up with the whole situation, but this time I could see into the eyes of the soldiers staring back at me and they looked very nervous. With the crowd worried I had not yet seen the gun rack clearly enough, they started pushing me right into the truck. For the soldiers, that was too much, and they rose to push me back out again. Again I was pushed in and again they pushed me out. There was no way out of this, so I raised my hands and called the crowd to order. 'I have seen guns! I have seen guns! I'll tell whole world! Now let me down! Now let me down!'

To massive cheers, I was let down again and I quickly slipped around the side of the truck. Bloody hell, this was a bit more involvement than I had planned for!

Just after that, CNN turned up, so I left it to them to do the reporting. Going back to the bridge, I could see that people were now gathered around the back of many more of the army trucks. Still, if each of the trucks had as many soldiers as the one I had just visited, a lot more people would be needed to keep them occupied for long.

Suddenly, a few people standing on the bridge with me started running in the other direction. I did the same and saw what they saw. It was beautiful – a huge motley procession coming from the other direction out of the city. Unlike the monotony of the army trucks, this parade was a bizarre procession of every type of motorized vehicle you can imagine. A crazy mixture of cars, trucks, lorries, buses, motorized bicycles, motorbikes with side-cars, disabled people's buggies and even energetic cyclists, it was proceeding up the road, waving banners and tooting horns as if it was Carnival. As it passed beneath us, we cheered. When it reached the convoy, bits of the procession broke off in groups to surround each truck.

The army was obviously gridlocked, so I started on the walk back home. As I made my way, I realized that similar scenes were happening all over Beijing. Army units had tried to penetrate the city along several main arteries and had been stopped at various stages by the trucks sent from Tiananmen Square and then by ordinary people who had come out of their homes to help. In some places, people were sitting and lying in front of the trucks to stop their progress, but it quickly became common practice to let down their tyres. The soldiers just sat there and tried to stare ahead, as if the traffic was bad that morning.

The crowds that surrounded the trucks for the weeks that followed were broadly representative of the city's population, and, as the stand-off continued that first night, more and more kindly ladies emerged to provide food and water to the soldiers. As they offered their hospitality, they grumbled about the soldiers coming with guns and repeated that the people love the People's Army. Many of the soldiers wept as they ate their dumplings and sipped their tea. They had been told it was a counter-revolution. As soon as I got back to my apartment, I called home. 'I know,' my mum said when I told her what I had seen; 'I saw it on the news.'

The stand-off continued, only reaching a threatening level on one of those early summer days when the evil sand winds roll in and Beijing turns yellow. As I stood at the monument in the centre of the square, I could see the clouds gathering in the north and the wind started to pick up. At that very moment, a procession of giant military helicopters flew in a column down the centre of Changan Avenue and stopped to hover at Tiananmen Gate above the portrait of Mao Zedong and on the imperial axis that runs through the city. They were awesomely massive, loud and totally untouchable. With the wind and sand now arriving behind them, they moved right over the square and dropped out bundles of propaganda that smashed open when they hit the ground and were whipped up into a swirling mass of paper. Thousands of students grabbed for the flyers in a frenzy, even as the student leaders behind me shouted to ignore them through their useless megaphones.

By the time groups from the Beijing Art College decided to up the ante even further by building a statue of democracy (that reminded everybody of the US Statue of Liberty) facing Mao's portrait along that same imperial axis, the executive decision had been made. It was just a matter of time.

I first heard the army had opened fire when a couple of Leeds students returned with that very news in the evening of 3 June. I was all for going to the square, and Leeds student Jane and North Korean Kim were also in, so we set off on bikes.

As we cycled towards the centre of town, we encountered groups at the crossroads discussing what was happening in Tiananmen Square. At the Xizhimen Bridge, half of them warned us not to go on, while the other half reminded us that, as foreigners, we had the responsibility to 'give world report' of what we saw. I had heard that before, but we all decided to continue.

As we worked our way southwards on the second ring road, we willed each other forward, agreeing to keep going only until we heard the gunfire for ourselves. After all, how could we report it before we knew it had really happened? It was only a couple of minutes later that we heard shots crackling in the distance. It was easy to discount the first distant volleys, but, as we moved closer, the intermittent sound became clearer and clearer.

Before we came to the Fuxingmen Bridge, where the second ring road crosses the Avenue of Everlasting Peace, which runs through the centre of Beijing, I could see that something was in flames on top of the bridge. When we reached the top of the slip road, we found a scene of destruction. Scattered across the bridge to our right were two or three burning buses and a barricade that had been smashed open through the middle. Debris lay all around, mangled bicycles and glass scarring the surface of the road. There was nobody out in the open, but many crowded along the sides, sheltering behind the line of trees that separates the main thoroughfare from the bicycle lane and the pavement. As we stood on the corner, I heard a rumbling noise, and an old tank, belching smoke from its exhaust, launched itself through the hole in the barricade and sped past towards the square.

After the tank had passed, we all looked at each other again. There could be no doubt that Beijing was being attacked by the army, and we all knew the best course would be to retreat. But we no longer needed to say what we all felt inside. Each of us was committed to going all the way to the square. There was no fear because, at least in my case, I had cleverly convinced myself that in this matter, as all things in China, I was a foreigner, detached and immune from the real impact of what was actually happening.

As we moved down the street, we could see blood on the ground, and slowly more of the local people who had been pinned at the side of the road started stepping gingerly forward from the shadows, looking anxiously back beyond us. A couple more tanks sped by, and we quickly followed everyone else by sheltering when they passed and moving on only when there was no sign of them.

A few hundred metres up the road, we came across a very different dynamic. Three troop carriers were bizarrely parked out on the road with canvas covers down and latched. An angry crowd was surrounding the back of the trucks, and we pulled up our bikes just 10 metres from the last one to watch. The crowd was becoming more animated, some people were carrying sticks and rocks, and all of them were spitting out venomous insults at the soldiers hidden inside. Behind us on the main road, hundreds more angry citizens were now emerging as well. Seeing the trucks exposed there, they also started marching towards them. Suddenly, the canvas cover on the last truck was raised, and I saw what is known as a general-purpose machine gun, set and ready to fire. The people right behind the truck scattered to the left and right immediately, so when the gunner opened fire with a first short burst, he hit people still advancing down the road 30 metres away. After another three of four bursts of fire into the fast-emptying street, all the soldiers jumped out of the trucks and surrounded them in a circle.

Everyone close to me, Jane and Kim included, had bolted over the small hedge at the side of the road and were now covering their heads. Still stupidly believing I was a foreigner and therefore not really to be counted at all, I was more preoccupied with making sure I did not lose or damage the bicycle I had borrowed from a Chinese student. I had already lost enough in the big demonstrations in May and I would not lose another now. Having carefully parked and locked the bike at the side of the road, I too hopped over the hedge and joined my friends on the ground. What an idiot. Poking my head over the hedge, I could see the soldiers standing in their circle with Chinese versions of the AK-47 at their hips. If someone nearby stood up to throw a rock or even move in what they thought was an aggressive manner, two or three of the soldiers opposite them opened fire horizontally, sending everyone back to the ground again, including one or two who did not get up again each time. Just opposite us, I could see a rather fat man who had been caught in the street and was now sheltering behind a spindly tree. His buttocks were bulging out from one side and his stomach from the other. It would have been amusing in a film, but he was genuinely petrified for his life and screaming at people not to throw rocks.

About 10 metres to my west, a middle-aged man had been hit by a bullet and was being cradled by his companion, a young man. He was crying and rocking back and forth, but this slowly changed into an anguished scream and then a mad, angry roar. I watched as he grabbed something and then stood up, running towards the soldiers and hurling a rock at them. The rock landed before it reached them and skidded under the trucks as the soldiers returned fire, and the young man also fell to the ground. By now, the fat man behind the tree was weeping openly, his calls for calm now desperate and hoarse.

Suddenly, and without any warning at all, all the soldiers ran away down the road towards the square. Within seconds, people were on their feet, and I saw a man cross over to the trucks and light paper under the fuel tanks of each one. It was not long before all three trucks were ablaze, and the people around were cheering at what they saw as revenge for the murders we had just witnessed.

Rejoining our bicycles, we debated whether we should now go back and again decided to carry on. Before we could do anything, we saw a single unarmed soldier, with his clothes ripped apart, running for his life towards us. He was being chased by an angry mob, and I could see the pure terror in his eyes as he sprinted past, not 3 metres from where I stood. Behind me, a second angry crowd was gathering. As soon as they saw the soldier, they advanced from the other direction, equally determined to catch and punish one of the perpetrators. With no option to escape to his right, the soldier made an incredible life-or-death decision. Hardly missing a step, he veered left and jumped straight into the line of burning trucks, disappearing into the flames. I quickly cycled back to behind the trucks and spotted him still running down the road on the other side. About 100 metres further on, sections of the crowd finally caught him, and I watched as he was wrestled to the ground and brutally murdered under a frenzied hail of clubs and stones.

Stunned by the sickening events all around, my thoughts turned back to the students in the square. If there were tanks and guns and murder out on the streets, what could it be like inside, where all the tanks and soldiers were heading? We continued our journey into the very heart of Beijing, our progress again disrupted by a couple of tanks trundling past at a much slower pace than before. There was more blood and there were more rocks and sticks lying around the streets, but when we arrived at the entrance to the Zhongnanhai compound, where China's top leaders reside, we came across an amazing scene. Throughout the demonstrations, the people I had seen gathering there had never crossed the white line that would have forced the ceremonial guard to take action. In the middle of this crazed night, with tanks and soldiers firing behind them, the people there now were doing exactly the same thing, sitting quietly along the white line.

Just beyond that entrance, the Avenue of Everlasting Peace opens out into a very wide thoroughfare that is flanked by the Great Hall of the People on one side and by the Forbidden City on the other. Tiananmen Square lies just behind the Great Hall, but there was no way for us to reach it. Having made our way to the first line of bystanders looking towards the square, I could make out an area of no-man's land ahead. At the far end of this eerily quiet space was a single impenetrable wall of tanks and soldiers.

For more than a few minutes, I argued with Kim and Jane that the violence we had seen was the result of a terrible mistake. Something had gone wrong with communications, and individual soldiers were now acting out of panic, inciting the people to avenge the deaths of their friends. Short of marching across the no-man's land to explain, the only other option was to try getting into the square from the back of the Great Hall of the People. We were standing right outside the Asian Games HQ, where I worked, so we headed off down a small *hutong* that I knew emerged at the south of the Great Hall. When we got there, the pavement was lined with agitated people, and we walked past them until we could see the square itself. Here, instead of the tanks we had seen on the main road, a single line of unarmed soldiers was linked together in a human chain.

It was clear that we could no longer join the students in the square, but there was also no doubt there were still some in there behind the soldiers because I could see flags and banners. Then the line of soldiers parted, and I saw two Caucasian foreigners being marched out of the square and up the steps to the Great Hall of the People. The people standing around were also watching and focused attention on Jane and me, warning us that, as they were now arresting foreigners, it was best if we made haste and reported what we had seen.

Neither of us wanted to be arrested, while the trouble Kim would get if he was identified would be unimaginable, so we made our way back along the *hutong* with an American journalist who was also standing nearby and decided to make an exit on the back of my bike. When we emerged close to the no-man's land we had first seen, there was still a stalemate. It was starting to get light, and we reluctantly headed back along the Avenue of Everlasting Peace. We did not get far. At the first junction, we were halted by the saddest procession in the world. As I later found out, large numbers of students in the square had been allowed to leave from an exit in the south and they were now winding their way back home to their colleges. The procession was a funeral march, and we dismounted as hundreds of crying faces with tattered banners and flags walked disconsolately past, weakly trying to muster the energy to shout the simple slogans of hope that had prompted this unforgivable treatment from their own grandparents. Despite their sorry state, they still had great pride in the ideals which they had represented for all those weeks, and I was filled with respect for their sacrifices.

Perhaps it was this defiance that convinced the army to wait until nearly all the students had turned onto the Avenue of Everlasting Peace before launching tear gas directly into the centre of the procession and 'storming the point' with tanks travelling at full speed with machine guns firing. As soon as the first gas canisters landed, I was jerked violently back to Chile and I quickly shouted for Jane and Kim to follow me down the side road from where the students had emerged. We ran with our bikes for about 30 metres, before I looked back to see a tank screaming through the mist, squashing the confused and disoriented students in the middle of the junction. More than anything I had seen that night, this seemed the ultimate crime, the ultimate betrayal. The peaceful students were leaving the square: why would you deliberately murder them now?

As the tear gas lifted, I could see the carnage at the end of the road, bodies lying there in the early-morning gloom. Very quickly, people came running past with injured companions, one shot in the shoulder, another with a gaping hole in his thigh. Then, the drivers of the same delivery tricycles that had been delivering soft drinks just days before headed into the mêlée, returning with people missing parts of their chest or their head laid out on the back. As the dead and injured streamed past, we all stood transfixed. Other distraught bystanders were also standing there, some numbed by the experience like me and others crying and screaming inconsolably.

Before we had time to react, we were approached by a group of people led by a woman who could speak to us only between great heaving sobs that racked her body every few seconds. The man propping her up angrily told us that her son was dead and that we were the only people who could tell the truth. She begged us to get out of that place immediately. Calling across to another bystander with a bicycle, the man asked him to lead us away before we were caught. Following his lead, we headed into the small *hutongs* that run parallel to the main east–west avenue. Although we were still just a few metres away from the scene of a horrible massacre, everything in the *hutongs* was silent, the calm broken only by the sounds of people releasing the first spit devil of the morning and the heating of morning kettles.

We finally broke out of this insulated dreamland where the *hutongs* meet the second ring road and we were back where we had started at Fuxingmen. Rather than travel north the way we had come, we decided to keep going west. It was now daylight, and all along the street we could see the devastation. At Muxidi, we came across another bus barricade, this one more recently created and still intact. There were people jumping up and down on top of it, and beyond them I could see soldiers sitting in an open-top carrier. Suddenly, all the soldiers in the trucks got up and ran away again. This time they were heading out of town. The people immediately jumped down from the barricade and made for the trucks. Inside, they found boxes of tear gas. As others scrambled for the contents, one man ran past me proudly clutching a military pistol. Now ransacked, the trucks were again torched. Then there was a huge explosion as the barricade was hit with a round from the main gun of a tank. The tank itself then proceeded to smash its way at high speed through the barrier and hurtle off towards the square.

We continued to make our way west, taking shelter as tanks roared past in both directions, soldiers now visible at the turret and carrying tear gas. When we stopped, I noticed that windows high up in several buildings had had their panes shot out. When we reached the China Central TV building, the other place I worked from time to time, we came across an army of regular unarmed soldiers wearing simple green fatigues. What was perplexing was that they were obviously being guarded by a second army, comprising standing soldiers wearing full combat gear. They seemed altogether much more professional and moved us on without smiles when we halted.

We finally arrived back at the university just as a weak sun was rising.

8

The Mourning After

Throughout the days that followed I was in shock, and no amount of alcohol could affect my mood. Like in Chile, I was left numb by the experience of civil strife, but this went much deeper as it affected people I knew and really cared about. With no access to outside news, I had no idea about the world's reaction, but I knew a terrible crime had been committed. The students did not deserve their fate, and the government's response had been wildly excessive. There could never again be any doubt just how much the central leadership was prepared to sacrifice in order to maintain stability. The government leaders would kill their own children rather than lose control, and this was the message that I realized the world must slowly now be discussing.

It was already time for some of the foreign students to leave anyway, and soon the evacuation started in earnest. The most anxious to get out of the campus to their embassy were the Polish students, not because they were scared, but because they wanted to vote, in their first free elections. One by one, the embassies arrived to take away their charges, and soon the university, to which I no longer belonged anyway, became quieter and hollower. The British students were visited by the embassy in a bus with Union Jacks plastered over it as the officials risked tank interception to travel across town.

Some of the British students were glad to accept their suggestion of temporary refuge in the embassy compound with its swimming pool and hurriedly packed overnight bags and their passports. Others were less ready to flee and argued that, unless it was compulsory, they would rather stay on campus. A couple of days later, the embassy had to make another visit to pick up a further group who had got cold feet, leaving just two rebels behind. For those who left on the second bus and those who had 'come for a swim' a couple of days before, it was the last time they would spend a night in their rooms. For most, evacuation to Hong Kong was followed by a swift return to London, where they became among the first shell-shocked eye witnesses around which the media and public rallied.

The emptying of the university made me realize it was time I returned to my own apartment and I tried to make contact with London. When I arrived in the hotel lobby, the doorman threw his arms up and started shouting for Mrs Deer, the office manager. Immediately, one of the reception staff scuttled off to the office, and I was led across the floor.

'Luo Wen,' she said despairingly, 'I thought you were dead! June 3 have persons see you towards square going,' she continued, 'but June 4, June 5 you not come back. You look! I just giving your parents write letter, ask them your clothes what do!'

True enough, the first few lines of an English letter lay open on the desk with a Chinese–English dictionary next to it. I expressed my apologies for causing her concern and headed up to my room. I tried calling the UK, but the international lines were down. I wrote a fax, a revolutionary tool that was replacing the telex, but the international lines were down. So I sent a telex asking what to do. The answer was that I should move from my small Chinese hotel to a large international one with better communications. If you lived on the west of town, that meant the Shangrila. I packed an overnight bag and set off on my bike. All was not normal at the Shangrila as the outbreak of military violence had happened at night, when most of the huge numbers of staff were at home. Given the strict curfew in place, nobody was coming to work, and so nobody who was there was allowed to go home.

The staff moved into the guest rooms, and room service was cancelled. Meal times were surreal. Although it is very common to see Chinese restaurant staff settle down to eat in their own restaurant at the end of a shift, I had never seen it in a western hotel before. With the fresh goods markets suspended, the buffet selection introduced for all meals got smaller and smaller each day, and the few guests, hotel managers, waiters and waitresses all just rolled in to serve themselves.

For reasons unknown to me, the Shangrila did still have international phone and fax communications and uninterrupted access to CNN. As I spent some time catching up on the American view of events, I realized it had been quite a week around the world. In addition to events in China and the Polish elections, millions in Iran had been out on the streets mourning the death of the Ayatollah Khomeni.

After just a day, I was tracked down by a diligent journalist from my local paper in England and gave an emotional interview that led the front page. Then I received the order from London that I should leave China by plane to any destination on any carrier. I went to the airline ticket counter, but it was closed. I knew that 'emergency' flights were being laid on for foreign nationals, so I enquired at the concierge how much it would cost to get a taxi to the airport, and they finally found a reluctant driver. He said it was more than his life was worth to attempt the journey, but if I really had to go he would need at least US$300. His was the only taxi that still had petrol, so I could take it or leave it.

Without anything like that much money and with no banks open, I decided I would have to go by bicycle and I set off back to my hotel to pick up some things. At the hotel, everything was very quiet, and the staff told me all the foreigners were gone and that they were very sorry that I had to go as well. As I came back down the stairs, one of the very friendly drivers attached to the hotel approached me and offered a ride to the airport for free. He told me he was so upset to be losing customers like me and didn't know if we would ever meet again. It was, he said, the least he could do. In return, I pulled out my remaining *renminbi* and gave them to him. I didn't know if I would be able to use it again either.

We picked our way around several army checkpoints, stopping each time until given a clear indication by the soldiers to proceed. When I arrived at the airport it was nearly empty, the bulk of the evacuations having been completed on the previous days. I was to join Josh on the Cathay flight to Hong Kong and was happy to see him there. He too had seen some of the violence from the other side of town and was now being evacuated by his company. When we boarded there was just a handful of us on the massive plane.

Among our fellow passengers were two Swiss backpackers, and, as they told us their story, I realized they were the same two I had seen being arrested in Tiananmen Square early on 4 June. It turned out they had taken the Trans-Siberian express from Europe and arrived in Beijing on the morning of 3 June. When they had set off, the events in Beijing looked like a youth party. They thought it was strange when they saw tanks at the station, but with no other plan they had gone straight to the square on arrival. Less than twenty-four hours later all hell broke loose, and they were finally arrested and marched into the Great Hall of the People, where I had seen them. They had been held until their release earlier that day and now they were travelling down to Hong Kong. They expected to be back home in Switzerland in a few days.

On arrival in Hong Kong, I was very kindly welcomed by Pat, a friend working for the trading firm Swire, and I was soon joined in his apartment by Jane, who had declined to return to the UK with the other students. Over the next weeks, we made contact with others displaced to Hong Kong by the events and waited, for what it was not clear. Bonded by our experience, we also found comfort in each other.

While the London office of CSL grappled with what to do with me as an unregistered employee, news came from David Risner at the BBC that I was not allowed to return to China officially or conduct any business to avoid any possible conflict with the BBC's news coverage. He told me not to worry, however: the BBC would still stand by my contract, and I was very grateful for his and Keith Owen's support.

The China story was still big news around the world, and when a friend of Pat's working for an airline returned to the apartment with a huge bunch of the weekend's papers from the UK I tucked in. After reading a variety of opinions and editorials, including a vitriolic attack on China by the *Observer*'s Jonathan Mirsky, I turned to 'other news' in the tabloids. On page 2 of one of them, I was greeted by a big headline about a BBC boss who had committed suicide by jumping off Centre Point in London. I looked closer and I was stunned. It was David Risner, who had only recently told me not to worry about my troubles. I do not know why he took that action, but I will always remember his support at that confused time in my life.

Our Yugoslavian friend Uncle Gregor was also in Hong Kong. For clandestine reasons, he needed the help of the Vatican to get himself back home. His way of getting into their good books was to provide some eye witnesses to the slaughter in Beijing who would share stories with the Catholic congregation. We went and did the show. Our accounts prompted crying in the audience, and Jane started having nightmares. I was still numb.

To help the evacuees deal with the post-traumatic stress, Hong

Kong's caring psychiatrists were offering free counselling. Since Jane and I were having such different reactions, we figured at least one of us was probably in need of some help so we went along one afternoon. I had the problem, the doctor told us, as my emotions would have to come out sometime, while Jane's nightmares would fade with time. The longer it took for me to release them, the more worrying it would become. Be ready, he told me, it will happen.

I waited, but nothing changed. I was even numb when the London office called to tell me that my contract had been terminated. I was no longer required, and it would be better if I disappeared. In fact, that was the spur I needed to move from the limbo in Hong Kong and get back to Beijing to catch up with friends and check on my life there. I had a double entry visa and so I headed back to Beijing.

Beijing was miserable. Armed soldiers stood at the crossroads of the intersections, and people's heads stayed down as they hurried about their business. The Chinese students were doing extra political lessons, and all the students in the graduating year had been sent back to their provinces in disgrace. The new first-year intake had turned up early for pre-enrolment boot camp.

I went back to my hotel to collect my things, but Mrs Deer told me that people had come to cancel the room and had taken all my stuff away. What? I went straight to CSL's office at the Friendship Hotel to see the manager but, when I turned up looking for answers, she was not there. The staff seemed pleased to see me, and I discovered there had been a flurry of telexes back and forth about how to deal with the problem of 'RS'. It turned out that I had never been registered in China and that I had been seen taking part in the democracy protests, an untenable position given the company's close links with the government. I copied the lot and waved goodbye to the staff.

With the universities emptied and the army omnipresent about town, the campus officials at my old university finally became concerned with me staying in the foreign students' dormitory, and it became essential to find alternative accommodation. For a couple of nights I stayed with an old friend who was harbouring one of the student artists who had created the Goddess of Democracy during the protests. His commitment had earned him a position on the wanted list, and, when the maid came to clean the bathroom, he was shoved into the kitchen.

A couple of days were enough for me, and I realized that there was little point in staying. I had been sacked by one company and was unable to do any work for the second. My series of articles on media in China was turning into one big feature spread on the media's coverage of Tiananmen Square, and there was little more to report. Just six months after setting off with such hope, I returned to England again to land on the doorstep of my long-suffering parents. I hadn't even had time for a game of football.

There was also still some unfinished business that came with me, both emotional and commercial. First, I had to resolve my situation with the *Observer*, the partner in CSL that was paying my salary and that would have to pay now that I was not wanted. Given that its China joint-venture was supporting the Beijing government, the *Observer*'s angry anti-China editorials seemed to me a little hypocritical. After a debate on Tiananmen Square at the Institute of Contemporary Arts in London, I privately asked the paper's journalist Jonathan Mirsky whether he was aware of this fact. He said that he wasn't. For one reason or another, the *Observer* got it into their heads that I had tipped off other papers about their relationships in Beijing and became worried that their activities might be exposed. Although I had never contacted anyone but their own journalist, the threat was deemed serious enough for a senior *Observer* executive to call my father late one Friday night. The fact he called my father, not me, was not a good start in my book, but it was explained that, should I ever mention any details about my work with the paper in China, the full wrath of its backer, Tiny Rowland, would come crashing down on us. We didn't want that, he said.

Over that weekend, I debated the pros and cons with my parents. China was still big news and such an exposé would no doubt be welcomed by competing titles. Money could be made, but what about the future? Would any company take the risk of employing a known whistle-blower? Would my bit of noise in Britain make any difference at all in China or just mean I was banned from going there as well?

In the end, I agreed to keep quiet and accepted nominal compensation for all the belongings that had been looted from my apartment. I didn't have much, and, without doubt, the most valuable item in the inventory was the silk suit given to me by Alex Higgins. As there was no receipt, they refused my claims for compensation. I even got in touch with Higgins. He remembered Josh and me, but he was unclear about the suit and didn't want to put himself in the middle of the argument. That was unusual for him, but it was also fair enough. I got nothing to compensate me for the loss of my life in China and even less for keeping quiet.

Although the student movement turned out to have a bloody ending, I am thankful I was in China at that time, not back in Leeds watching Kate Adie's version on the BBC. In particular, I was a proud witness to the incredible month in Chinese history when the people stood up in unison to cheer their peaceful young heroes as they pursued what was rightfully theirs.

While I sat back down, wondering what to do, Josh had decided that enough was enough and managed to get himself quietly reinstated at Leeds University, sponsored by his company. It was the right move for him, but the only thing I knew about my own future was that I did not want to return to university in Britain but find another way back to China immediately.

The events in China had acted like a trigger, with similar sentiment across the Soviet Union causing it to fall apart at the seams. In November 1989, the Berlin Wall was breached for the first time. Although foreigners were still being shepherded into East Berlin through Checkpoint Charlie, the German people were now taking advantage of an open border. I followed the story with growing interest as the people power movement was so similar to that in China months before.

As I watched sadly from afar, the feeling of despair around China was symbolically reflected in the eyes of the people by the abject performance of the Chinese football team. In October 1989, at the qualifiers for the World Cup, China managed to snatch defeat from the jaws of victory twice in a row, conceding two late goals in the last three minutes. These disasters are remembered as the two 'black three minutes' in Chinese football, and there was no doubt the whole year was cloaked in darkness.

Meanwhile, I was ever conscious that I had still not achieved the emotional release I needed after Tiananmen. It finally happened one night at a cosy pub in England and it took me totally by surprise. I was having a beer with my best childhood friends, Paul, James, Nick and Jan. We weren't talking about China at all, but as I took in the crackling log fire and saw our friends Rachel and Kim smiling behind the old oak bar, I was hit with a feeling of being totally protected, totally safe. This strong feeling of comfort and human warmth grew and grew until it overcame me completely, and I burst into a flood of screaming tears as images of tanks and blood and dead people and smoke and crying students and fire and anger catapulted themselves from deep inside my stomach. I could feel it coming but I was powerless to stop it. Rushing outside, I stumbled across to a bench outside a church and let it all come tumbling out. For a quarter of an hour, I just cried like I was being sick, releasing each deeply buried thought with a gut-wrenching groan and empty wails until the memories were exhausted. So that's what the shrink meant.

By Christmas, East Germany was finished, and Jane and I decided we had to go to Berlin ourselves, had to take part in the historic events as the people reunited. It would not only be an adventure, but might help us deal with what we both still believed deeply was unfinished business in China. Totally ill-equipped (my mate Rob only had time to grab his slippers), the three of us joined a sold-out train from Waterloo and spent the whole freezing journey in the draughty corridor.

In Berlin, we met up with friends from Beijing and were provided with a fantastic apartment. We started with a visit to the East through Checkpoint Charlie, which was soon to be removed. *Nächste Bahnhoff, Friedrichstrasse!* As we emerged into the East, the first thing I could see at the end of the road was bizarrely familiar. It was a large Chinese restaurant with signposts in red. We went straight inside and learned from the staff that it was a restaurant established by the Beijing Hotel as a symbol of China's friendship with the East German people. More specifically, it was a symbolic gift to Prime Minister Krenz, whose personal support for the crackdown in Tiananmen Square was so highly regarded back in Beijing.

With Vietnamese and several other Communist workers then based in East Germany hopping and skipping their ways across the border to the West, the workers in the Chinese restaurant were here on state business and were being watched every day. We talked sombrely with the staff as we ate our meal and then continued to explore the dark and drab half of the city.

The highlight of the festive period was Silvesternacht (New

Year's Eve), and it took me straight back to Beijing in ways I had not expected. First, our host asked if we wanted to see a riot. How could you predict that, Jane wondered? It was easy, he told us, there was one every year in Kreuzberg. Not quite believing him, we all headed off down to that district and stood around with lots of other people. As it approached midnight, police trucks started moving into the area and took up positions in the square.

Just before midnight, I started noticing people collecting little piles of stones and rocks at the side of the road. On the stroke of twelve, the crowd pulled down their hats into face masks, the police vans disgorged fully armed riot police, and tear gas was thrown into the crowd as they charged. Hey, wait a second, this was a serious riot – the only things missing were guns and tanks. Without any delay, we headed off down the street and finally managed to squeeze inside a small bar that was rammed with others fleeing the mayhem and the tear gas. Finally, the fighting sapped the energy of the crowd and the police, and we emerged to the rock-strewn streets. Where to next, asked our German friend.

'How about somewhere where people are happy this evening?' Jane asked. That was no problem either, and soon we were making our way to the Brandenburg Gate. When we had come past the day before it was still separated from us by a huge section of the Wall, and we had joined people in chipping away bits of coloured masonry as mementos. Tonight, a section of the Wall had been opened, and people were streaming through into the East in a smiling, bubbling river of excited heads. We joined the stream and finally worked our way through the gap. We were in. As we walked away from the Wall, I looked back, and my sense of achievement was rocked for a second. Plastered across the East German side of this symbolic barrier of the Cold War were the words 'Saatchi & Saatchi – First Over the Wall'.

My attention was then grabbed by some audacious amateur

climbers who were doing their best to get on to the Gate itself, to mount the magnificent sculptures at the top. In a rush to join them, others were now scaling some scaffolding erected for the TV cameras. Without warning, the scaffolding suddenly collapsed, and we saw lots of people thrown off from far too high. I winced as the last ones to fall landed on those below and picked themselves up. There was no truck to whisk them away.

In the other direction, millions more elated people were exploring the great public buildings along Unter den Linden. In a surging tide of bodies, we were lifted towards the Great Palace of the Republic. The doors were open, and people were running in and out, those exiting burdened with pillaged items, from office papers to banquet decorations. We encountered the same scenes all down the wide avenue, and, for the first time, I felt a key difference with the student movement in Beijing. Whereas the vacuum created by the demise of the East German government could be filled by the West German government, if the students in China had sacked the Great Hall of the People they would not have known what to do the next day.

On our way back through the gap in the wall, the ecstatic East German guards at the already redundant border control were struggling to cope with the thousands of passports being voluntarily presented to them for the first time. Everyone wanted to record the momentous occasion by getting a last East German exit stamp reading '1.1.90', and the guards were happy to oblige. I also carried back with me a selection of the small painted chippings I had taken from the Berlin Wall. Each time I have offered one to a Chinese friend, it has been gladly received with great respect.

I returned from Berlin with new hope in 'people power' and immediately set about registering my own company. To keep it general, I called it Oriental Relations Limited, or ORL, and my focus was to extend the work I had previously been involved with, namely commercial sponsorship of sports events and production and distribution of media content. I had touched on these areas before Tiananmen and I saw them as the best ways to facilitate meaningful exchange between the closed and manipulated Communist Chinese media and the open and manipulated media of the western world.

I had no money, no clients and an office in my bedroom at my parents' house. I was an angry and skinny twenty-two-year-old consultant in an industry that barely existed. I grew a beard, which made me look twenty-five, but it didn't improve market conditions. I bought a book called *How to Be a Successful Consultant*. This excellent introduction told me that getting my name in print was one good way to build the reputation on which successful consultants trade their expertise. It didn't seem to be a problem writing for *Television Week*, so I became an early overseas subscriber to the official *China Daily*, the Communist Party-owned English propaganda newspaper.

I divided my areas of interest into relevant categories and religiously went through each edition, cutting out and pasting the relevant articles into big scrapbooks. My parents must have wondered what I was doing in my bedroom, but I found that, after just a few weeks, I had amassed a huge amount of filed material, including such official facts and figures as were available, across all the major areas in which I thought British people should be engaging with China. Not surprisingly, the news was all good, but when I got my hands on some professional western reports I noted that they all used the same statistical sources that the *China Daily* summarized so neatly.

With some widely accepted Communist base material, I started contacting trade publications to see if they wanted feature articles on China. Some of them did, so I turned to my scrapbooks and crafted the bones of feature articles for a bizarre cross-section of titles aimed at readers with very different feelings about China. I interviewed my old colleague Mr Mile concerning China's chances in the Asian Games for *Athletic Weekly* and then delved into the murky arena of childcare for *Disability Now*, visiting an infamous Shanghai orphanage that later caused controversy when a secret film was shot there. Despite the poor conditions and primitive care, I felt that the people working in the orphanage were totally dedicated to the children, most of whom had physical disabilities and had been discarded by their parents. They just needed more resources.

By way of contrast, on the very next day, I was invited to tour the newly opened Shanghai golf course for *Golf Monthly*. As I wrote how a Chinese researcher had recently proved China invented the game, I also had to introduce the lavish course designed by Robert Trent Junior and the legions of young female caddies working out of a ridiculous ersatz European clubhouse.

Energized by my trip but confused by the differing stories I had covered, I started trying to encourage British businesses to consider how sponsorship (in its widest form) might help them achieve defined business objectives in China and help people at the same time. I passionately believed in this route and approached the Sino-British Trade Council. After bothering the trade promotion body for months, I finally received £2,000 from United Biscuits, one of its key corporate members.

For this nominal amount, I spent months preparing the first comprehensive British report on sponsorship opportunities in China across sports, culture, arts, education, environment and other social issues. Although a synopsis of the report appeared in the *China Britain Trade Review*, not a single substantial lead resulted. China was still too controversial, and I was knocked sideways by this lack of response. Even United Biscuits, one of the pioneers of Business in the Community in the UK, had little appetite for similar projects in China, which it saw as a low-cost manufacturing base for mainly export business. It would take many years before Corporate Social Responsibility became relevant in China, and it would be western consumers who demanded the changes.

With the opening of the company taxing my mind, I decided it was time to get some exercise and joined the local football club. It was the first time I had done so in England for many years. The only thing that had changed was me. At the first session, the coach sat us all down in a circle and asked us to shout out our names as he pointed his way around and allocated positions for the first trial. When it finally came to me, I shouted my name and position, and the coach replied, 'OK, Brian, you can be left . . . out.' It is one of the oldest jokes in the book, but also a reflection of where I felt I was living; I might have been in England, but I was spending all day writing about China. I was so disillusioned that I didn't bother to tell the coach or my teammates my real name and played as 'Brian' every week. When my mother and Jane came to watch a game they couldn't stop laughing, and I told them it was only because I would not be playing there for long.

I knew I had to get back to China, and my first opportunity came with the Shanghai TV Festival in late 1990. On my way to cover the event for *Television Week*, I managed to catch up with some Chinese friends at a party in Beijing. While my memories had been on pause since June 1989, the rest of Beijing had been dealing with the post-Tiananmen reality every day for more than a year. Of course they weren't talking about it any more – what was the point? It was far better to just shut up and get on with trying to make a living. They were right. I would never forget, but it was time to move on.

9

The Beautiful Game

By the start of 1991, I had been a China consultant for a year and was still in the UK trying to build enough media and cultural exchange business to fund a move back to China. It was very tough going and, still following my consulting book's suggestion to get my name in print, I was always on the look-out for a good story. One day I noted in my faithful *China Daily* that Guangzhou was to host the first Women's World Cup.

It was the first time China would host a world-level international football tournament and a chance to check out the best women players at their first world party, so I decided to go along with Jane, who had long complained at the absence of women's football on television. We were duly accredited as foreign journalists for English title *When Saturday Comes*. As I found it impossible to lace my piece with the same level of ironic wit shown by many of the other contributors, my story was never filed.

Before we arrived in Guangzhou, we were contacted by the organizing committee with our itinerary and the contact details for our personal guide. His name was Lucifer, and I wondered what could have possessed him to choose that name. While it is compulsory for foreigners to take Chinese names because nobody can write our names in Chinese (even after years of study), Chinese people taking English names is usually a voluntary process. Many give themselves first names when their work starts involving interaction with foreigners.

So it was with some trepidation that we arrived in Guangzhou to be met by a guide Jane considered the devil himself, but who I thought was more likely to be one of his students. And that's what he turned out to be. The poor lad had been christened Lucifer by a young English teacher from America who taught at his school but was gone now. 'Have problem?' he asked. When I explained, he agreed to change his name, but only when his new box of name cards ran out, which suggested he still didn't really understand.

Apart from finding out that Americans can be very cruel, the trip to the Women's World Cup taught me some important lessons, starting with the brutal realization that the biggest problem in women's football is men. Although barring me, and all other men, from seeking forgiveness for our sins at the World Cup team meetings didn't seem the right way to build bridges, Jane did attend and what she heard wasn't pretty. She heard that some men, and all Italians like her father, viewed women's football as a voyeuristic chance to see tits, legs and arses and not as sporting encounters involving athletes. The Italy team, it was said, made it to China only because the big clubs invested in the game to please the lecherous chairmen. The Nigerian team told of regular matches that drew 200 or 300 male spectators: not bad, until they explained they came to laugh at them and sometimes throw rocks. In England (where the ban on women playing on official FA grounds was incredibly only lifted in 1971), Germany and Australia, I heard that development was being driven by the lesbian community and was based on the hardcore drinking model of the men's game in those countries. The Brasilians, on the other hand, had plenty of opportunities to play football on the same decrepit pitches as their brothers, but found it hard mentally to adapt to their nation's belief that they should be automatic world champions. As a result, they played like a team of paranoid Ronaldinhos, dribbling in circles and then losing the ball in their famous gold shirts. I found out that each team's route to the finals had been hampered by men to varying degrees, and that these prejudices had led to women's football emerging along very different lines in different places.

The reasons why the USA, China and the Scandinavian nations started the 1990s with the leading teams in world women's football were also fascinating and for very different reasons. The country to benefit most from the late development of serious women's football around the world was the USA, still a bit player in the men's game at that time. The fact women didn't really play football anywhere meant that this huge, rich nation was playing on its first level football field, its 150-year disadvantage in the men's game irrelevant. With soccer moms and kids choosing the game in increasing numbers, the USA was already the most powerful force in the women's game and tipped to win the inaugural world championships.

One of the main challenges came from the hosts, a country that could not be more different in its approach to education and sports. Unlike the USA, where football was developing among girls because it is a great game, the development of women's football in China was part of the state plan. The first women's football team was established at a factory in Xian in 1979, and the province of Shaanxi is widely credited with the first developments in the women's game at municipal and provincial levels. Indeed, when China held its first national competition in Beijing in 1982, the Shaanxi team emerged victorious. With the blessing of FIFA and the AFC, China hosted its first women's tournament in Guangzhou in 1983 with Liaoning, Guangdong and Japan taking the top three positions. Two years later, the National Sports Commission gave women's football formal sport status by holding a national championship for thirty-six teams, with Tianjin emerging as champions.

China had the first chance to test itself in international competition at the sixth Asian Women's Championships in 1986. At last, China had football champions to look up to as the Chinese team swept to victory without a single loss, scoring twenty-three goals along the way. This success was reflected in women's football being included at the national sports championships for the first time in 1987.

The players I was now seeing represent China at the first Women's World Cup were athletes from the pockets of women's football activity that had grown from these efforts. Like the game in general, the aim was not to provide healthy exercise for millions of girls, but to produce a team to win the World Cup it was now hosting. To that end, the 1990 Asian Games in Beijing, at which the Chinese women's team emerged as champions, had provided the perfect preparation. In China, there was no sexist angle, no commercial angle, no community angle. It was a plan enjoyed by the women who were playing, but made entirely by men for political reasons.

As far as I could gather, the best men from the viewpoint of women footballers lived in Scandinavia, a place where real crowds already came to games to appreciate the skills of the players and to watch the sporting competition. But, among all these stories, for me the most shocking news came from the teams that were not in Guangzhou at all. Not teams like England and Scotland that failed to qualify on merit, but teams from those countries in which women are not allowed to play football at all. To me, the words 'You are not allowed to play football' were usually followed by the words 'in the kitchen' or even 'in the car', not with a full stop.

The idea that half the population in several countries weren't allowed to play football ever seemed impossible, and I set off to the Women's World Cup press conference with a few questions for FIFA. It was my first FIFA press conference, and everything seemed in order until the Women's Committee took up the vacant places on the platform next to Pelé, who was a guest, and the moderator: they were all men. When the mike reached me, I held back my original question and just asked, 'Why are there no women on the Women's Committee?' Pelé laughed and looked at the officials on either side.

It turned out that, since the Women's Committee had been formed only recently, the correct gender appointments had yet to be made. Although this raised the question of why this small oversight wasn't addressed when FIFA first thought of the brilliant idea of a World Cup for women. I had only one question left. I asked the panel how it was that several countries in the Middle East which deny women their full rights to play football on religious grounds can still remain full members of FIFA.

The answer was shocking and shifted my view of football's governing body. According to FIFA, women had no right to play football. Although many other forms of discrimination were covered, including racial, religious and political, discrimination on the grounds of sex was not. Privately, a now senior FIFA official explained to me that a number of Gulf states were big sponsors of men's football at junior levels, where FIFA needed funding. I found this situation doubly shocking since the Middle East was one of the regions said to be taking some TV coverage of the women's tournament. Who was watching and why? Were they like the Italians on Jane's list, but only when other countries' women were on display?

I noted recently that sex is now included in the list of discriminations that FIFA statutes forbid among its member nations. The only problem is that all the same countries that still refuse or restrict a woman's inalienable human right to kick a football are still happy members of the FIFA club. I am not sure if it is worse to have no protection or protection that is not enforced. I left the press conference with a keen new understanding of the reality of football outside China. It wasn't pretty.

At the briefing for the foreign versus local journalists match that is always a welcome part of any World Cup, we were told to meet for breakfast at a leisurely 9.30 the next morning and travel to the Zhujiang (Pearl River) Beer Factory, the sponsors of the match. It sounded good, but I was still a relative novice when it came to the Chinese concept of an invitation match.

It was 7.30 when synchronized phone calls woke us to say the bus was leaving in fifteen minutes and we should hurry not to miss it. The rest of our team hadn't looked so hot when I saw them the day before, and the lack of sleep and breakfast didn't help today. Lucifer helpfully warned we wouldn't have a hope in hell against any opposition which had the advantage of sleep and sustenance.

At the end of a bouncing journey through the province, we arrived at the beer factory, which was very white and very big. Not quite sure what to expect, we were led into one of the buildings to be introduced to our first unknown activity. Walking through the door that magically opened in front of us, we emerged into a huge hall. It seemed like the whole factory was there to see us, cheering and clapping as we entered stage left.

The first activity was the 'Which special guest can fastest drink finish one bottle Zhujiang beer' contest, some rounds of which had to be replayed due to rule changes that nobody could understand. This was followed by three-legged races. 'Now foreign friends split (into) pairs, every pair use rope make four legs change (into) three legs, then please running (to) end, drink Zhujiang beer.' It was confusing for the competitors and thus a firm favourite with the crowd.

When we had completed several more games involving us necking the full range of Zhujiang cans and bottles in front of their makers, I tried to engage the leaders in the drinking, but it was suddenly all over. The audience stopped laughing and filed out of the room silently, no doubt to brew more party beer. Guided by short Zhujiang beer people in white hats, we exited stage right and were led meekly to our bus and dispatched to our next appointment, a lunch banquet for both the teams. It was being hosted by our friends at Zhujiang beer.

Guangdong cuisine is not one of my favourites, but that was one of the best meals I had ever had, involving an unfeasible number of courses with a ridiculous array of dishes. I realized this was just an official meal, but a good one given the high level of government support for this World Cup.

I recognized a couple of the Chinese journalists from the media centre, and they enthusiastically helped me wash down the meal with more bottles of Zhujiang. Unlike in Britain where 'Dry your glasses' means 'Get the fuck out of my pub', in China it means 'Cheers' and applies to every ceremonious clinking of glasses among people having a good time. I forgot about the football match, but our opposition didn't.

'You play what position?' we were each asked in turn. Identifying me as a forward, the journalist next to me continued the line of questioning, '100 metres, you run how quick?'

I have never been much of a runner, posting 15.6 seconds in my last recorded 100 metres at school (completed under duress). I was sure I could run faster with a ball than without one, so I said, 'Not have ball, I run roughly 15.6.'

'15.6!' he replied hysterically, '15.6 not count fast!'

Laughing, he turned to his friends and pointed at me, 'Ay yah, you guess guess, 100 metres he run how fast,' immediately adding, '15.6' before anyone had time to guess. As it slowly dawned on them that they all had achieved faster times than I had, the laughter and the sense of relief seemed to grow.

'Ay yah,' I retorted to the table at large, 'you did not listen clear. I said "not have ball" run 15.6. Have ball, that not same. Have ball, run 12.4!' That shut them up and as they tried to get their heads around how I could take three seconds off my time by kicking a ball along, I went for the kill.

'If have ball, (and) also have opponent, I can run 10.2! If have ball, also have two opponents, one time I run wind-assisted 9.76.' Then I burped, but not on purpose.

When they could force us to consume no more, we shook our wobbly hands with our Chinese hosts and were led out, this time by tall, beautiful women wearing traditional *qipao* dresses without white hats. Since they knew it was impossible to travel far from Zhujiang beer city without a toilet stop, they led us directly to the washrooms and advised us to take matters in hand first. I thought that was a nice touch.

We were then shepherded onto the bus for a ride that was just long enough to send a drunk and stuffed football team to sleep. When we were woken minutes later, we found we were at the stadium. As we swung into the complex, I could see in the distance a team in white taking a group photo on the pitch and I thought it was one of the women's teams gathering before the next round of World Cup matches.

Once the bus had parked, we wandered up to the entrance beneath the main stand following some smiling young volunteers. There we were greeted by Zhujiang beer officials, who presented us with bold white kit sponsored by Zhujiang beer that came out of a big box. It was possibly the most uncomfortable, and certainly the smallest, kit I have ever worn: the shirt restricted most vertical arm movement and made it hard to breathe and run at the same time. The shorts left nothing to the imagination and the socks were so stiff they could have been given directly to people with broken legs. At least I had my football boots, so I thought I would be able to play OK. The organizers also gave us small wooden shin pads with painful edges on the inside and then they brought out a big box of plimsols and told us to change into them because football boots weren't allowed. On top of my growing worries about FIFA and women playing football, this was the rule to beat all rules.

Laughing a little hysterically, I asked the official to explain why China had banned football boots and decided to force everyone to wear bedroom slippers instead. Fortunately, he was able to enlighten me. In recent years, many people in China had been injured by people wearing football boots, so it was decided by the CFA that it would be safer if everybody apart from provincial and national teams wore the same soft gym shoes.

I wasn't happy, but the alternative was to miss the game. So, dressed in this absurdly tight, scratchy football kit with Zhujiang on the front and wearing a pair of what felt like ballet shoes, I headed out to the pitch loaded with beer and seafood to be greeted by another thousand cheering beer workers; it was a real day out for them.

The foreigners team was made up of several journalists who wrote about football and one who played it. She was on the Canadian team which had failed to qualify, but had made the trip as a journalist. We combined well in the first half and scored to go ahead, but it became harder to operate as the beer and food took their toll. Half the team, myself included, regurgitated the banquet at half-time, and our drunken stupor was giving way to the realization that we had been cruelly tricked from the very first phone call that morning. This was now a serious matter of principle; we had to win this game.

For most of the second half we were, with our Canadian striker outpacing the Chinese male defence every time I pumped long balls into the corners. That part was OK, but the shirt restriction meant I couldn't move much after I passed it and there was nobody else in support. With fifteen minutes to go, it looked as if we were home when I split the defence, and the Canadian was through on goal. Whistle. I knew it couldn't be offside, because there was a defender on the other edge of the area picking his nose and the keeper was still on his line.

I thought banning football boots was a little cheeky, but what happened next took the prawn crackers. Having blown his whistle, the referee waved the entire Chinese team off the pitch. As they left the field, they were replaced by a team of fresh substitutes. All eleven of them. Amid fevered protests from our side, the referee explained that, since it was a great honour for China to have this match, it was only fair that as many people as possible had a chance to take part. I suppose there is a kind of logic to that, and it is something that I would always remember when having future diplomatic matches in China.

Since none of the members of the new Chinese team had been at the drinking games or the banquet, I figured they had probably slept in and enjoyed a light pasta breakfast before final training. They scored two goals in the closing minutes to win the match and the crowd went wild – China had won with all the odds stacked in their favour.

'Of course', Lucifer told me with an evil glint in his eye, 'if you early rise from bed, not eat breakfast, drink very much beer, eat very much food, wear very small clothes, take very dangerous shoes and only bring one team, you how able in China win friendship match?'

Before I left Guangzhou, I decided I had better buy a pair of regulation gym shoes for myself. Maybe I could show them to UEFA and get a similar ban on football boots instituted on health and safety grounds across Europe – I could make a fortune. Unfortunately, most Chinese shops still operated on the customer-last principle that lies at the heart of Communist retail strategy. When

I finally located a suitable pair, I pointed at the ones in the display cabinet that were my size and asked how much they were.

The first of three assistants itching to help replied with an accusatory grimace, 'Sell finished.'

'No problem, these OK,' I smiled, pointing at the display.

The second assistant then stepped forward and, without uncrossing her arms, said, 'Not sell.'

'Why?' I replied. When the third assistant stepped forward with a dismissive sneer, I sensed a conspiracy.

'Not sell,' she repeated trying to sound irritated, before adding, 'if other person want, then we what do?'

That she couldn't sell them because someone else might later want them was obviously ludicrous, so I responded immediately. 'I want buy now. If you have other person come, you tell them already sell finished, good not good?'

'Not good,' they all replied in harmony.

I could see this was going nowhere, but before leaving I appealed one last time to some deeper sense of logic. 'OK, I know you not sell, but I beg you, this pair shoes, you from counter take out. This way, customers know you have no shoes. Fine (or) not fine!'

'Not fine! Not allowed touch counter,' they all said as I beat a hasty retreat.

While big state shops took a little longer to change, restaurants were already on the way and there were also thousands of *xiao-maibu* (seeow my boo) (small sell departments) privately run by families that were open for hundreds of daily items. They were happy to run out and get anything they didn't carry in-store and would wake up at any time of night to serve you. If you wanted the display model that was fine too. It was clear in which direction business in China was going.

•

After returning to Britain from the Women's World Cup, I knew the UK was just too far away from China to build meaningful relations and was taking too long to re-engage with China following Tiananmen Square. It was also clear that the game of football needed some help, especially in China, although I didn't yet know how I might contribute.

Events in Tiananmen Square had deeply affected people in Hong Kong and this was dominating British thoughts at the time. The fear was hardly surprising, given that the colony was set to be handed back to China in just a few years under the deal negotiated by Mrs Thatcher and Deng Xiaoping. Despite the crisis in confidence, Hong Kong still represented the best option for my small company, and I moved there in spring 1992, following Jane, who had now graduated from Leeds. Setting up in my bedroom in a flat shared with Big John from Shanghai and his girlfriend, Julie, I continued to liaise with sponsors and my old friends in Beijing and Shanghai.

The move also provided a good opportunity to get back into playing football under my own name, and John and I soon joined a floating team called Manor United that played seven-a-side at the small concrete stadium pitch in Wanchai. After some months learning again how to deal with the flesh wounds that come with gravelly concrete pitches, I came to see those games as the highlight of my week, a chance to get lost in the game, to forget everything else for a couple of hours. Even the tower blocks disappeared.

Soon I was asked to join a team playing at the old Hong Kong Football Club. The pace of the game was very fast and it was only in the fortieth minute that I announced my debut by meeting a wayward corner with a huge outside-left-foot volley that bent outrageously around the keeper and shaved the head of the defender on the line before hitting the roof of the net. It was the first and about the only time I touched the ball in that game.

Finally I got the sponsorship break I needed when UEFA agents ISL needed help with the 1992 European Championships. Working with a local agent, I secured Jialing motorcycles as the sponsor for the series on CCTV and made enough money to continue for a few months. It wasn't much, but it helped me make friends with Mr Ma Guoli, the wise man in charge of CCTV Sports and, ultimately, the man responsible for making sure the world could watch the 2008 Olympics on TV.

In November 1992, Chinese viewers' interest in football was also excited by their own team's performance, as Team China progressed from the group stages of the Asian Cup in Hiroshima, only falling at the semi-final stages in an excellent 3-2 match against Japan. China might have beaten the United Arab Emirates on penalties to take third, but the latest loss to Japan was a hard pill to swallow.

I didn't really like Hong Kong with its strange Cantonese language and people who were so busy making money there was no time to tell you the time. I didn't really like many of the westerners living in Hong Kong either. Like in Brasil, I found it was playing football that provided the best chance to spend quality time with other people. Once the team got too drunk or sordid, I could leave without anyone remembering.

Unlike in Beijing, where there were thousands immersed in the language and culture and millions of chilled-out locals, in Hong Kong there were stressed locals and thousands of Britons making money while they were young enough to spend it in clubs. Most of them could have woken up in Singapore for all they cared. Out on a couple of the islands a more reasonable form of insanity was to be found, but that was its own kind of hell for long-term residents.

Up in my tiny flat in a nondescript block redeemed only by the little football pitch below it where John and I often played with the local kids, I had to move my foam bed up against the wall to use a desk I had built using adult Meccano and cheap wood board. There, looking out over endless high-rise blocks, I tried to make sense of where I had been and work out how to get out of Hong Kong.

Since launching a media career by behaving like an amateur TV star and teaching journalists to ask basic questions, I had been involved in everything from establishing campus football teams and off-campus parties to looking after outrageous celebrities, family and friends and encountering incredible rules about simple things like football. As my months dragged on, I started attending media and sports conferences and always left wondering why I was in Hong Kong at all. Nobody really knew what was happening and, somehow, all the best things happened much deeper inside China.

Three years after dropping out of university, I had accomplished my main goal of working for myself. I had learned Chinese and managed to develop a way of interacting and negotiating that seemed to work. I had seen deeper insights into the way that Chinese people live and work and I had shared the most intimate relationship of all with a Chinese woman, proving beyond doubt that people are all the same, despite the barriers between us.

I had distributed TV shows for very little money but that were seen by hundreds of millions of people and I had travelled through the middle and all around the coastal edge of China, entertaining local people with my foreign nose and cheeky Chinese answers. Almost without exception, I knew I loved it all, so why was I sitting on the sidelines?

I could wait around in steamy Hong Kong writing about what was happening in China or I could go and make it happen and still write about it. My relationship with Jane wasn't as comfortable as it should have been, and weekends at her small hut on Lantau

Island became strained. In the end, we decided to call it a day. Free from personal ties and with no boss to please, I never doubted that it would all make sense one day and I resolved to head back to Beijing as soon as possible.

Part Two

10

Method in the Multicultural Madness

Large swathes of China and a billion hidden people lie beyond the imagination of the outside world, and, for a long time, the billion people in China had no idea about the rest of us either. But, while that is still true for most of the western world, the Chinese people have learned an awful lot about us, most of it through the media. The ways in which the Party selected and controlled this information flow was intriguing to me, and I had been fascinated ever since I saw myself clowning around on TV as a student.

Although the Chinese government made good progress in extending its propaganda networks through relay stations and, in the 1990s, satellite, there were still a couple of hundred million people who couldn't tune into CCTV coverage of Italian Serie A if they wanted. They didn't have electricity. Still, this left over 800 million who could watch TV, including a few hundred million who lived in cities. Over 200 of these cities established local state broadcasters to complement the provincial state broadcasters already being run at the regional level and the state-owned CCTV at the national level.

The city stations also became interested in European professional football, creating further depth of coverage with extensive rebroadcasts, highlights packages and other feature shows cobbled together from archive materials. In line with the growth of football on TV, state radio joined the fun with new sports shows while thousands of newspapers introduced new columns, supplements and finally stand-alone sports titles.

The potential to educate China about the rest of the world that had first intrigued me was still compelling, but I knew that the rates China paid for foreign programmes were centrally controlled, and that trying to create innovative, challenging television inside China was virtually impossible. Stuck in Hong Kong, I was feeling too distant from the heart of the action in Beijing and when I received a call from Beijing TV's Mr Tiger with news of the upcoming visit of his new president, Mr Fluid, I sensed my chance.

When we met in November 1992, an enthusiastic Mr Fluid told me he wanted me to return with them to Beijing immediately and build the international business of Beijing TV into a major commercial organization by the end of the year. It was ridiculously ambitious, but I started working on these grand ideas. Although CCTV had national coverage, BTV was much more open to adopting international practices, and Mr Fluid and Mr Tiger were suggesting that I take on a much wider brief.

I returned to Beijing in spring 1993 as Beijing was making its first bid for the Olympic Games. Building on my experiences with the Asian Games and CCTV in the late 1980s, a series of articles in trade publications and my work raising sponsorship for international football rights, Mr Fluid secured for me a new role in Chinese broadcasting, not polishing English scripts, but actually building the International Department with Mr Tiger. Given the sensitivity around media in China, it was a huge leap of trust on his part, and I was immensely proud to be given this opportunity.

Like CCTV, BTV had been instructed by the government to add foreign-language services as its contribution to an open Beijing, and this was the first focus of my work. When I first arrived on a fixed-term consultancy agreement, I was put to work on two weekend slots for English programmes, a strand known as *Beijing*

Weekend. I quickly changed the name of the show to *Olympic Weekend* and set about creating mini-strands that would reach out to audiences in a way that CCTV's English service had failed to do since Ms Touch's *Focus* programme was cancelled in 1989.

There was only one problem, and I created it for myself. I suggested that one of the ways BTV could freshen up the shows was by moving on from the idea that foreigners only appeared speaking Chinese in variety shows to letting them present other shows, behave more like journalists and work as reporters alongside their Chinese colleagues. Mr Tiger thought this was an excellent idea and immediately instructed me to be the first foreign presenter. This was not what I expected or wanted, but he told me there was no time to conduct the citywide auditions with which I wanted to launch the new shows. So it was that I was dispatched on my first report for *Olympic Weekend* – covering the visit of an award-winning Finnish women's choir touring Beijing.

With no formal TV journalist experience, I managed to work myself into a state of great agitation as I tried to give an introduction with the choir rehearsing in the background. Added to the sharp TV lights and oppressive heat in the theatre anyway, the fear factor conspired to help me start sweating profusely. Released by the heat and pumped by my nerves, the sweat erupted like a broken dam, forcing the cameraman to jump back from the viewfinder and shake his head at the producer. 'Too shiny,' he said. Somebody kindly produced a tissue and I gratefully stuck it to my forehead and dabbed away. When I removed it, small white patches were left on my face. I couldn't see them, but the cameraman's laughter gave it away.

Having proved to Mr Tiger that I had severe limits as his online talent, I begged him to be allowed to get involved with sports. Luckily he agreed, and the first series he let me produce and present was called *Olympic Dreams*. It concentrated on a subject I felt much more important – discovering and promoting examples of the Olympic spirit among ordinary people in Beijing. Unfortunately, I couldn't find many, as people who 'did sports' were all at sports institutes. As a result, most of the films revolved around the international community and visitors to Beijing.

Among my special features was a profile of one of the world's strongest men, the Finn Riku Kiri. Brought to Beijing to promote his assault on the world title, Riku got quite upset when the Chinese 'strongmen' sent to challenge him were unable to pull the truck and refused to carry their iron briefcases. They were just trying to save face, and Riku was so angry that he picked the briefcases up and ran off with them. I got on well with Riku and his wife, the fifth-strongest woman in the world, and had great fun helping them change money at the local market. Everybody at the market welcomed us, and nobody tried to rip us off when we converted dollars into *renminbi*. Before he left China, the giant Finn lifted me onto his shoulders, so I could end my piece with the line 'This is Rowan reporting for *Olympic Dreams* on top of the world's strongest man'. Mr Tiger chuckled when he censored the piece back at Beijing TV but made sure to tell the Chinese journalists not to mimic such stunts, which would totally undermine the responsibility of the state media to remain calm and on Party message.

Over that summer, BTV let me loose with their camera crews all over Beijing, and it seemed very much like the best job in the world. I was fitting in very well with everyone at BTV and, through one of China's top cinematographers, I also met Beth, a beautiful American student in China for a short-term course, and my faith in women was fully restored.

I also wanted to get football into the series, and one of the features focused on amateur football and, in particular, Peking Strollers FC, the team that I joined on my return. It is impossible for me to remember all the players who didn't pass to me, but Roland from British Airways was the one who always went right with his clearances when I was in acres of space on the left.

Since I had left in 1989, there had been something of a revolution brewing in the foreign amateur football scene in Beijing, and several foreign teams were forming and playing in regular friendlies. The timing was right for the next step, and I was delighted to be involved as grassroots football finally burst out from the foreign community in 1994. The man at the pump was a heavy metal German student called Robert. Building on a similar league in Tokyo, and based in the foreign students' stronghold of Yuyan Xueyuan, the largest campus for foreign students in Beijing, he started the International Friendship Football Club and set up an IFFC league for foreign student and embassy teams as well as local teams such as the Rock Stars. Now renamed Red Star Beijing, they were still just as likely to lose their tempers, and Old Brittle had decided to hang up his boots.

Playing games at universities in the west of Beijing, the IFFC was one of the first times that individual initiative had been seen in the country's football circles for decades. So radical was the move that it soon came to the attention of the Beijing Football Association (BFA) that quite large numbers of people, and certainly more than ten at a time, were meeting to play the game they regulated.

Together with Robert, I went down to the BFA to discuss the registration of the IFFC and to get support for his amateur league. Our argument was simple: football brings together people from all over the world, and nobody should be allowed to stop us. Greeting us at the sixties-style headquarters was the affable competitions manager, Mr Open. He knowingly told us that the BFA had had lots of trouble with amateur football and had cancelled the city's amateur cup because of fighting. The safety of the players and officials was of utmost importance, especially foreign friends. But, he smiled, as long as we were civilized and followed his strong advice that only foreign teams participate, we could have permission for Robert's IFFC to become an 'amateur team' under the BFA. By dubious extension, the IFFC was also 'allowed' to organize its own league and cup competitions. It was a highly symbolic development, bearing all the hallmarks of the game that had taken hold in so many countries around the world a century earlier. It was independent, it was voluntary, it was strictly amateur, it was multinational and multicultural and it needed squads of twenty or more dedicated part-timers to work properly.

The only thing missing was consistently competent referees. Although they were the same ones we used anyway, the BFA insisted they should supply the referees, which cost a bit more. There was also an annual registration fee, making the IFFC a net contributor to government coffers in its efforts to promote the grassroots game.

The league was rudimentary in the early stages, and we found ourselves playing on various dirt pitches of dubious quality dotted around Beijing. Just as Mr Open had suggested, the 'safety' of players and officials was a key concern. At one early edition of the IFFC's mini World Cup played on grass at the Table Tennis Institute, I was relaxing with other members of Beijing Strollers between games when we witnessed a 'safety' incident the likes of which none of us had ever seen before. During an ill-tempered match featuring the Rock Stars, a particularly vicious tackle resulted in the referee pulling out a red card for the offending long-haired rocker. Picking himself off the floor as his opponent lay whimpering, the musician seemed resigned to his fate and started walking off the pitch. Then, without any warning, he snapped. Maybe something was said. Turning, as if to shake a marker, he started sprinting towards the referee. Dumbstruck, the ref just stood there open-mouthed as the hairy rocker released a mighty scream and launched himself at the official, sending him flying to the ground. A second later, the rocker was on his feet again, pummelling the ref on the floor with his hair gyrating as in a guitar solo. It had all happened so fast that nobody else had moved. Before the rocker's teammates could pull him off, the ref had curled up into the foetal position and was pleading with him to stop. As the torrent of blows eased, I could see him twist to reach into his pocket. Twisting again so he was looking right up at his ferocious attacker, he pulled out a card. It was yellow. Satisfied with the referee's 'revised' decision, the rocker flicked his hair over his head and went back to his position on the wing. The ref got up, and the game continued. It was my turn to be dumbfounded.

In many ways, the fledgling IFFC, with its outrageous characters, frequent fights and legendary amateur teams like Fortuna 94, Inter, French L-Equipe, Afrika, Flying Dutchman and BW Korea, looked incredibly similar in shape and form to the last time a bunch of foreign amateurs had started playing football in China.

After going absent without leave for a thousand years, football came back to its ancient home only when the modern game was introduced to the mainland via Hong Kong and Shanghai at the end of the nineteenth century. Unlike golf and tennis, which also travelled to the Far East with the British titled classes, and cricket (which got lost in India), football was the only team game for workers, albeit foreign ones with privilege. According to the selfless operators of China's most patient football website, sinosoc.com, the first documented match using Football Association rules in mainland China was played in Shanghai in 1879, when the Shanghai Athletic Club faced an Engineers XI.

In 1887, exactly 100 years before I first turned up looking for a club and couldn't find one, the amateur players in Shanghai formally established the Shanghai Football Club. While it took German Robert just a couple of years to establish our league in Beijing, the lazy bastards in Shanghai didn't get it together until 1907. What the hell were they playing at for twenty years? The answer is they needed a sponsor. Just as I was able to help develop the IFFC league with timely support from Scottish beer brand Tennents (which got everything else wrong and soon retreated from China), it was the globetrotting whisky magnate and sophisticated social marketer Sir Thomas Dewar who donated the shield for that first league a century ago in Shanghai.

Dewar was one of modern sport's first commercial sponsors and he encouraged and rewarded healthy competition and high performance everywhere he travelled in his kilt. 'Minds', he once remarked, 'are like parachutes: they work best when open.' I wonder what he would have made of Mao Zedong's later assertion that the Chinese people were an open parachute on which anything could be written. In 1898, Dewar had started the Sheriff of London's Charity Shield, laying the foundation for what became known in England as the Community Shield. An annual match between the best professional and amateur teams, it featured the largest trophy in football history, a shield standing six feet tall. Dewar dictated that the proceeds from his Shield match be allocated to worthy causes, helping consolidate one of the most important community principles of football. But, it was already too late for amateurs to play professionals in England, and the increasing dominance of the professional teams led to the series being cancelled in 1905. Dewar, however, persevered, carving out his page in the history of football around the world and kick-starting the game out of the steamy bars of Shanghai.

Although it was initially dominated by the British, other established football drinking nations, led by the Portuguese, soon joined the action. Similar teams and leagues emerged up the coast in the port of Tianjin, in German-conquered Qingdao and in the southern city of Guangzhou. By the 1920s, invaders from several countries had established amateur football teams in these coastal cities, and the leagues started attracting Chinese talent. This led the Nationalist government to include the China Football Association (CFA) as an organ under the China National Amateur Athletic Federation that was established in 1924 in Nanjing. This marked the then Chinese government's formal recognition of football, not just as a sport, but as a significant measure of national standing and a handy political tool. The late restaurateur Ken Lo represented China at tennis in the 1930s and he once told me that the Chinese footballers, tennis players and golfers of his, and earlier, generations were a formidable force in Asia.

As the only team game to gain a foothold in the mainland and firmly rooted among the working classes, it was football that had the most direct impact of any sport on the world view of the generation of young educated Chinese who would later come to rule China. But, crucially, playing football was limited only to young people in universities and colleges and to the Chinese entrepreneur class who were closely involved with the foreign-controlled treaty ports.

With the Japanese invasion and civil war ripping the country apart, the game failed to take root among the masses as it had across Europe and South America. Nevertheless, the major cities continued to produce players, and the Federation, not the CFA, affiliated with the Asian Football Confederation in 1931, leading to China's appearance at the 1936 Berlin Olympics. Of course, the host of that event had his own ideas about how to play the game, and the Shanghai league, which was slowly bringing amateur Chinese and foreign players together, was unable to continue once world war broke out in the Pacific.

As soon as the Second World War ended with Japan's surrender, the ecstatic wealthy residents of Shanghai rushed back to their football pitches, tennis courts and the golf course to celebrate. The football league that resumed in 1946 featured a brilliant mix of Chinese, Asian and European teams, including Eastern, Northeastern, Korean SC, Italiano and, amazingly, Jewish Recreation. However, the euphoria did not last long, with standard Sunday league handbag interruptions quickly degenerating into mass brawls, during which national pride always seemed to be at stake. I hate to judge, but, given my experiences with amateur leagues in the 1990s, Chinese teams must have borne their share of the responsibility back then. However, unlike the 1990s, in the 1940s they had just got rid of the Japanese, and the same bloody big-nose foreigners were still in charge of bits of the country and most of the trade. Surely the disciplinary committee would take that provocation into consideration should they be tried today. Unfortunately, that same sense of injustice is still alive and kicking in the new millennium, when China is fast becoming a superpower. As a result of the mass brawls, the post-war Shanghai mixed league became virtually impossible to organize, and the non-Chinese teams soon left to form their own International Soccer League, taking many of the best Chinese players with them.

Meanwhile, the rest of the world was recovering from the Second World War, and it was decided that the Olympic Games would resume in London in 1948. Football was one of the sports that the failing Nationalist government allowed to prepare for the tournament, but it was facing defeat in the civil war, and the total budget allocated to the whole delegation was just US$25,000. To try to make up the deficit, the Chinese football team played a total of thirty-two warm-up matches during a four-month tour before they arrived in London. This included games in Hong Kong, Saigon, Bangkok, Singapore, Rangoon and Calcutta. To save more money, they took four tons of food with them to the UK. Although they failed to win any medals at the London Olympics and had to borrow money to pay for their return home, the delegation returned to China with fond memories of the welcome they had received in London, including visiting Londoners' homes and a reception at Buckingham Palace.

The following year, impending Communist victory in China caused a stampede of emigration from the westernized cities along the east coast, scattering China's top sporting talent right the way across Asia, Europe and North America.

By September 1993, China's international sports relationships had changed considerably, and Beijing waited with bated *qi* (chee), or breath, as the International Olympic Committee made its decision on the host nation for the 2000 Olympic Games. It was the biggest sporting prize ever dangled in front of Chinese eyes, but was Beijing ready?

Closely involved in the media side of the bid, when the result was due to be announced I was at the Sichuan TV Festival with a delegation from European TV stations and, due to my scheduling error, my parents. In Europe, I would have had to cancel one of these responsibilities, but not in China, where people are more than willing to help out their friends if possible. When I first realized my parents were coming the same week, instead of rescheduling, I rang the organizing committee to ask if, as I was not married, I could bring my parents instead? They said 'yes' and added them to the international awards jury, with VIP tours around Chengdu and to magnificent sites such as the Le Shan Big Buddha.

As we all gathered around the TV to hear the Olympic result, everyone jumped in the air when the IOC announcer said 'Beijing', only to continue with the names of the other competing cities.

When it finally emerged that Sydney, not Beijing, had won I knew there would be despondency at Beijing TV. When I returned, there were more than a few snide remarks about the UK's vote delivered by Princess Anne. It was this vote, it was believed, which tipped the balance. After all, what could you expect from the Commonwealth buddies?

As I explained happily to those who would listen, I had held a personal grudge against Princess Anne since childhood, and the experience had even given me republican tendencies. Perhaps I should explain. When I was very young, she agreed to take a detour through our village on her way to an official function. I remember how excited everybody was meant to be at school; we even had a special lesson during which we made Union Jacks to wave at her. At the appointed time, we all trooped down to the main road and assembled obediently along the pavement holding our flags. What seemed like several hours later, a police convoy came screaming past at 60 miles per hour. Somewhere in the middle was a big black car. I think I spotted the Princess's nose as it flew past. Then we all walked back to school. I remember thinking what a waste of time and, as I recounted the story, it seemed to have resonance with my colleagues at Beijing TV. They were, after all, the people whose job it was to report national fervour when they saw only mild interest or the other way round. Neither were they strangers to having playtime interrupted to mark the visits of senior leaders.

Despite the loss of the Olympics, our attempts to produce more relevant programming and the introduction of fully bilingual shows to extend the audience beyond the English-speaking community resulted in better ratings. It was decided that not only would we continue our work, but it would be expanded to a daily schedule in seven languages. Although there was no scope for football programmes in English, I was invited to join the Beijing TV football team. Organized by the trade union, it had been formed to play in an annual competition scheduled by the Beijing Radio, Film and TV Bureau for all the media units under its control.

Having proved myself in the warm-up sessions and realized that few of the players were much better than me, I was confident of making an impression and turned up for the first match expecting to score goals. On the first weekend, I was told I wasn't allowed to play at all . . . all season. The opposition, Radio Beijing, accused me of being a foreign ringer and refused to take the field, despite the fact that I really was an employee of Beijing TV and their team included a couple of Chinese ringers of their own, a typical ploy used by Chinese amateur teams at all levels to gain an unfair advantage.

Of course, Beijing TV was on my side, and by the following season the problems had been ironed out and I was cleared to play in line with my honest claim to amateur status. I didn't play the first week either. Over the intervening years, I had forgotten that the CFA had banned football boots from amateur competition. Nobody in the foreigners' games ever complained, but now I was again being offered someone else's gym shoes to wear. This time, my anger was exacerbated by the fact that I didn't even have studs, but a pair of black Reeboks that I used for five-a-side and that were also OK for grass in dry conditions. I refused to take the field.

Like all the other modern rules of Chinese football, the ban on boots was made of bamboo and so could be bent in all directions without breaking. In a great effort to allow me the tools with which to win the cup, Beijing TV adopted a different tactic, presenting my boots for special clearance well before the final check by the officials. By explaining that they were FIFA-approved for amateur matches, most referees let it slide, and there was nothing to stop me performing as our coach knew I could. I doubt any money changed hands, but if a couple of steamed dumplings found their way into the ref's pocket, they got me cheap. In the first match, I was withdrawn at half-time, having scored five – a left-foot curler, a right-foot curler then a header followed by right and left volleys. And so it continued through the rest of the rounds as Beijing TV swept to a victory against pre-tournament favourites Beijing Audio-Visual Company. I scored so many goals; it was a record that could be equalled only in legends or against even weaker opposition.

With my loyalty to Beijing TV secured on the field with the state media cup, my official appointment as the first foreign expert and the official birth of *Beijing Bilingual* in January 1994 followed. This provided me with the chance to create several new shows and work my way deeper inside a system which I found was run by people very like myself, people who wanted to move forward and were open to learning. As I introduced western ideas, so they told me about Chinese ways. While I still looked different from most of my friends there, very quickly I started losing the feeling that I was an outsider. Playing football regularly with the BTV team and appearing on various shows, I was soon accepted as a colleague, our shared experiences at work bonding us in ways that made my 'foreigner' status increasingly irrelevant.

Apart from the friendships that grew each day we shared the challenges of producing new content, this experience of working in China, for the state, in the most sensitive part of the Party apparatus, also gave me an unusually prominent public role helping to shape the cultural messages reaching the capital city through television, the most important weapon in the late twentieth-century propagandist's armoury.

Our early successes included *Musicmakers*, the first MTV-style show on Chinese TV. That show finally evolved into a cooperation with the USA's MTV when it was finally allowed in by the Chinese government, but much of the international content for the early shows came from the *UK Chart Show* bought from my friend Adam at Yorkshire TV, part of the ITV network in the UK. Although the show was cleared for broadcast to children in Britain on Saturday mornings, only a fraction of the videos passed Party censorship scrutiny in Beijing. In fact, when we started the show, designed to introduce modern music culture in all its wonderful forms, we were not allowed to show people with long or coloured hair or messy clothes, big crowds at concerts, suggestive dancers or disco, bar or night-club scenes. Some weeks, there was virtually nothing useable. It was clear how careful our efforts needed to be to remain within acceptable political boundaries and yet there was an unspoken agreement to keep trying. The strategy for moving forward was a matter not so much of taking small steps, but shuffling sideways then forward in a series of imperceptible movements. With 'below the radar' stealth, we slowly pushed out the parameters.

Another such show was *English Bridge* (and later the Chinese version *Bridge*), the first talk show to bring foreign and Chinese studio audiences together to discuss social issues. These shows pushed the boundaries of what could be discussed openly, helping people think in new ways. Among the memorable topics that excited strong public debate and an official Party warning was 'Payment by instalments: good or not good?', a question we posed when hire-purchase was first introduced to China. In that episode, elder Chinese argued that they would not purchase anything until they could pay for it in full, while many foreigners suggested that we should enjoy material wealth now by paying in instalments. As always in such public debates, younger Chinese participants were conflicted by their duty to their elders and the enticing 'borrow to enjoy now' concepts of the capitalist West.

Such shows revealed big differences across generations and put us at the leading edge of what was permissible on state television.

In order to continue addressing such hot social topics, we had to mix the schedule with softer cultural subjects like 'How do you do?', which looked at the different ways people greet each other around the world. In that episode, the less than tactile Chinese audience learned that in several cultures protocol required men to kiss and embrace other men. An Arabian guest revealed that there was no contact at all between unmarried men and women in his culture. As a shy but polite Englishman, I explained that I preferred to shake hands with other men and, possibly, air kiss a known-to-be-friendly woman – but never the other way round. The Chinese audience seemed to think handshakes all round was the correct protocol.

Apart from challenging the censors with cultural contrasts and pop music, BTV also gave me the opportunity to produce and present my own regular weekly show. It was the first time a big-nose foreigner had been given such responsibility inside the state TV system, and, after a lot of thought about various genres, I went for news. As I had first seen at CCTV, news in China is manufactured by the state and distributed by the state media, so there was below-zero chance I would be allowed to do hard news stories. International business, however, was a branch of the news still largely unexplored in depth and it would provide excellent opportunities to meet with potential sponsors.

BTV President Fluid was fully behind me, and, when *Bilingual Business Report* launched in early 1994, it was the first show in Beijing to follow China's rapidly expanding international business exchanges from both sides of the story. While I interviewed senior leaders from the foreign side in major deals, my Chinese reporter, pen name Robert Pearson, got the lowdown from the Chinese side. I was quite happy doing interviews, but I absolutely hated the studio work. With no teleprompter, I found it impossible to remember the lines I had written and I have never approved enough of my own appearance to spend the time required of people constantly in the public eye. As a result, my performances were uniquely wooden and unnatural, while my hair went from very short to very long over a number of consecutive episodes, before suddenly becoming very short again. In addition, so strange-looking are foreigners that it is still a recurring feature of Chinese TV not to give us much make-up. The overall effect certainly wasn't *Newsnight*, but given the paucity of in-house productions, I broadcast to 30 million potential viewers at primetime on Friday with three repeats over the weekend, including Saturday night primetime. The show also managed several big interviews with leaders from Fortune 500 companies, including Bill Gates.

Soon I was creating new segments to handle the growing number of foreign brands offering sponsorship after their bosses were featured on the show. Among these was *Auto Test*, launched with Shell. It involved me and other reporters travelling miles out to the Beijing test track to put the latest imported models through their paces. Since our sponsor's product was used by all cars, if I didn't like them, I said so. The response was immediate, and soon we were inundated with offers from foreign car manufacturers and their PR agencies. I am not into cars, but money talked at the top, and I was instructed to expand the amount of airtime devoted to that industry. I turned *Auto Test* into *Auto Express* and started to lose interest.

Finally, we cut a deal with an outside production company who paid BTV good money to take over the segment. *Auto Express* was still on the show, but it was off my hands. The original business news and feature section continued in line with my own quest to learn as much as possible about business in China. I produced a series of industry features in which I asked the same set of questions to the heads of several companies in the same sector. It was fun reviewing their answers, realizing that nobody knew what was going on, and then showing the public the results.

Without thinking, I also started getting involved in areas that I would have been better off ignoring completely. Although company deals were fair game, government involvement in bilateral trade drifted me into choppy political waters. At a China–EU press conference I watched as China's fierce minister of trade, Madame Wu Yi, brilliantly accused EU Commissioner Leon Brittan of being British, not European, on the question of Hong Kong's return. I thought it would be a very good idea to interview him.

There was such a small foreign community in Beijing that it was easy to call up my friend Alice at the European Commission delegation and schedule a time to conduct the interview. Very kindly, the ambassador agreed to let me use his office at the embassy. By chance, my old friend Paul was visiting and, since he was a cameraman who had worked with BBC and ITN, I invited him to come along and help organize the shoot. Along with cameraman Wang, we jumped in a car and made our way across town.

At the embassy, we were escorted into the office to set up the camera and lights. Immediately, Paul went into action, totally rearranging one corner of the room to suit our requirements. Wang, who was more used to a point-and-shoot model, was shocked, but no package I ever did for BTV was framed so well.

Happy with our effort, we returned to the editing suite, and the interview was broadcast the following week with no complications. Emboldened by this success at ministerial level, I didn't worry too much when the Israeli embassy called to say their minister of trade would be available for an interview during an upcoming visit and suggested a time. The repercussions were immediate. When the Israeli embassy provided the Chinese Ministry of Foreign Affairs with the minister's proposed trip schedule, one appointment in particular leaped out at them: Thursday, 3 p.m., interview with Beijing TV. That didn't look right. In fact, it broke every rule in the book. What the f**k was

Beijing TV doing? They knew the score, and it certainly didn't include interviewing foreign government ministers. In fact, Beijing TV would never do any interview with a foreign official unless expressly requested to do so by the Foreign Affairs Department at the correct level. But, there it was in black and white – from the Israelis! The Foreign Affairs Ministry called the Beijing Municipal Government. The Beijing Municipal Government called the Beijing TV president's office. The president called the chief editor. The chief editor called the director of the International Department. The director called me. They had found their culprit and neutralized my interview without delay. Who else could it possibly have been?

The following Monday, I was instructed to attend the departmental political briefing, a weekly event that I had previously been excused as a foreign atheist with no political affiliations. It was a self-criticism session, and I stood up to acknowledge the grave mistake I had made as the rest of my colleagues giggled under their breaths. I promised never to do it again and repeated the correct procedures for interviews with foreign government officials. Don't do them.

Satisfied that it was an unforced error on my part rather than a direct plot to undermine the government, the director started the reverse process of explanation with a report into the incident and my subsequent penance. The report was passed up the system until it arrived back at the Foreign Ministry, and all was well again. Just like self-criticisms at university, I looked at the process as a welcome learning experience.

As in the late 1980s, Josh and I were still into the party scene and we were always on the look-out for better venues. We had visited the little Friendship Store in the Sanlitun area back in 1988 as a possible place to expand operations into the more lucrative embassy district, and the current manager, Mr Find, had since turned it into an English pub called the Poachers Inn. Mr Find had been involved in China's early international trade activities in the 1980s and had travelled to the UK. There he fell in love with the English pub and, years later, having abandoned the pressure of trading for a quieter life in Beijing, he set up the Poachers Inn and was looking for foreign friends to fill it.

I found the place again while frantically searching for a bar in which to watch the 1993 FA Cup final with Big John. At that time in Beijing there were hundreds of little bars with TV sets, but without fail every one was tuned to karaoke and designed for illicit canoodling in little booths. When we arrived during the first half, the Poachers Inn had pirated scarves of English football clubs on its exposed wooden beams, including West Ham, and even a wicked old barman called Lao Li, who grumbled perpetually about life as he poured the pints.

After we had found Mr Find, which wasn't hard, as he stands well over six feet tall and is shaven-headed, we decided this was the place. With competition only from boring hotel discos and karaoke handjob bars, the Poachers flopped entirely when nobody believed the free beer offer the first night of our cooperative launch. The few who did turn up found an empty hall that looked like a peasant birthday party that had finished. The solution was to actually hold a big birthday party for Josh, who had more friends than anyone in Beijing, and our friend Barbara. That did the trick, and an entire era of low-cost international entertainment was launched. The Poachers Inn was an institution, one of the first bars to open in Sanlitun and the only dance hall to remain open consistently through a period when bar openings were most often followed by bar closings, as the owners fell foul of one government department or the other. As I could not commit to running the Poachers, I did not join Josh in entering a business relationship to share the profits with Mr Find and I was more than happy clinging to my role as unofficial chairman, with no formal duties and a permanent drink ready at the bar.

For a free and single young person in his twenties, it was the perfect life. Thursday to Saturday evenings hanging out at the best party in town with Mr Find and Josh's partners, Alex and Nick, and the rest of the week playing football with both Chinese and foreign teams and reporting on various interesting happenings, including the opening of the Poachers. Even better, I was able to write about the media developments I was helping to create for a couple of trade papers. No longer did I need to cut out the *China Daily*.

After some time, my onscreen work with Beijing TV had so exposed me to the poor public that Mr Fluid and the other powers that be considered me safe enough to be let loose on live TV, doing something that for me would provide the best TV experience of all.

11

The Football Pundits

The FA Cup final was a show I had watched faithfully as a student when Wimbledon had beaten Liverpool in 1988 and again when Liverpool beat Everton on the night Beijing imposed martial law in 1989. It was an introduction to the BTV Sports Department, broadcasters of the FA Cup, that led me most directly into the life of struggle that befalls anyone who cares about football too much in China. BTV's English football presenter, Mr Song, who also played in goal for the BTV team, suggested that I appear as a guest on his weekly highlights show as an introduction to possible live broadcasts. At last, it was a chance for a simple fan with no football qualifications to contribute to the public football debate in a way that *Match of the Day* would quite rightly never have allowed.

I was thrown in at the deep end for a casual supporter with Queens Park Rangers versus Norwich in 1993, and I found it very hard to contribute much. For example, I don't remember the score. The first problem was that I was reading the game in English. By the time I came up with the appropriate Chinese comment, the incident was gone. It sounds stupid when you miss the play, so I kept my mouth shut. That's not ideal either.

My second problem was also language-related. Since Chinese has no alphabet, the only way foreign names can be rendered is by assigning them Chinese characters that approximate to either the sound or the meaning. So, for example, in Chinese, Liverpool is known as *Li-Wu-Pu* (lee-woo-poo) and Newcastle as *Niu-Ka* (new car). Those are the easy ones. After a little time, most of them became familiar, even ones translated according to meaning that sounded completely different. Here is a small selection from my rather warped crib sheet of English clubs:

Arsenal	Pander to Multiple Payments
Aston Villa	Tie Up, Drag Out
Bolton	Gamble That Stopped
Chelsea	Cut That West
Fulham	Wealthy Force Nanny
Liverpool	Profitable Thing Riverside
Manchester United	Graceful United
Newcastle	Cow Card Ugly
Reading	Thunderous (Meat) Cubes
Sheffield United	Thanks Humble United
Spurs	Crazy Irritation
Watford	Irrigation Special Blessing
Wigan	Hold Together Ridge

It wasn't just the teams; every single player, substitute, match and club official, all the VIPs, the stands, even the grounds must have Chinese names as well. Remembering them was an impossible project.

In normal circumstances, the state-owned Xinhua News Agency decides the official names. So, if you, or your team, have ever made the news in China, you already have official Chinese names. Just don't ask me what they are. These days, you can go to mychinaname.com, run by a charming man called Florian from Germany who is trying to reclaim the right for all of us to choose our own names in Chinese. His first success was to change the Chinese names of the 2007 Women's World Cup-winning German team.

My third problem with football commentary in Chinese was

still language-related and concerned the translation of common football phrases, never an easy thing. One of my favourite throw-away lines is, 'He'll never score with a haircut like that', a colourful observation that illustrates what has just happened (he's messed up) and reflects his lack of skill and fashion sense all in one. Unfortunately, in Chinese it can come across like it sounds – his haircut makes it impossible for him to score. There are several such gems, often loaded with irony and sarcasm in English, that take on a different meaning in Chinese, but I went ahead and gave them a go anyway. And so it was that 'It's a game of two halves' entered the Chinese football lexicon.

Unlike in many countries, most matches on Chinese TV are commentated by the team in the studio, and it has only been on rare occasions that we have been able to commentate live from the ground. Except for ad breaks, this means being on 'live' audio for 120 minutes, or even longer if the match goes to extra-time and penalties. This can get very tiring, and it was sometimes necessary to leave the studio several times to clear one's throat.

As soon as I started doing the show regularly, I realized that the audience for football was much wider and more diverse than my English-based business show and more and happier people wanted to engage me in conversation on the street. Except when I was particularly tired, I welcomed these approaches and was pleased to offer my predictions for the coming round of matches. I always asked the fans whether they played football themselves and, with every negative response, I would admonish them. If they claimed they were too busy, I told them that the busier you are, the more important relaxing through football becomes. If they claimed they were too old, I told them we had players over fifty playing in our team.

After a couple of seasons, other football-loving foreigners who spoke Chinese started asking if they could also realize a lifetime's dream and commentate on their favourite club on TV. Following my lead, they all gave their pet phrases a run out at one time or another. Of all our guests, none was more loved by the audience than Calum, a Scottish journalist and Nottingham Forest supporter who once provoked the wrath of the Scottish Nationalist Party by commentating on the Scottish Cup final in a poorly accessorized kilt. His two favourite catchphrases were 'He is over the moon' and 'He must feel as sick as a parrot', phrases that are still confusing people today.

The most efficient guest in terms of analysis was my old Leeds classmate Barry, who often travelled up to Beijing on business from his base in Shanghai. Not a convinced football fan, he called me one weekend to see what I was doing that night. I said I was going to watch Chelsea v. Liverpool with some friends, and we agreed to meet. At the TV studio, I brushed away his charges of trickery, and we agreed with Song that we would both do the live show. In line with Chinese entertainment values, it was decided that, as I was from London, I would take a Chelsea position, which meant that Barry, who was from Birmingham, would be a Liverpool fan.

During the opening segment, it all went well. Although Barry declined to make any comments ahead of the game, he did offer 'Liverpool, 2-0' as his match prediction when pushed by Song. Sure enough, Liverpool took full control and moved into a comfortable 2-0 lead. However, Barry was struggling with the speed of the action, as I had done on my first outing, and declined to speak a single word during the first half. When the show returned to the studio at half-time, Song turned to Barry to congratulate him on his team's performance and his earlier prediction. 'You should very happy,' he said. 'You said 2-0, your prediction very accurate.'

Looking a little glum, Barry then shocked Song, the audience at home and me, by making only his second comment of the match. 'Liverpool finished. Chelsea win 4-2.' Again, he lowered his head and declined to elaborate further. Unbelievably, we sat and watched as Chelsea first reversed the deficit and then went into the lead, before scoring again to run out 4-2 winners. Again, the whole of the second half was not troubled by a single Barry comment.

At the end of the game, it came back to the studio, and once again Song turned to him. Shaking his head, he said, 'You are prediction champion,' and went on to explain to the viewers how only true fans can sense the way a match is going to go in the first and the second half. Barry remained straight-faced throughout and spoke he not a word. At the end, he just said, 'Thank thank you,' and left the studio for the first and last time. Surely, never in the history of live TV sports commentary has a studio guest so accurately and so succinctly shared his reading of the coming drama without needlessly interrupting it with obvious comments.

Another interesting development in the mid-1990s was the introduction of live phone-ins, providing Chinese fans with a chance to give their views about the match and, quite often, the commentators. I frequently incurred the mock wrath of fans of the big clubs by suggesting that neutral supporters should always support the underdog. One night, Song went to the phone lines for comment at half-time, and I heard a voice I recognized. It was my American friend Chris, otherwise known as Superbird. He was watching rugby with some other friends and they had flicked over at half-time to see how I was getting on. The phone number was there on the screen, so he gave me a call, and we had a ridiculous conversation, mainly because he didn't know who was playing. After promising to catch up later, we said goodbye, and a bemused Song and I carried on with the show. However, somewhere in Beijing, other people were less than amused as it dawned on them that a foreigner in the studio was talking on live TV with another foreigner in an unknown location. Live phone-ins were conspicuous by their absence the following season, and SMS messages would ultimately allow presenters to filter audience feedback completely.

With every week promising new drama, football commentary was fun, and the positive shouts of encouragement I started getting from people on the street made it even easier to get to know the real people behind the inscrutable masks. Another door was opened, and football was the key. I was also far more relaxed in the football studio than the business studio, so I finally ditched *Bilingual Business Report* (and my interest in post-production) and devoted my part-time on-screen career to adding partisan commentary and analysis of my favourite game on one of the most popular shows.

Sport was the driver of commercial sponsorship, and this was another key part of my work with BTV that I enjoyed immensely. During the mid-1990s, my American partner, John, and I introduced several new programmes and sponsors to the schedules. Just as I had developed *Auto Express* for car buyers, so we launched *Michelin Motorsports World*, the first dedicated motorsports magazine show for petrolheads.

Not entirely by coincidence, it was also about this time that I suggested to Beijing TV that they should give me a car like everyone else. That proved harder. The main problem was that foreigners from embassies and foreign-invested companies drove cars with black number plates, while Chinese people drove cars with blue number plates. Since Beijing TV was not allowed black number plates, I was a driver without a car. No car, no licence; no licence, no car. After several requests were turned down, it was finally agreed that the matter would be raised at the annual banquet marking Beijing TV's cooperation with the Transport Police on the highly rated daily production *Traffic News*. I filled in the relevant documents, and they were placed in an open envelope. Once the leaders were happily engaged in the dinner, the matter was quietly raised, and the chief of police wrote 'agreed' on the papers followed by his signature. The following week, the envelope worked its way back to our department, and Mr Tiger said he would appoint somebody to take it to the police station. 'I go,' I said, conscious that the various annual procedures that they had to do for me were annoying additions to their jobs. Having finally made it to the correct police station, I handed over my envelope to the officer behind the counter. Although he looked primed to issue the administrative 'no' before asking my business, he took it and read the message.

'No way do,' he said, handing back the envelope.

'You what meaning?' I asked, still confident that the signature would do the trick.

'Leader too high,' he replied, 'I not have power (enough) approve. You go opposite, look for Zhang Director.'

Sometimes, it was possible to have a permission note from a leader so important that the others wouldn't believe it. Having received reconfirmation from Director Zhang, I returned to the desk officer. He was deeply unhappy that he was giving me a licence and explained that I was several stamps away from the full complement. For a start, my work unit didn't have a licence for black-plate cars. That is as may have been, but I walked out with my Chinese driving licence, and it was not long before I was introduced to the bog-standard red Volkswagen Jetta that was being churned out by the Sino-German joint-venture for the people to drive.

I drove in Beijing for several years before it became intolerable and I finally realized I had the dishonourable distinction of helping fuel the car explosion through my TV shows. Luckily, I was only once involved in a crash while behind the wheel. Since nobody was injured and the taxi driver who hit me was more embarrassed than the eight singing footballers in my car at the time, it need not be explored here.

If you were a foreigner in a black-plate car, traffic police in Beijing were basically friends. If you were a foreigner in a black-plate car with the character for 'embassy' on it, the traffic police were so friendly that they automatically turned in the opposite direction whenever you did an illegal high-speed manoeuvre. In my normal blue-plate car, which had its side and back windows blacked out by a friend at BTV who borrowed it for a couple of weeks to cavort with his lover, I could not easily be identified as a foreigner. In fact, the combination of blue plate and cheap car suggested to guards at the diplomatic compounds that I was actually a national minority from Xinjiang, and I was refused entry on more than one occasion.

I was also regularly stopped at police night checks on the Xizhimen bridge. Once it had been established that I was the foreigner from the football show on TV, the frequency of the stops increased, and I became a bit of entertainment for very friendly policemen on a boring Saturday night. Despite the frustration, I usually enjoyed these exchanges, as they were genuinely interested in talking football.

On the rare occasion that I broke the traffic laws, the policeman would normally see that I was foreign and let it slide. Occasionally they couldn't. Once, as I was trying to go left when not allowed, I was faced by a bank of angry cyclists. The policeman was standing right there and he could hardly ignore my breaching of the rules in front of so many witnesses. Following his instructions, I pulled over and took my driving licence and my car papers across all the traffic to the middle of the junction, where he was now standing on his small podium. He looked down at me, and I smiled up at him. Then he stepped off his pedestal and smartly saluted me. As police are servants of the people, this is common practice in China and should be immediately introduced in Britain. He then took my documents and, studying them only briefly, he looked at me again. I continued my smile.

'You understand (or) not understand Chinese?' he offered me by way of introduction.

As I thought about my answer, I realized there were several. I could answer that I understood Chinese well and then try and plead my case as an ignorant and stupid alien. I could say I understood a little and try to make him laugh at my funny intonation. Finally, I could pretend not to understand at all. I really wasn't sure which strategy to adopt so I decided to ask him.

'I pretend not understand, OK?' I said in my best local accent and looked at him for genuine advice.

'Of course, not can pretend!' he replied, the huge grin on his face betraying the impossibility of his own situation. Only once did a policeman not wave me away, but he did when I really did pretend not to understand at all.

While usually enjoying the privilege of this special status, only a few weeks later I was playing devil's advocate and supporting the common driver. I had always wondered how government officials and the police could justify driving flashy imported cars, and one Saturday afternoon I was driving along the third ring road and came up behind a black government Mercedes. There wasn't much traffic, and, as I moved past it, I noticed that there was a man driving and a young boy sitting next to him. It was probably his son, and they were going for a weekend drive. A couple of miles further up the road, I saw in my rear-view mirror that the same car was now speeding up behind me, flashing its lights, and I wondered what critical government business this father and son team had suddenly discovered. Like any decent British driver, I did not take kindly to people abusing their powers on the road and I refused to move into the inside lane. The Merc then started hooting and using swaying movements to indicate its intense interest in getting past me. A siren started. No way, you can only use your official status in times of professional emergency, not when you are bored or want to show off to your son. I continued to refuse to bow to his pressure. As we exited the third ring road, he sped around my inside and raced to the traffic lights, where he screeched to a halt across the road. Before I had come to a stop in front of his car, he had already jumped out and was shouting at me.

Several cyclists and pedestrians immediately sensed an incident and gathered round. It was only when I got out that they realized I was a foreigner, which made the intrigue even more compelling. The man didn't seem to care and ranted and raved about his importance, about the absolute requirement for everyone to get out the way the minute he applied his siren. I listened calmly, and when he had almost shouted himself out, I asked for the chance to respond. As I had found out many times before, if there is one wonderful thing about a Chinese crowd in a petty argument, it is that they often genuinely consider the respective cases and side with the innocent party.

'In my country,' I said, 'the people most not like is leaders use government cars do private business! I ask you, today afternoon, you and your son have what urgent business require you interrupt people's normal lives?'

When the crowd saw he had no answer, they looked at each other, then burst into rounds of applause and shouts of 'Foreigner speaks well.' Seeing that he had lost the popular vote, the man stormed off back to his car, slammed the door and sped away. It might have been a small victory, but it also showed my growing confidence that, if I always made sure to 'speak with reason', there was no argument that could not be won with the support of the people.

Apart from teaching Chinese viewers how to drive very fast in our Michelin show, John and I also worked to improve Chinese coverage of great sporting events, including securing sponsorship to pay for live commentary teams. Our first success came with Wimbledon tennis, and live commentary from the Centre Court of the world's premiere tournament became a feature of regional TV coverage.

I had been a keen tennis player in my youth and even worked one summer holiday as a junior instructor. Because of this, BTV's commentator, Wang Yi, tempted me to take the microphone at Wimbledon, but analysing a tennis match requires a very different vocabulary, focusing on psychology, mental pressures and inner emotions. Talking about haircuts wasn't as funny. It was football, with its larger-than-life range of characters and its history and fierce rivalries, that interested me more.

Finally, in 1995, I managed to organize the sponsorship required to travel to the UK with crews from Beijing TV, Oriental TV (Shanghai) and Guangdong TV. The plan was to produce a special series of in-depth features, to do China's first live on-location commentaries of the FA Cup semi-finals and to meet with the Arsenal team ahead of its historic visit to Beijing that summer.

There is a law that says whenever you lead a group of people into interesting places unknown, they will wander off. It is the same with Chinese TV crews, and I had three of them in tow when the first ones got lost at Heathrow airport. After a frantic search, we were all transferred successfully to two huge apartments close to Green Park, where we settled in for a two-week stay investigating the great, the good and the ugly underbelly of English football for an expectant audience back in China.

After banging on during live matches about football culture, this was my first chance to show the game that lay behind the screen, and my UK partners, Airtime, had helped design a schedule that ensured we covered everything from the England team to the Sunday leagues. Led by the senior producer Old Sauce, we were a tightly knit group of Chinese football explorers into the unknown.

The first episode in our five-part series was on the England team, led by coach Terry Venables, the first person to have played for every level of the national team. It was a promising time: the following year England would be hosting the European Championships as modern football finally came home. We travelled to Bisham Abbey to drop in on an England training session for the friendly against Uruguay scheduled for the following week. The place was full of British journalists doing a normal day's work, so our group of eight Chinese and a Londoner who needed a haircut stood out like a red scarf on the blue side of town.

Our England piece also included a day at Wembley, taking in the above-mentioned friendly. Although we had permission, it wasn't easy getting three ancient broadcast cameras into the stadium that night. When one of the cameramen decided to get some quick shots of the players warming up, his little red light sparked fury from the representative of the rights holders.

As the players plodded their way through a tedious 0-0 draw, one of the friendly stewards that we had interviewed earlier about volunteers at football matches came over to stand next to our seats and leaned forward.

'He's a right tosser!' he shouted over the crowd's whistles.

'I'm sorry,' I replied, 'what did you say?'

'John Barnes,' he said, 'he's a right tosser,' before standing up and shouting 'Tosser' again, much louder, as Barnes once more failed to make progress. The rest of my Chinese team was now intrigued by my conversation and asked me to explain.

'If a player play very bad, fans call him "tosser"!' I said, and the message was passed along the line. To the great delight of the steward, a couple of our team indicated their agreement by shouting

'Tosser' a few times of their own towards the pitch. From that day on, the elite members of our group still affectionately refer to each other as 'tosser', an affable term of abuse between friends that not every culture in the world could tolerate.

Next on our list of football stories was Manchester United. We were meant to arrive in time to film the players training and interview Dr Ferguson, but the driver got lost and we were late. When we finally arrived, all the players and the manager had gone home. The crew complained that the driver was a real 'tosser', but I tried to get them to focus on the club – the real story we were there to follow.

Hugely successful and very profitable, Manchester United was as big as it got in England when it came to the club model. From the very first moment, you knew you were somewhere special. We interviewed Mr Edwards, the chairman, in one of the executive boxes overlooking the pitch and walked the hallowed turf with the head groundsman. At the megastore, we were shown round by a wonderful old man in a club blazer who had been at the club for many years. The whole operation was inspiring in a commercial kind of way, and the Chinese group was blown away by the awesome range of products on sale. Much memorabilia was acquired, some of it made in China, but special for having been purchased on site.

Once the national team and top club reports were filmed, it was time to travel further down the football pyramid. Millwall in London was the perfect place to go. Our interview with veteran chairman Reg Burr was illuminating, and his commitment to the club made a real impression on Old Sauce and the others who came on that shoot. We followed club staff as they went out into the community to bring football to schools with kids who spoke over thirty different languages. It showed what a positive impact football could have away from the bright lights. It was our favourite episode, the one that we felt should have most resonance in China, where there was no link at all.

On one of the weekends we spent in the UK, I took the production teams to Clapham Common in south London to meet up with some of my English friends and have a friendly kick-around. After the game, Old Sauce kindly invited everyone for a traditional drink of beer, but we had to tell him England had a very strict policy. On Sundays, it was even stricter, and all the famous pubs were closed until seven o'clock in the evening. All my English friends felt very ashamed that we could not invite our guests for a beer and cursed the government for having this policy.

The physical highlight of our investigative tour came at the Sunday league match we were invited to attend by the FA rep helping with our trip. It was classic stuff, played on a sloping, muddy pitch close to a wooden clubhouse next to a row of houses. Even better, Song, who had given up as goalkeeper for the Beijing TV team, was invited to play in goal. He was even given Peter Shilton's England jersey to wear during the match and told that if he kept a clean sheet, he could keep the jersey, a prize above all others on that trip.

Song wasn't the best goalie even with his glasses on, but without them, he was hopeless. Amazingly, he still hadn't conceded by half-time, and his team was even in the lead. I sincerely doubted his luck could continue, but I blinked again as the opposition hit the post and then hit Song, the ball ricocheting for a corner. Finally, a foul in the area led to a penalty, and I feared his dream shirt would be returning to its owner. As he stood there, wearing Shilton's massive shirt and a pair of equally large gloves, I could see him squinting to try and bring the ball into focus. The striker started his run-up and launched his foot at the ball. Song just stood there absolutely still. He hadn't seen the ball move at all. It had flown right over the top of the goal and landed in a nearby garden.

Turning to pick the ball out of the net, he was suddenly surrounded by his cheering teammates, the most unlikely hero. The
match was won easily without a single goal conceded, and the shirt
was his to keep. But, while his exploits had been filmed, I doubted
how much natural sound we would be able to use. From the start
to the end, the most frequently heard sound was 'fuck'. Ranging
from the admiring 'You fucking beauty' when a teammate scored,
to the angry 'You fucking wanker' when somebody dived, the full
range of nuances was represented during that game. 'Get fucking
back,' the captain had shouted at the start and he had finished with
'Great fucking game, lads!'

We had covered the England team but missed the chance to
meet with the Manchester United players, so the crew was still on
the hunt for some big names. We did bump into Steve Bruce at the
FA in Lancaster Gate, but he was there for a disciplinary hearing
and didn't want to be interviewed.

We finished our travels in England at Arsenal, the great English
club that was expected to visit China that summer for an exhibition match against the Beijing Guoan team. While we were filming
Arsenal's impressive junior training programmes, we walked
passed a small cabinet, and inside was a football shirt. Written
across the top were the words 'Come on my old China'. Old Sauce
asked me what the words meant, and Song wanted to know why
they were written on a football shirt in a cabinet at Arsenal.

It took a long time for me to explain that in Cockney rhyming
slang, the word China means 'mate', but we all found this very
interesting, and everyone agreed that Londoners were most wise
in their choice of words. The tour had already brought us much
closer together, and this just made for an even better atmosphere
as we returned to Arsenal at the weekend to meet the players and
watch the game against Norwich.

We were given pitchside access and met with club captain Tony

Adams as the team warmed up for the match. He stopped to give us an interview, and, given the expected match in China, I asked him how much Arsenal knew about the Beijing team. He told me Arsenal had once played in Singapore, so they had a pretty good idea what to expect. Those would turn out to be famous last words, but Arsenal thrashed Norwich that day, creating a new Chinese phrase for our little group. To be 'truly Norwich' was not a compliment.

12

Instant Football Noodles

By the mid-1990s, tens of millions of people in China could provide you with a pretty good list of Europe's major cities based on the names of the football clubs that play there. By contrast, the choice of 'designated football cities' in China is based on political decisions. Just as China's commercial TV industry is said to have launched in 1979 with a single ad placed on Shanghai TV, the symbolic birth of football sponsorship in China came in 1984, when Baiyunshan Pharmaceuticals was announced as the proud sponsor of the Guangzhou football team. The rest of the country followed suit, and hundreds of clubs were formed with the largesse of football-friendly leaders enjoying the benefits of the latest wonderful western concept, the marketing budget. Not for the first time in its football history, China had the chance to start a grassroots revolution, and this one spread like wildfire. But, like fire, it soon burned out. First, the revolution didn't go nearly wide enough before turning inwards again in the search for elite stars. While the nation should have been providing basic football facilities for all, the richer work units simply built private pitches for their new stars, and the poorer ones gave up altogether.

With the fuel of quasi-commercial funding, competition between leading provincial teams hotted up even more. The first CFA Cup was launched in 1984 with the top twelve teams being designated as 'A' teams for the following season. Then, just months before the Heysel stadium disaster forced European, and British, football into a period of deep reflection, China also had to face the horror of needless deaths linked to the game. At the end of a rain-soaked match between the Yunnan team and a visiting Hungarian team in Kunming, a stampede combined with poor management resulted in the death of eight people and injuries to over 100.

It was the strongest football region in China, Liaoning, that first 'jumped into the sea' of private enterprise. In 1988, it was announced in the port of Dalian that the Liaoning government's provincial team was actually – shock horror – a football club, just like the shiny ones in Europe. China held its collective breath, but the central authorities let it pass, and it was so. Not for the first time, a process that had taken several decades in Europe and South America was compressed into just a few years in China. But, following acceptance of the ideological division of professional from amateur and the de facto establishment of commercial clubs, there was one difference – China still had no amateur clubs, no pyramid.

In the 1989–90 season the Liaoning team (now sponsored by Eastern Pharmaceuticals) took part in the Asian Club Championships in Tokyo and emerged as champions, seemingly justifying the moves towards professional clubs. The success at club level continued, with Chinese teams walking away as champions over the first three years of the annual Asian Cup Winners Cup competition established by the CFA at the invitation of the regional AFC.

With new forms of sponsorship in abundance, in 1992 the CFA held a conference near Beijing that was designed to put China on a new route to success. It was announced that the central authorities had given the green light for football to act as an experiment; it was to be released into the market for the first time in Chinese sports history. With the existing provincial league competition cancelled for the National Games, the CFA took the opportunity to run a test event in Guangdong for the top club teams, with similar events in Chongqing and Nanning for the second-level teams. That there was work to be done was only emphasized when the national team failed to make the 1994 World Cup finals, this time losing to Yemen.

Despite that reality check, at a meeting in Chengdu, the minister in charge of sports laid out a ten-year vision for Chinese football. As if there was not enough pressure already, he proposed that China reach the World Cup finals by 1998 and the top sixteen in the world by 2002. To realize this executive order, and with support from soft drinks manufacturer Jianlibao, the CFA decided to kidnap the country's top twenty-two young players and send them into exile in Brasil for five years. Surely that would do the trick.

With the future seemingly taken care of, at the end of 1993 the CFA met again in Dalian and finally laid down the guidelines for a new national league that would enable Chinese football to reach the scale and importance achieved by the major European leagues. This time, the CFA decided it would follow international methods, with clubs receiving a division of the gate receipts and other revenues.

The plan was to release the emerging professional clubs from state control, and the first club to be formally established as a self-governing legal entity was Shanghai Shenhua FC. The model for club ownership was based on Germany, where there are strong examples of corporate ownership of football clubs. However, unlike Bayer, which built an employee football club that grew into the Bayer Leverkeusen we know today, in China the relationship between sponsoring corporations and clubs had very little to do with employees and all to do with a very cosy government–big business agenda. Built from the government squads in the football cities, the best clubs played their home matches at their respective government-owned stadia and were funded through naming sponsorships with major enterprises from that region.

Marlboro cigarettes and International Management Group were also behind the Great Leap Forward-sized plan, and it was announced the clubs would compete in the Marlboro league, which would be covered widely on TV. I have joined many others in calling for the details of that deal to be made public, but they never have, and rumours of excessive commissions continue to this day.

For a short time, the China 'A' league looked OK, with a combined TV audience of nearly 500 million and average attendances topping 20,000. Quite fortunately, the chances of success were boosted by China's decision to introduce a five-day working week. Given the number of people involved, this policy created billions of hours of new leisure time every weekend.

Advertising interest was also high, as big international and domestic brands followed simple logic and flocked to the untested property. Temporarily seduced by the hype, I even persuaded my Peking Strollers teammate Dom at Saatchi & Saatchi to bring his athlete's foot cream client to the party by sponsoring Beijing TV's live coverage of the new league.

The league worked for the first couple of seasons, and Rupert Murdoch was soon seduced. In an attempt to achieve a Sky TV-like hijacking of the Chinese TV market using domestic football as the weapon, Murdoch's newly acquired Star TV network agreed to air exclusive matches on its Asia regional channel. Unfortunately for Star TV, it had not accounted for the strong political lobbying power of the regional TV stations, which were set to lose out, and each local station won back the right to broadcast the matches involving their own local teams. This left Rupert with the regional Asian rights to the Chinese league. What interest, the press speculated, would viewers in any other country have in Chinese domestic football? None.

The establishment of professional clubs in China did open the way for many more of the biggest clubs in world football to make off-season tours, but it was only with the inception of the professional league that fans in Beijing and other cities had even the illusion of home pride to defend. These promotional tours and the blanket TV coverage of European leagues created another great paradox of football in China, the concept of supporting a number of rival teams at the same time, and the practice of swapping favourite clubs on a monthly or seasonal basis. Indeed, so dominant is the serial supporter in China that it is quite rare to find a fan with a real unflinching loyalty to one team – win or lose. I certainly don't want to discount the dedicated fans of certain clubs like AC Milan, Liverpool and Manchester United, but this was the impression I got from talking to many people. The main problem with this situation is that fly-by-night supporters do not build into loyal customers who are guaranteed to keep spending every year, and all football clubs need them.

There are, of course, also some benefits to this approach. First of all, your team will always be winning and, when it stops, you can just choose another one. Likewise, if you like a certain player, you can transfer your club affections as he moves around. Many fans in China will have spent last summer watching the 2008 European Championships, using them to help choose the stars whose clubs they would support over the following year.

After our in-depth feature on Arsenal during our trip to the UK, where we received Tony Adams' insight on Arsenal's preparations for its game against Beijing, the Gunners finally arrived in China ready to defend the English club record of never having lost in China. Even Watford had beaten China and, considering that record, I also fell into the trap of predicting an easy Arsenal victory on live TV.

In the end, the Beijing team repeated its famous 1994 victory over AC Milan by beating Arsenal 2-1, the game memorable for Ian Wright's early departure and goalkeeper David Seaman falling over and breaking his ankle. It left only captain Adams as the hero, and, since the Chinese fans had rarely seen a passionate ninety-minute performance like it before, they rewarded him with a standing ovation. Beijing's wins over AC Milan and Arsenal and the China team's earlier dispatch of Sampdoria and Columbia initiated a period known by Chinese fans as *Gongti Bu Bai* (gong tee boo bye), which means 'Workers Stadium – Unbeatable!' A draw with South Korea's Hyundai Horang-I preserved that record into 1996.

Like the crowd of Zhujiang beer workers who had cheered when two teams of Chinese journalists beat the foreign reporters' team at the Women's World Cup, the crowds at the Workers Stadium were able to willingly suspend their disbelief. They wanted so desperately to believe their team was high-quality, they 'forgot' that the foreign teams were on commercial holidays at the end of tough seasons.

Unhealthy tendencies were also emerging in the domestic game, with petulant players and corruptible referees becoming an increasing feature of the rumour mill building around the China 'A' league. Finally, in October 1995, it spilled out in front of the watching fans and media. In a match between the Sichuan All-stars and the Yanbian Moderns, the Yanbian team complained about unfair refereeing and refused to play properly, losing 6-0 and sparking further riots.

The corruption issues were not properly rooted out, and the introduction of a 'Super Cup' between the winners of the league and the Cup that winter felt like a hollow affair. For a start, where was the charitable spirit of the Community Shield on which it was meant to be based? Sadly, such concerns about the lack of community spirit melted away far too easily as China notched up a 7-1 victory over Macao, a 7-0 win over the Philippines and a 2-0 win over Hong Kong at the Asian Cup qualifiers in January and February 1996.

By the time spring arrived, after just three victories and a draw against visiting foreign teams and wins over some minnows in regional competition, the Beijing public had fully embraced the 'Workers Stadium – Unbeatable' slogan and were preparing for another year of happy team-whipping through the tour season. I was not the only commentator worried that fans were getting carried away, and the coach of the Beijing Guoan team warned publicly that friendly matches were not necessarily good for Chinese teams.

Meanwhile, Manchester United was proving why it was already regarded as the most professional marketing operation in football by not coming to China. Very interested in the market, it was also the most wary and turned down all opportunities to visit on tour. Instead, it sent the merchandising division to follow up on an approach I had made to all the leading clubs on behalf of Beijing TV and its viewers. In return for official prizes, we plastered MUFC merchandise around the studio and ran a Manchester United competition on live coverage of the English Premier League every week, even when it was not featured. Manchester United won the league and Cup double that year, and so the series climaxed with a special studio show, during which the most dedicated fans were presented with their prizes. It cost United some old merchandise, but provided Chinese fans with the first chance to 'touch' a great club.

While United was brand-building through the media, a number of top clubs and national teams were scheduled to visit China in summer 1996. It would turn out to be one of the first times that both ugly sides of Chinese football fans would be laid bare in the Workers Stadium for all to see. The first target of the fanciful belief that China was unbeatable at home was a huge star who had recently won the World Cup.

13

We're Unbeatable, Shabby!

In 1996, the first opposition to come to Beijing for a friendly tour was the Brasilian club Flamengo, a leading club from the nation that had won the 1994 World Cup in the USA. Romario, the World Footballer of the Year that same year, was the star looking to thrill his many Chinese fans. No doubt semi-believing the public hype that they couldn't lose, the Beijing team looked comfortable with the ball, and soon the crowd was heralding each clever touch with the shout '*Niu bi*'(new bee), which translates literally as 'cow's vagina', but is actually the equivalent of 'the dog's bollocks' in vernacular English. Chinese footballers have rarely known such vocal crowd support.

But, at the same time as they were cheering on their own 'unbeatable' team in another match that meant very little to most observers, they were also ready to show their ugly side. I almost thought I was back in Europe, but the chanting was different. The difference was clear when I looked round at the intelligent young lady whom I had convinced to attend the match with me. She was a football match virgin, and it was a highly risky place for a date.

As Beijing again moved into the lead, the shouts of 'Niu bi' for the Chinese players were supplemented by shouts of '*Sha bi*' (shabby) whenever Romario touched the ball. It means 'Stupid c**t'. Luckily she didn't understand, so I ignored it. But the next time Romario got the ball, the whole stadium joined in. There were more than 50,000 people group chanting the most disgusting insult at one of the game's biggest stars. He wasn't even playing that badly. Then the moment I dreaded: she leaned over and asked me what it meant.

'Stupid c**t', I shouted back, shrugging my shoulders. Another potential fan was lost to the game, but why should I lie for them? Cheered on by this ugly support, Beijing beat Flamengo 3-2, and everyone told Romario that *sha bi* meant superstar in Chinese.

Following the dispatch of all-comers in friendlies for nearly two seasons, the international football excitement in Beijing got even hotter that summer. To everyone's surprise, it was announced that the England team we had interviewed in the UK would come to play China in a full international on the eve of the European Championships. Several members of the press in the UK were against the idea of England travelling so far just before a major tournament, especially to play a team that had absolutely nothing in common with the upcoming European opposition. But, while concerns about the state of the pitch filled pages in British newspapers, for China it was the biggest game in modern times.

Not only would England be the strongest national team ever to play in China, but they came with a full senior squad, highly rated players who were not on a summer holiday, but all desperately fighting to impress manager Terry Venables. Given the crowd's growing arrogance, I really hoped England would teach China a lesson, burst the false bubble and force people to understand that, if China was serious about international football at the highest level, there was a long way to go back down the pyramid.

The build-up started the week before England arrived with a special live England TV football quiz show presented by Song and our co-commentator on the English football show, Mr Sole. Along with a 100-strong studio audience, I gladly joined as a special guest with a famous football journalist and a Chinese footballer. The show consisted of a number of questions relating to

England and English football, and the three guests and the studio audience were asked to contribute to each round.

The first question was about Pelé; more specifically it asked whether Pelé had ever played at Wembley. With the other guests divided on the answer, the cameras turned to me. I didn't know, I was born after the 1966 World Cup, but I guessed that he probably didn't play because he was injured and I couldn't recall Brasil visiting England during that famous period for both nations. 'Sorry,' I said, hedging my bets, 'Pelé kicking football time, still not have . . . me.'

Strangely, the crowd dissolved into laughter and gave me a huge round of applause. I wasn't sure why, but it relaxed me. Next, we were asked to look at the screens and we were shown a black-and-white clip of a game from England many decades before and told a little about the heritage of the game. During the match, a donkey walked onto the pitch, and we chuckled as the players tried to push it back off. At the end, Mr Sole asked, 'In this kind situation, referee should do what?'

This time he went to the audience for answers first, and one joker came back with 'Should give donkey red card.' Damn, that was going to be my line. With a little time to think, I was ready when it came round to me. 'I agree that gentleman's answer,' I said, 'but because this is donkey's first offence, should be yellow card.' Once again, the audience creased up. And so it continued through the show, my every comment eliciting whoops of laughter from the audience without me quite knowing why. Maybe everyone was just excited about England coming.

At the end of the show, we were asked our predictions for the big China v. England match. When I called it as I saw it – a clear England win with no chance of a Chinese goal – the audience went silent, and so I quickly added that the result was less important than bringing the two countries closer together. Polite applause.

With such an important match in town, the BTV Sports department was buzzing, and I made sure I was at the heart of the action, even receiving permission to become an accredited Chinese sports journalist, something that would not have been possible without my TV profile. I still carry that pass in my wallet.

Our coverage of the team's visit started at the airport, the first time I had used the VIP wing. Sailing around the normal airport procedures just like in the 1980s, we came directly to the gate where the BA flight was expected and set up the camera. A few minutes after the plane parked, we saw the first passengers coming up the gangway. At the front was Gazza. I knew he was pissed because he was bright red and was being propped up by Bryan Robson. As the group came closer, I moved forward with microphone in hand.

'Gazza, what are your first thoughts in China, got a message for the Chinese fans?'

As he tried to focus on me, he slurred out the words, 'We're only here for the fucking money,' and was dragged off by his teammates.

'He say what?' the producer asked me, noticing my obvious shock.

'Say not clearly, not can use,' I replied, fearing that his comments might still be heard on the report as there would be nobody to translate. It was quite common for TV stations to just make up the Chinese translation of foreigners' comments. Before you complain, I have seen it done the other way round as well.

After his inauspicious start, Gazza had sobered up by the time that he and Venables appeared at the official press conference. Full of confidence and buzzing, he told the Chinese press that he was here to perform on the field, to show the Chinese what it was to be a world-class player at the top of his game.

As I had first learned at CCTV, Chinese journalists are not the right people to ask penetrating and searching questions. In fact, they seldom ask any questions at all. Many are the times I have watched press conferences conclude without a single question being asked. It is embarrassing for the people on the stage, and that's why I always try to ask one. It's also cheap publicity, because questions from foreigners are always given more TV time on the news. For that same reason, some foreign journalists don't like asking questions at Chinese press conferences either. In this case there was a large contingent of hardened British football hacks in the room, and they pressed for inside information about how the game might affect selections for the Euro Championships. By contrast, the first question from the Chinese side was absolutely typical.

'Gascoigne Mister, you like (or) not like Chinese food?'

I closed my eyes, expecting Gazza to react with an Alex Higgins-style stunt. But he was all smiles as he politely declared his love of Chinese food and then amply illustrated the fact by licking his lips and holding up his thumbs. Having seen several world-class players turn up for friendlies the previous year and fail to impress, I really hoped Gazza would live up to his word and show some of the skill that made him one of the most exciting players of his generation.

Ever since the Women's World Cup in 1991, I had wanted to stamp out the lager-influenced memory of the international journalist match so, through a family friend in the UK, I contacted one of the football journalists travelling with the England team from Britain. The day before the big match, it was agreed we would have a Chinese media versus British media friendship football match. When I went to pick up the England journalist team from their hotel, I noted that most of them were a little overweight and seemed likely to have eaten all the proverbial pies. While they were no doubt much more savvy players than the Chinese team led by

Song, the extra weight they carried might make it an interesting match.

My first surprise was to find that Martin Tyler, the famous voice of football commentary in England, was also in the squad. Although he wasn't going to play, he had agreed to come along and offer encouragement from the touchline. I asked if everyone was there and suggested we leave for the pitch, but we had to wait for a couple more players. When the lift doors opened, far from two more podgy journalists, two very fit men emerged: Trevor Brooking and Trevor Francis. I am a West Ham fan, and Trevor Brooking was my childhood hero, and everyone knew the other Trevor was the first million-pound footballer.

Loaded into the bus, we made the journey across town to the Asian Games Village to meet up with the Chinese team. Mainly drawn from the local media, including my teammates at Beijing TV, they were busy warming up on the pitch. I decided to play for the Chinese team, but the English team was short a player, so I brought along a young British student called Keith Bradbury who, along with Jonathan, his partner in crime, was working as an intern at my media company during his study year in Beijing.

As soon as the England–China journalists' match started, it was clear that the English team, with the two Trevors marshalling the midfield and Martin Tyler shouting instructions from the touchline, was the far stronger, and the goals started flying in from left and right. Before long it was 6-0, but amazingly our team continued to play with smiles, holding back the urge to cheat, foul or just walk off. They were giving me and themselves real 'face'; it truly was a friendly and played in an excellent spirit.

Just as I was thinking we would never score, Trevor Brooking decided to take a spell in goal, which surely must increase our chances. When I received a long throw from the keeper, I turned with the ball at my feet and saw the two Trevors in front of me. Dribbling past Francis, I launched a low shot towards the left corner. We all stood and watched as the ball crept inside the post, leaving Brooking stranded on the line. Turning to me, the first Trevor said, 'Nice goal, Rowan,' and the second Trevor came across to offer his congratulations as well. There it was, the pinnacle moment of my previously unrecognized football career. If you don't believe me, you can ask Martin Tyler.

On the night of the big match, Beijing was at fever pitch. The whole area around the Workers Stadium was buzzing as 60,000 fans made their way to the ground. As many had predicted, this was no exhibition, and England moved easily into the lead with a goal from Nick Barmby. With my journalist card getting me into the ground and my foreign face through the inner cordon, I was standing right on the touchline next to Venables and I had the chance to answer a question I had long wondered about. With all the noise in the stadium, could the players really receive and react to instructions from the bench during the game? You bet they could. Venables spent the whole match issuing instructions to the players, the central defenders relaying messages to the players on the other side. It was like an orchestra. In particular, I remember he kept repeating one particular instruction – 'Take him on!' – to Steve McManaman, who was playing wide on the left. But, McManaman didn't take his man on, but instead kept turning back, holding and returning the ball to the nearest defender. Venables was not happy.

There was only one player whom I never heard Venables coach from the side: Gazza. It might have been because he wouldn't have taken any notice, but more likely it was because Venables knew exactly what he was doing. With a bright-red face after just a few minutes, Gazza ran, tackled, dribbled and passed like a man possessed, scoring a brilliant second-half solo goal and taking the central role in everything positive England tried. His body looked totally knackered, but his brain continued to ignore it all the way through the ninety minutes. This was what China needed to see – grit and determination, but also the great joy of a player living his vocation.

While appreciating England's commanding performance, the crowd quickly focused their attention on the Chinese team, and the whole atmosphere changed. With England cruising at 2-0 and looking for a third rather than allowing their hosts a consolation goal, the crowd started picking up a chant that had started at one end. Soon the whole stadium had joined in. 'Qi Wusheng, out,' they shouted at the Chinese coach, who was already cowering in the dugout. By then, I was standing close to the England substitutes bench, where David Platt was among the players becoming increasingly confused by the chanting.

'What are they shouting?' he asked me as the chant rang out again even louder.

'They are calling for the coach to be sacked,' I replied. 'They have disowned their team.'

Platt's face was a picture of incredulity. 'What!' he replied, 'China has only had a professional league for three years. We have had a pro league for over 100 years. If the Chinese fans give up in a match like this, China will never get anywhere in football.' That about sums it up, I told him.

A little later, the crowd showed that they fully appreciated the impact of sarcasm and began cheering each time England passed the ball and booing each time China touched it. To be a Chinese player on that day must have felt like a screaming hell. In the end, England won just 3-0, and the Chinese fans, who a few weeks before had been shouting 'Stupid c**t' at Romario, were now traipsing back home swearing at the utter pointlessness of China having a football team at all. If there were stupid c**ts around that night, they were again in the stands.

When the match finished, we sprang into action, and I got the BTV crew in next to the England manager before CCTV had picked up their cameras. Ha! With the interviews in the bag and the teams retired, I walked to the middle of the pitch and called the BBC World Service to give them a previously requested match report. Such was my excitement that I can't remember what I said, but I think I got the score right.

The Workers Stadium claim was in tatters, and Beijing Guoan subsequently turned out to record losses to Napoli (3-0) and Maradona's Boca Juniors (2-1). That troubled star's main contribution while in Beijing was to rudely proposition the female BTV presenter we dispatched to interview him.

The lesson that England taught China in 1996 might have hurt the fair-weather fans and may have plunged Chinese football into another crisis of confidence, but I knew that the result was the just one. Until China sorted out its football from the bottom to the top, it did not help to build false hopes. England, along with all the teams that regularly beat them, were in a different class, and I started to think that football in China needed serious help from the outside.

A few days later, the China team escaped to Europe, where it was soundly beaten by Holland. This was followed by a draw with Uruguay and a loss to Paraguay with home and away defeats to South Korea thrown in. The bubble had truly burst. At the 1996 Asian Cup in the United Arab Emirates, China did make it through to the quarter-finals but lost to Saudi Arabia. It was a 4-3 thriller in which the Saudis overturned a Chinese two-goal lead. That defeat partly reflected, and fully confirmed, the lack of confidence the Chinese players had in the fluctuating support back home.

·

As the English football season moved into the key Christmas period at the end of 1996, my mind started turning over everything related to football and media and China, or was it China, media and football. Or Chinese football media? What actually was my life all about? Was I there just to help serve up the popcorn diet of European football on TV that had become the real opium of the masses, instead of addressing the real issues?

I loved China and had many friends who appreciated the game, but the mass response I was seeing around football was ugly and made it difficult to completely immerse myself in the culture. All the competing ideas in my mind were conspiring to drive me further and further back in football history to try and find a place and a time that Chinese people might recognize, a point around which people could base their understanding that, all things being equal, football really should be the people's game of China.

14

Planning for Revolution

As I was wrestling with the issues of how I might contribute to solving the problems in Chinese football, my sleep became disturbed by a series of strange dreams. To be more accurate, one strange dream that kept recurring. In the dream, I was called to a meeting with China's paramount leader, Deng Xiaoping. It was the type of dream you remember clearly in the morning, and the detail was reinforced each subsequent time it happened.

Although I met Deng in a couple of different places, most of the dreams took place while I was sitting at an English wooden pub table in a Beijing garden. It was summer in the late afternoon, and the sun was shining. I knew it was China because I could see the red of imperial walls between the trees in the distance, and the grass 'lawns' were actually thousands of individually planted tufts – totally useless for playing football. As I sat there looking around, I saw elderly Chinese people in the distance, some strolling with hands clasped behind their backs and others sitting at benches, chatting. I was a bit nervous the first time, having been called there to meet Deng, but the warmth of the sun and the relaxing surroundings were very calming. When he appeared, he was in a wheelchair that was being slowly pushed by a grey man in a formal blue Chinese suit. A blanket covered Deng's lap, and he wore a cap, a scarf and a coat, despite the weather. His assistant's look told me that Deng was frail and must not get overtired, and then the assistant was gone. Each time, we sat there for what felt like five to ten minutes before the assistant reappeared and wheeled Deng away. I sensed we were having a conversation, but he never spoke a word to me, and I have no recollection of what was discussed. It was very strange and it kept on happening.

In early 1997, the dreams suddenly stopped, and so did Deng. Just around Chinese Spring Festival, the general architect of reform died in Beijing, just missing his long-held wish to step foot in Hong Kong once it had returned to China. I remember when he died, because I was rushed to hospital in Australia with the most serious illness of my life. It had a very long name, but when you boiled it down, one of my testicles (let me keep some secrets) had expanded to several times the size of the other and then turned hard, black and numb.

'Strewth,' said the Aussie GP who examined it to his secretary, 'cancel my appointments, I am taking this bloke to the hospital.'

Luckily it was not what we both then feared, and the specialist's long name for it was followed by a recovery programme that involved spending a few days lying in hospital being drip fed a concoction of antibiotics. The only pain was watching Australian TV. As I sat through some appalling reports on the life of the man who had brought hundreds of millions into the modern world, I called them to complain – they couldn't even get his name right. Despite these irritations, I am delighted that 'the ball most precious' recovered its normal shape and function, but not before all the nurses in the hospital had come to have a look and make the appropriate down-under jokes.

Rejuvenated by enforced rest in Australia, I returned to Beijing in the spring of 1997 with a revolutionary football plan forming in my mind; I knew that everything was pointing to radical grassroots action. As China's domestic football disasters continued to unfold, I realized there was only one way to achieve sustainable progress at the higher levels as everyone wanted so desperately. It was obvious. After a couple of years of reasonable performance, the cracks in the Chinese professional football experiment had appeared, and the veneer of football modernity had started to warp. The top-down model was not working and it never could.

After a promising start, China's attempts to qualify for the World Cup finals in France in 1998 went badly wrong with a 3-2 home loss to Qatar, and it looked as if the team might fail to abide by the minister's suggested performance path five years earlier. So, while China and the world was looking forward to the birth of what had already been billed as the 'Chinese millennium', and the economy was reinforcing that view with incredible sustained growth, China's football league was dying a slow death.

The real game that had yet to be born was already being abused, but, as far as the powers in China were concerned, the only solution was to tinker with the professional clubs and their elite academies. The clubs picked for the Marlboro jamboree could claim no real emotional attachments with their potential fan base; they had not grown out of the community but appeared by magic government decree and had been sponsored by state and quasi-independent corporations with outstanding political relationships.

The money being invested was enough to build tens of thousands of community football pitches for the people, but the people were becoming addicted to cigarettes rather than the game. In some cases, the name of the sponsor, and therefore the club, changed every couple of years. Over the ten years of the first professional first division, only one team, Shanghai Shenhua, did not change its name. To seal the lack of emotional links between club and community, the clubs were renting government-owned grounds on match days, playing in echoing concrete places with no club connections or atmosphere. Few efforts were being made to engage with potential fans, and mechanisms that clubs employ all over the world were being ignored.

When I filmed with Beijing TV at Manchester United, there were over 700 items of merchandise available in their megastore. To compete, the other local club, Manchester City, operated a strong local community programme that I also filmed in action some years later. By comparison, Beijing Guoan FC, the Chinese capital's flagship club, only needed a token store, since its range of official items stretched to just seven and it had not bothered building any links with the community beyond the search for professional players. Even its shirt sponsor, Nike, turned the rules of the replica kit market on its head, making only enough shirts for the club itself. It refused to retail the replica kit, seeing a very limited market for authentic memorabilia and fearing a rash of cheap rip-offs.

Meanwhile, the training 'academies' set up by the economically liberated clubs combined the worst of the East European and South American models and were later taken out of their control by the kindly Education Ministry. Well-meaning though that organization may have been, it knew nothing about football and was not linked to all the other parts that make up the football pyramid.

In a shocking exposure of what happens when talented children slip through the cracks, in June 1997, the group of poor Jianlibao youngsters who had been sent to Brasil five years earlier returned home. Rather than the dream they were promised, they had spent most of their time in a small village playing against local amateur clubs. It is hard to imagine what they felt like when they touched down in their own country again, but the emotional shock could not have been good for their young minds. The new-look China youth team built around those players headed off with the great hopes of the nation to the World Championships. It was only after they were knocked out at the first group stage that the psychological problems of the 'Jianlibao Model' became a topic of heated discussion.

As if to rub it in, when the Beijing Guoan team finally gave in to the pressure for foreign players and fielded its three recently imported 'stars' for the first time that July, it ran out 9-1 winners against the mighty Shanghai Shenhua. The foreign trio scored eight of them, setting a new record win in the league. China's first 'golden goal'? Scored by a Spanish speaking Paraguayan. The first player at a Chinese club to play in the World Cup? The same man.

In September 1997, I passed my first decade in China by holding a tenth birthday party for Luo Wen, my Chinese name and now well established as the Chinese me. The difficulties involved in organizing an event that could be enjoyed together by foreign and Chinese friends from university, work or through football were multiple. I knew that many of my important Chinese guests would prefer to come early, be fed by 7 p.m. at the latest and leave at around 9 p.m. Most of the westerners, however, would prefer to come late, eat nothing until after midnight snacks and then hang around to the early hours.

In a desperate attempt to try and avoid having two parties, I created a number of small performances that required mixed guest participation through the night. Knowing that Chinese people love raffles, I also handed out little tickets with numbers for a special prize competition to be drawn at 10 p.m. which I judged to be the optimum cross-over time. It was only when a few Chinese friends approached me about eleven to ask when the draw was being held that I realized it had actually worked. There were no prizes, so I apologized, and the remaining Chinese guests, with the exception of the football players, who were already quite drunk, all left for home.

This approach to my ten-year China milestone reflected my belief that what we all share is greater than what we don't, but it also revealed that Rowan and Luo Wen had to be quite distinct characters to operate effectively in their respective camps. With the exception of close friendships, football was the only place that a single person could fully emerge. On one side, I was still the person my parents had raised, with English values about queuing and a western scientific approach to analysing the external world. On the other side, I was thinking more and more like a Chinese person, always considering the impact of my actions in terms of my relationships with others. Whereas Rowan got angry that foreigners had to pay more than Chinese people to visit the same tourist sites, Luo Wen visited the same sites as part of official domestic TV delegations with all expenses graciously paid by the hosts.

The result of this confused status was that the public Luo Wen had slowly become like an alter ego, a masked version of myself who was open to performing in public in Chinese in a way that Rowan was never comfortable doing in English. As I was always dealing with people for whom English was not the first language, I even found myself adopting their accents and vocabulary as I tried instinctively to aid their understanding. This was not necessarily a healthy development, but, by creating a second mindset that worked in a very different language, I was able to keep rationalizing my life in China.

The month after my Chinese tenth birthday, China's campaign to reach the 1998 World Cup ended with elimination at the qualifying stage, plunging the whole country into national mourning and another long lament about the ills of the game. I was sick of this fatalistic response. Since nobody had done anything serious about grassroots football in China for the decade I had been playing it, I thought it might as well be me, or rather the combined forces of Rowan and Luo Wen.

English football was still very popular on TV, and my public profile and official position at Beijing TV (the core propaganda arm of all local ministries) provided not just a head start but an inside start when it came to arranging meetings and dealing with various departments. Because TV stations are Party mouthpieces, each programme department works extremely closely with the relevant government organization. Just as the *Traffic News* is a cooperation with the transport police, so the Education Department works to promote the policies of the Education Ministry, and so on. As an official Beijing TV worker, I found Luo Wen had friends everywhere.

At the same time, my own media activities were also growing with my partner, John, as international distributors sought new markets and advertising agencies came charging into China following their clients. This meant an increasing need for trade services, and I saw an opportunity to build on my provision of feature articles to the trade press. These articles slowly developed into *China Media Monitor*, edited by my old classmate Big John, the first independent monthly executive briefing on Chinese media.

It was a very sensitive area to be dealing with, but I was confident I had good enough relationships at the Ministry and TV stations to launch the service at the 1997 Sichuan TV Festival, incorporating the company in Hong Kong as CMM Intelligence Limited the following year. This move created China's first independent media trade services company and it proved to me that, by working quietly inside the system, I could build the trust needed to effect change in even the most sensitive of sectors. At the beginning, 100 per cent of the company's Chinese clients were government-owned, and these players still dominate the media sector today.

By default, my on-screen TV work led me into more TV work, in turn exposing my various lengths of hair to wider audiences of tacky game shows on regional and national channels. While I much prefer talk shows when my views have at least as much prominence as my big nose, I also appeared in kitsch spectaculars dressed in fantastic Chinese outfits, either over-painted in white or with my blemishes rudely exposed without any make-up at all. While embarrassing for the English part of me, these various experiences all served to protect Luo Wen within the system and lower the traditional barriers around me as a foreigner.

I was also spending time with my then Chinese girlfriend, Nina (names merged). Like football, this private part of my life also helped me dispel the distinctions between the 'foreign' and 'Chinese' influences in my mind, while bringing the differences between East and West into even sharper focus. There was still some underlying jealousy about foreigners with Chinese girlfriends, and this forced us to be low-key, especially as there was a real risk that our relationship would affect Nina's very public career if it became known. This meant spending time at home rather than going out, which was fine by me. When we did venture out, we ate in small restaurants in unfashionable parts of town. From time to time, taxi drivers would swear at Nina or even refuse to give us a lift, but, in the flush of love, we greeted these small frustrations with cries of 'Revolution!' and we even managed to travel to Europe on holiday. Everywhere we went, we explored deeper into each other's cultures, testing each other in fierce debates on traditional values and exchanging views that revealed more than either of us had expected.

My first lesson was to be taught that Chinese women are not just highly skilled in the marital art of *sajiao* (sa jeeow), they are world leaders. *Sajiao* translates roughly as 'coquettish' or, as Nina described it, 'woman tools'. There are a wide range of *sajiao* moves from silly giggling and overly expressive eye and body movements to a series of small whimpering noises and feminine grunts that can convey everything from anger to satisfaction. Like Nina, more and more intelligent women in China were abandoning this crude but perennially effective way to wind Chinese men around their fingers, but *sajiao* remains a critical skill across the country. To show me what she meant, Nina performed some simple moves, and I immediately recognized it: it was the stereotypical behaviour seen at all levels of the media and across the huge 'personal services' industry. While initially flattering to a man who wants to be the boss, a woman who adopts predominantly *sajiao* tactics can quickly become irritating, especially when failure to get her way leads to childlike tantrums. Nina was a fiercely independent woman and, if she adopted *sajiao* (and she certainly could), it was either as a private joke with me or as part of a ruthless manipulation of gullible Chinese men in her business career.

Apart from revealing these secrets, she also educated me in the Chinese art of negotiation, and I became adept at playing the social games that were not even required of me as a foreigner. As always, I retained the right to feign ignorance, as I did about several subjects that cropped up in our heart-to-heart discussions from time to time. Even the most aggressively modern Chinese women retain a highly practical nature, and I have watched many friends who fought hard to build careers happily abandon them with no regrets to marry and have a child soon after their thirtieth birthday. In many cases, this plan precedes the discovery of a suitable partner, and so it was with Nina.

When the subject of weddings was raised in general conversation, we discovered that the Chinese and English traditions were in direct opposition. I tried to explain that a traditional English wedding was paid for by the bride's family, but she immediately adopted a fatally wounded expression that was pure *sajiao* tradecraft.

'Not good,' she said, 'China wedding have man pay! China wedding must have man pay!' She then launched into a very comical high-pitched scream of torture.

'Not good,' I retorted, only half in jest. 'British wedding must have woman pay'.

Knowing exactly what she would say next, I quickly added, 'We how can make *my* mother pay money, all British people all laugh (at) her! Lose face.'

'Who say with you marry, stupid,' she replied, accepting defeat by playfully punching me in the stomach with a neat move her father had taught her. In turn, this allowed me to seal the 'banter-weight' victory by responding with a small Chinese phrase she taught me herself. It says that, for a woman, 'to insult is to like, to hit is to love'.

A healthy sex life does wonders for the spirit, and, armed with Nina's negotiating diploma, I felt confident in tackling China's football problems. Greater London, with roughly the same population as Beijing, had up to 3,000 grass football pitches dotted all over the place, with over seventy full-size pitches at the famous Hackney Marshes alone. In Beijing, there were thirty in total. Most of these were in universities, and that figure included the public stadia and the national football training pitches near the Temple of Heaven. There were others hidden deep inside military compounds, but it was only while playing for Beijing TV that I was occasionally smuggled in to train, so they didn't really count.

This shocking discovery raised many more questions than answers. I wanted to know why some of the land around Beijing couldn't be converted into football pitches. As I thought about it more, the more it seemed plausible for selected groups of Chinese farmers to stop producing rice and grow grass for football pitches instead.

To find out just how crazy that was, I consulted my agricultural adviser, Professor Joshua Muldavin, a gentle American giant who has spent many years living in the Chinese countryside. He informed me that the average annual income from 10 mu of agricultural land (the size of a football pitch) was about RMB 1,200 (about a hundred quid), the same as renting one of Beijing's grass football pitches for two hours! With a quick calculation of how many games could be played on a single pitch over a year, it didn't take a genius to realize that any farmers I could get on board would be delighted with the returns. It was perfect; I could regenerate the countryside and correct development imbalances by bringing urban money back to the peasants – the most literal of grassroots revolutions. It sounded like a good dream to chase, and I decided to dedicate my weekends to building a symbolic football pitch.

With the help of Joshua's then father-in-law, Professor Good, a retired official from the Beijing Sports Institute, I started scouting for potential land on the outskirts of the city. The good professor was very enthusiastic and decided that helping me would be a useful occupation in his retirement. It was simple, really, he said, the closer we came to the city, the more expensive the land.

As I considered the relative benefits of distance against price, I reflected that early football grounds like Bramall Lane (1862), St James' Park (1880) and Anfield (1884) all found their homes on land in the suburbs of cities that have since grown around them. In Europe, for every amateur ground that has grown into a stadium along with the professional growth of its club, there are thousands of smaller clubs that did not grow but that have also found themselves on land that is now attracting property developers. Trying to find land to start an amateur football club at the turn of the twenty-first century in the capital of the fastest-growing economy in the world presented very different challenges.

I visited several strange places with Professor Good and friends from Beijing TV, meeting many wonderful people who couldn't help me along the way. This included the owners of the Beijing horse-racing track. This was a bizarre project, since gambling is illegal, but it had excellent potential for football pitches, as evidenced at Hong Kong's Happy Valley. Horse-racing could not take off without gambling, but I stuck around to see how it worked. In order to remain open, the managers told me that several tricks had to be employed. This included not allowing any betting until the fourth race (once any senior government leaders had left) and then calling it 'guess the winner'. Given the audience had never seen horse-racing before, it was also necessary to introduce an educational element, including studying 'the form'. In the first race I saw, the announcer introduced the field. At the end of the procession came what looked like a Shetland pony with a massive jockey on board. To my great amusement, the announcer instructed the crowd to look for the smaller horse with the large jockey and explained that this was one you might not want to 'guess as the winner'. Sure enough, the other horses had been rubbed down and stabled before my pick entered the final furlong.

The entire infrastructure, including the grandstand, was in place, making the horse-racing track an excellent example of what happens in China when people with money decide to invest in something that they have not researched. All over the countryside around Beijing, the huge and grotesque results of massive wasted leisure investment were plain for all to see.

I just wanted land to build a first football pitch, but Professor Good saw a bigger opportunity and kept taking me to industrial work units, the leaders of which were more than happy to lease large tracts of land at the right rate. None of them proved viable for one reason or another. In one place, way out of Beijing, the ambitious owner offered to give me land for forty pitches. In his own version of madness, he had already built a hotel and now needed some guests. I appreciated his offer, but there were less than forty amateur teams in the whole city outside the work unit system, so this would have been putting the ball before the boot.

To build a football model that could sustain itself, China first had to deal with a big dilemma that it seemed to have created for itself.

This is summed up by just two little characters, *yi* (yee) and *wu* (woo). In my trusty Chinese–English dictionary, the combination *yiwu* has two principal meanings: the first is 'compulsory'; the second is 'voluntary'. *Yiwu* is brilliant for that achievement alone, blending a total contradiction in English terms into a single concept. It refers to 'social obligations', that awkward set of activities that you don't have to do, but that you have to do really, even if you don't want to. We all have them, but in China they extend to collective activities like planting trees or giving blood, which is where I first met them. Being an active member of an amateur football club was definitely an *yiwu*. In fact, you could describe most clubs as 'voluntary organizations with compulsory responsibilities' and remain on fairly safe ground. The problem in China was that nobody wanted to pay club subscriptions or match fees, and the work units that used to organize sports were fast shedding themselves of all kinds of social responsibilities.

In an effort to find a compromise between distance and rent and to satisfy the needs of my own little group of foreign and Chinese teams first, I ended up back at the very first place Professor Good had led me, a small walled plot out the back of a chicken farm in northern Beijing. Not far from the expressway to the Great Wall, the land was owned by the Dongbeiwang State Farm and consisted of a pig sty and two unused fish ponds. The space was just about big enough for a full-sized pitch, and I could see the finished product. It had a small clubhouse at one end and a car park at the other, just like home.

Right next door was a Sino-Japanese salad cream factory, but the land Professor Good earmarked had never earned any economic returns since making money had become fashionable a decade earlier. At a meeting with the State Farm, I was introduced to a wonderful man called Mr Plum. He had a smile as big as his belly and was a TV football fanatic who followed Liverpool. He greeted me as an old friend and told me that I was a much funnier commentator than Song. After sharing cigarettes and tea, it became clear that Big Plum, as I already called him, was prepared to give me the land at a non-commercial rate, but that I needed to come up with the money to build the pitch. His assistant, Small Plum, although not related, was in full agreement.

That certainly was a fair deal, but I still had no money for rent or to build the pitch and I was nervous about my business investing money away from the media sector without clear returns. Leaving the money problem for later, I sought the advice of other friends who were well disposed towards football and each of whom had expertise in relevant sectors in China.

Unlike my birthday, it wasn't suitable to bring everyone together at one time, and so, while I met with foreign friends together, my Chinese meetings were usually private. The revolutionary band whom I called to the first secret football campaign meeting in a bar called Frank's Place opposite the Workers Stadium represented several decades of experience working in China and a wealth of knowledge about the subtle disciplines of modern commercial warfare that I would need to succeed.

There was one from real estate, another who had set up an agricultural business, a commercial lawyer, my football-loving British co-commentator Calum and my old friend Josh, who, without any licences of his own at all, was successfully running the Poachers Inn, still the best foreign pub/disco in Beijing, with Mr Find. Mr Find also advised me, but the only Chinese person present that day was Professor Fruit, a long-time friend and my local partner in the advertising and TV distribution business. Personifying the changes in China, he taught political studies at the Party school and ran a commercial publishing business. I had watched with amazement as he became 'lost in music' on his visits to the Poachers Inn, and he is an all-round gentleman and loyal *gemenr* (ger mer), or mate.

Between them, they managed to convince me after visiting the site that, whatever the apparent romance of the project, there were simply too many obstacles to running it as a business. The lawyer advised I would have to register a joint-venture in a restricted sector for foreigners and would need at least US$100,000 in capital investment. The real-estate expert suggested there were over thirty different documents to complete, and permissions from several ministries would have to be won. Someone raised issues about the ownership of land in the so-called green belt around Beijing. The agricultural expert questioned the suitability of the plot for my purposes and asked awkward questions about drainage, soil quality and water supplies.

Even Professor Fruit agreed that significant due diligence would be required before any football parties could be considered. I returned to Small Plum to ask some further questions and, as I trundled out a list of demands for further clarity, he proceeded to lay out completely vague answers. When I asked for a scale map of the actual plot we were taking over and its boundaries, he drew them for me on a piece of paper. When I enquired how long the first agreement would last, he replied, 'Several years,' and declined to be more specific.

In the end, I just could not bring myself to take the plunge and I had no option but to put the project on the back-burner. But I never lost interest in this quirky little bit of waste land, and intermittent enquiries via Professor Good revealed that it continued to lie idle over the following year. Unlike the land, I didn't lie idle. I knew that, if I wanted to spark a successful football revolution, I had to spend more time analysing what had happened to football in China under the Communist Party, to try to untangle the historical progression of a game in which everybody was so desperate to succeed, but that nobody was taking seriously. Even for an England fan, it made for grim reading.

15

A Chinese Guide to Football Suicide

Whereas in Europe, the romantic vision is of football associations that formed because there were players who formed teams and teams that became clubs that sought strength in unity, the history of football in New China was started, and continues today to be written, by distant rulers in Beijing. The intense suspicion about any type of 'meeting' and the need for approval for everything that I had first encountered at university and that had become routine for me at BTV was still hard for me to take in. In terms of football at least, it was also impossible for me to accept in my heart. It's my game, after all.

The reasons behind China's stubborn refusal to let football grow organically lie deep in its political history. The Communist Party started redefining and remodelling all sports as soon as the People's Republic was established in 1949. The Party was the only organization that was allowed to be organized 'voluntarily' at local levels. Mao's government saw sport, like the media, as a political tool and it immediately set out to exploit and shape sports as mechanisms to extend social control and to achieve international respectability.

One of the most important international sports, football, was at the top of the list of games that could help build relations with China's European Communist allies. With the country still led by the People's Liberation Army (affectionately PLA), the army team, known as Ba Yi (which means August 1st, or 8-1), was the first to play an 'international' match in October 1951. It was just two years after Mao's historic address from the rostrum at Tiananmen Gate, and the occasion was an invitation tournament in Czechoslovakia. The honoured opposition was the Bulgarian People's Army. If the Bulgarians hadn't 'scored' a last goal, 8-1 would have lost 8-1. That would have been the supreme insult, but 9-1 didn't look too good either. Naturally, the shock of the defeat stirred the Communist leadership into action, and the PLA quickly went around strengthening its squad by holding New China's first national football competition in the port of Tianjin. The only foreigners invited to the party were Hungarian advisers, which wasn't a bad choice at the time.

In line with China's geographical administrative divisions, there were six regional teams in that first modern domestic competition. There were also two other teams – the PLA and the Railway Department. That the army was involved was no surprise, but just like the bloke with two left feet who has a car, the invitation to the Railway Administration had more practical roots – after all, the others had to get there somehow. That initial tournament resulted in the picking of New China's first international squad and then the formation of representative teams by the regional governments.

It was not until 1952, three years after the Communist Liberation, that this top-down Party and army-controlled system was civilianized with the establishment of the China National Sports Commission. To take control down to lower levels, subsidiary commissions within the government structure were created at provincial and municipal levels.

In a decision that fundamentally changed football in China, FIFA chose to recognize the new Communist National Sports Commission as the official representative of the game, allowing it to take up the membership originally granted to the former

Nationalist government. Since nobody was playing football at the time, the people didn't even notice. The people's game was now the government's game, and FIFA had given its blessing. Given the size of China's population, it was a steal of preposterous proportions. All other voices were silenced before they had a chance to speak.

With the National Sports Commission charged with developing elite athletes and teams, it wasn't long before a bona fide China national team turned out in a friendly against Finland. Despite the hopes of the nation, it lost 4-0. China's second set of matches came against North Korea in 1953 in Hong Kong. In the first game, China again lost 4-0, but won out 4-2 in the second match two days later. It was New China's first ever victory.

This landmark was followed by the first attendance of Communist Chinese sports ministry officials at a FIFA Congress. Held in Paris, it provided New China with a chance to smooth away any lingering suggestions that football might be independent of the government and the Party. Back at home, few people even knew the meeting had taken place, and even fewer were involved in the process.

With world football unable to operate in China except through the government, the Sports Commission concentrated efforts on speeding up the success of the national team. Forty years before China sent its youth team to Brasil, it had sent a total of thirty-five young players, at great expense, to Hungary. They came back two years later with Josef Ember, China's first foreign coach, but the World Cup is still in the post.

The coordination of football for everyone whose talent could not bring glory to the nation was given across to what the government calls 'workers' unions', the division that organized the football team at Beijing TV. They are really Party-organized workers associations, dealing with social affairs within major work units. With the patronage of football-loving leaders (something that China does share with the world), the 'top' level of amateur football started to flourish under this system, with hundreds of semi-pro level teams funded by state work units feeding players into the provincial squads. This led to the establishment of the first ten-team national league in 1954.

Confident that they had control over the game internationally and domestically, the central authorities were only then bold enough to establish a subsidiary organ of the Sports Commission that sounded like it had something to do with football. Establishing what was a toothless China Football Association (CFA) succeeded in pushing FIFA's relationship (and influence) further down the chain of command. It had very little to do with building a football pyramid and very much to do with the demand that 'the' football team become a winning symbol of ideological superiority.

Football was such a good game for making friends that, between 1954 and 1957, China played an amazing 166 matches, mostly against Asian and European Communist countries, losing 91 of them. Among this incredible fixture list was the first multinational tournament held in Beijing that featured the national teams of neighbouring North Korea and Vietnam.

This was also a period of high political tension across the Taiwan straits, and at the thirtieth FIFA Congress in Lisbon in 1956, the CFA deputy president was instructed to complain formally about the recognition of Taiwan that had created the impression of 'two Chinas', an impossible scenario in Beijing. When Taiwan withdrew from the qualifying round of the 1958 World Cup finals, China was able to compete. Although China lost 2-0 to Indonesia in the first match of the two-leg tie, it won 4-3 in the return, forcing the teams to meet in Burma of all places for the play-off. With the Indonesians requiring only a draw to qualify on goal difference, China was unable to find the net even once. It was the kind of national failure at the crucial moment I knew only too well as an Englishman.

Although FIFA and the People's Republic of China tried to patch up their problems with the 'Taiwan question' by certifying China's first batch of FIFA-registered referees a few months later, the political characters were already on the wall. At the following Congress in Stockholm, the Chinese representatives again walked out, this time announcing they were not coming back. Back in China, the state newspapers which had launched new football editions started using the space to depict football as run by FIFA as a 'bourgeois vice', and many of us today would be tempted to agree.

With the Cold War nicely chilled, there was plenty of foreign opposition, and resignation from FIFA didn't stop China playing internationals or trying to build out a structure from under the national obsession. The national team turned out hundreds more times between 1958 and 1961, again mostly against teams across the Soviet Union and as hosts to visiting African and Asian nations.

International competition was considered separately from the development of the national league structure, and Mao's disastrous Great Leap Forward then killed the league. The movement designed to leapfrog the country into the modern age actually catapulted China back from whence it had come. Football, like much else in civil life, disappeared for three years, and the whole movement created unneeded challenges for the people to overcome again.

In an amazing example of central team selection, the political conditions for the return of the game in 1962 were heralded not by a new competition or league, but by the Ministry-published sports paper, *Sports Paper*, choosing the top twenty-two players in China. The failure of that national team in its first international foray (it lost to Uruguay Universities) prompted another massive rethink deep inside the Sports Commission. The resulting plan was typically appalling for the long-term development of the game in China, but might not be a bad idea today at some of the European clubs where a number of stars have become overpaid underperformers.

On central instructions, the CFA decided that the entire national effort to become a strong football nation would be based on the principle of 'Three Froms, One Big'. The three 'Froms' were three practices 'from which' China could succeed, and the one 'Big' was the powerful force that would result, the secret to reaching the levels of the great world teams of the 1950s and 1960s. The first practice was 'From hard or strenuous (training)'. It was believed rightly that China would never win the World Cup if everyone sat around drinking rice wine and eating dumplings. The second practice was 'From strict or rigorous (training)'. This sounded quite similar, but no team can expect to emerge triumphant over a long competition without putting in extra hours. The third 'from' practice that the CFA proclaimed football workers at all levels must implement without delay was 'From lots of competitive (training)'. The third revolutionary practice was basically 'playing lots of football'. At this stage, the players had the message, but the CFA weren't finished. It was only by combining the 'hard and strenuous training' with the 'strict and rigorous training' and the 'competitive training' that they could end up with the 'Big' force. In an amazing defiance of common sense, the CFA solution for the Chinese team's failure to compete meaningfully at international level was to subject the players in the current squad to a massive, unprecedented and unremitting regime of more training. Not even the least knowledgeable of today's big-money chairmen is stupid enough to think he can train a weak team to victory.

Filled with this myopic national vision, the league was resurrected in 1964. This time it was at least part of a new sports drive that included a central government edict for young men in their millions to take up the game. Supported by the central government and the Ministry of Education, this clarion call to action, including the designation of ten cities as football development centres, may have been inspired by the same political urges, but it was also a clear decision to unleash a wider-based grassroots campaign.

That same year, a Brasilian club became the first from a major football nation to visit China (for a training session), and it looked for the briefest of moments that change really might be afoot. Indeed, Chinese football would have been very different today if that campaign had been continued. After just two years, the embryonic amateur football sector crashed and burned just like the rest of China's social fabrics as the Cultural Revolution turned millions of should-be young football lovers into the angry executioners (and excommunicated) of Mao's great ego trip. Like elites from every walk of life, football coaches and players could not escape the vicious political purges of the times, and over 1,000 players and 100 coaches were denied the chance to pursue their vocation; many were sent for re-education through hard labour in the countryside.

It was only as Mao's health deteriorated in the early 1970s that certain leaders started looking at alternatives to the rigid state planning system and management of resources. The idea that market forces could be brought to bear was starting to gain shape. Ahead of such radical moves, pieces were carefully and slowly put into place. Well established as one of the smoothest roads to global rehabilitation, international sport continued to preface China's moves, and various games notched up notable diplomatic scalps credited to Mao, including a nice game of 'ping-pong' with Richard Nixon's America.

For football, the beginning of the end of the Cultural Revolution came in 1973 with a competition for five key ball sports in

Beijing and the relaunch of the national league after an absence of seven years. That same year, the Chinese national team played its first overseas invitational match, a 1-1 draw with the freedom-loving nation of Albania. In May 1974, with the support of the football-loving magnate Henry Fok, China participated in the Asian Cup qualifiers. Again playing its games in Hong Kong, it recorded victories against North Korea, Brunei, Hong Kong and Japan, before losing to North Korea 2-0, still enough to make it to the finals in Iran in 1976.

The political long-ball game wasn't quite over, and China chose that occasion to reignite the argument about Taiwan's national status. That same year, the Chinese team was training in Yugoslavia when the World Cup started. When the head coach, Nian Weisi, received an urgent telegram from Beijing, it said that they 'should not support FIFA' under any circumstances, including watching the World Cup on TV.

Back at home, the 1975 national football competition in Beijing ended in a draw between the Guangdong and Liaoning teams. Instead of a replay, they shared the trophy. For most people in the world of football, this is a most unsatisfactory result for the game and the poor trophy. It was just another example that the game itself was not actually that important to an administration in which different factions were fighting for control of the ailing Mao's legacy.

One of my first memories of China was seeing the trial of Mao's ranting wife, Jiang Qing, and her Gang of Four on the television news. They were fighting for control when great revolutionary leader Premier Zhou Enlai passed away in 1976 and accused their rivals, including Deng Xiaoping, of instigating the 'Tiananmen Incident', during which people had expressed their love for Zhou.

Amid all this political turmoil, China still managed to participate in the Asian Cup that June, losing to Kuwait, drawing with

Malaysia and losing to the hosts Iran. Chinese pride was only salvaged with a final win against Iraq, but there could be little doubt of the importance attached to maintaining a presence in international sporting competitions.

Finally, on 9 September 1976, Mao Zedong left the scene he had dominated for much of the twentieth century. Following a final battle between the Gang of Four and other leaders, Jiang Qing was arrested and Deng Xiaoping began his final rehabilitation. Amazingly, less than two months after Mao's death, it was decided that people could start to smile again, and football provided the occasion, with Australia becoming the first foreign nation to tour, recording a 2-0 victory over the Chinese national team.

Football was vital to the new leaders, and, just a year after Mao's death, China held a twelve-team international tournament in Beijing and Shanghai, including nine teams from overseas. They were selected carefully; the Chinese youth team won the competition and China's first team came fourth. Just as football had led Chinese diplomacy in the 1950s with the Communist world, so the new Chinese leadership used football to build relations with the West.

Normally, that might have caused a problem in the USA, but that country was also tinkering with soccer, so the timing was perfect. The first western club to come to China was the New York Cosmos in 1977. Led by football superstars Pelé and Beckenbauer, it played a historic match in Beijing (a careful 1-1 draw), and a second match in Shanghai, which China won 2-1. For those playing diplomatic football, it was the perfect result. The following month the Chinese team toured the USA and Caribbean, recording a 1-1 draw in the first match in the USA, but losing 1-0 and 2-1 in the following games. A 3-0 victory over Jamaica was the only consolation, but the political results were positive.

As China pushed for readmission to the world football family, the landmark visit of the Cosmos *galácticos* was followed the next year by the arrival of the other great football team of that era, West Bromwich Albion. It would be many years before I finally answered the question as to why that particular club had broken the ice. Irrespective of the club involved, there is a rule that what happens on tour stays on tour. Little ever does, and there are various jokes about the English team's visit to the Great Wall that are now embedded in football folklore. The one I like best involves manager big Ron Atkinson turning to a young Bryan Robson and saying, 'I bet you can't bend it round that one.'

At the end of 1978, China was back in international competition at the Asian Games in Thailand. Posting early wins against Qatar and Saudi Arabia, it then lost to Iraq and South Korea. The PRC team did, however, beat Thailand and Malaysia to win a place in the third-place play-off, where it avenged its earlier defeat to Iraq by one goal to nil. This was a reasonable result, and immediately afterwards the Chinese headed for the next Asian Cup qualifiers in the Philippines, where it set itself up with victories over the hosts and then Macao. Although China lost the final match to South Korea, it was just enough to qualify again.

The new-look China team wasn't shy about going on relationship-building tours either, visiting an incredible forty-seven different countries to play football at the end of the 1970s. Among these was a European tour in 1979 that took China to the UK for a return match against West Brom and games against Celtic, Chelsea and Middlesbrough, the northern English city remembered fondly in Communist Asia as hosts to the North Korean team that famously beat Italy in the 1966 World Cup.

After leaving the IOC and FIFA in the 1950s, China finally returned to the fold, and football's world body once again sold the game to the Chinese government. This time, the level at which FIFA engaged with Chinese football was firmly set at the CFA level, deep inside the bureaucratic sports apparatus that had ultimate control. The CFA was finally ratified in 1980 with FIFA's demand that Taiwan change its name to 'Chinese Taipei' and give up any reference to the 'Republic of China'.

Having again given the token CFA clearance to run the game, FIFA could only sit back and watch as the National Sports Commission, not the CFA, presented a report on improving the technical levels of Chinese football not to FIFA, but to China's State Council. The plan was passed, and the same year it was agreed that sixteen cities were to be designated as special 'football' centres.

Meanwhile, China's readmission to world football was not going well on the pitch; mainly because it meant real competition against teams that also wanted to win. When the Chinese team took part in the qualifying rounds for the 1980 Olympic Games, it lost to mighty Singapore. At the Asian Cup in Kuwait, the confidence of a 6-0 win over Bangladesh and creditable 2-2 draw with Iran came to nothing as China recorded losses to Syria and North Korea.

However, at the end of 1980, the national team took out the tiny European colonies of Macau and Hong Kong and then old foe Japan, before beating North Korea 4-2 in extra time to win the right to participate in the Asian qualifiers for the World Cup, and the people rejoiced. China's onward route to qualification for the finals saw it come up against New Zealand, Kuwait and Saudi Arabia. With just a single point from its two matches against New Zealand, China needed a confidence win against Kuwait, which it got with a 3-0 scoreline. Next up was Saudi Arabia.

Trailing 2-0, the Chinese team staged its first ever international comeback, winning the game 4-2 and prompting ecstatic students to burn their bed quilts with joy. Secondary schools even made the subject of 'From 0-2 to 4-2' the subject of exam essays. Unfortunately, the excitement was short-lived because, despite a further victory over Saudi Arabia, losses to Kuwait and then New Zealand sent China back to the drawing board again.

The same year, several authorities, including the Ministry of Education, once again joined hands to launch football into primary and secondary schools in the special football centres, first with the 'Sprout Cup' for the best kids in primary schools and the 'Hope Cup' for the top players at middle schools. This was followed by the first elite training camps and the launch of the 'Child Cup' for outstanding under-14s and, in 1983, the 'Baby Cup' (or Bay bee Bay) for the very best under-10s.

These initiatives all pointed towards an understanding at higher levels of the government about the importance of playing from a young age, but there was a massive and fundamental flaw in implementation. The words 'special', 'outstanding', 'elite', 'very best', 'top' and 'hope' gave it away. While all this effort should have been directed horizontally towards popularizing the game among all kids, it was built vertically solely to extract the best ones. That might, and worryingly does, work for China in terms of gold medals in many sports with narrower appeal, but it doesn't work in football, where all the leading nations are lucky enough to draw from a massive natural pool of talent swimming in a sea of football clubs established over generations to cater for every level.

Playing football should not require removal from society and the sacrifice of a balanced education. In fact it should be the opposite – without sport as part of normal life it is often hard for many kids to find that balance. But, like the rest of Chinese sport, the new junior academies were built along the Soviet-inspired factory model, complete with high injection and rejection rates, and only basic levels of education or career support for young athletes that could not make it.

It was painfully clear that the ethical values that had been instilled by the ancient Chinese through the game of *cuju* were long forgotten by the time real choices could be made. Even worse, as soon as the academies started receiving central government attention and, crucially, funding it was everybody for themselves. Immediately, the old trick of falsifying production statistics to win bonuses was applied to a new product – talented children.

Unscrupulous parents, teachers, coaches, officials, institutions and politicians all joined in to exploit the fragile potential of their own children and they all have to share a collective guilt as the first generation that could, during an opening period of peace and growing prosperity, finally have chosen to spread the game as widely as possible. Instead, it was elite or it was nothing. The fraud most commonly took the form of altering children's ages to gain an advantage in local, regional and national competitions and so win bonus funding. In one case, a player in an under-15 match was found to be twenty-two and registered at a professional club! I wonder how much the fourth official got paid that day? That particular incident happened in 2005.

Despite these issues, the government continued to invest in its vertical programmes throughout the 1980s, and desperate people continued to cheat to get kids into the system. It could only end in embarrassment when Chinese teams met international opponents who played by the rules. And it still does. It was only when the players that made it to the national team despite this system returned to Singapore for the Asian Cup in 1984 and ended as runners-up to Saudi Arabia that Chinese fans felt some semblance of regional face had been won. That same year, China won a much bigger prize, the right to take back Hong Kong from Britain. In the context of its recent football history, the ugly 'May 19th Incident' that had followed China's 1985 defeat to Hong Kong in a qualifier seemed that little bit more understandable from the fans' point of view.

When Beijing, Tianjin, Shanghai and Dalian hosted the first under-17 World Championships, the Chinese team did well to emerge from its group matches against Guinea, the USA and Bolivia. However, it fell at the next hurdle to West Germany, as Nigeria swept to the title in an early sign of the promise to come from that continent.

Looking beyond the world of elite sports development, by the time I first arrived in the late 1980s, the opening and reform policies were at last encouraging China's by now timid amateur and semi-pro footballers to re-emerge from the shadows. Like Britain, Germany, Italy, Russia and other football nations 100 plus years before, the massive industrial enterprises (some the size of towns) were again starting to play a central role in developing prototype clubs.

However, in a process that was being repeated time and again, the ultimate aim in China was totally elitist, and it was these vertically structured clubs that would ultimately become involved in Chinese football's own version of the Great Leap Forward, the collapse of which was partly responsible for spurring me to action a decade later.

In an effort to achieve success at the ultimate level, the CFA held its first selection activity for national football coaches in 1991 in Kunming. The coach of the China Olympic team was finally appointed to run the full national squad but, just six months later, he resigned, and China became the first country to compete internationally without a recognized coach on the bench.

The realization that domestic coaches had neither the experience nor the character to succeed at international level encouraged China to go shopping again. Herr Klaus Schlappner was deemed to be the answer and he duly arrived from Germany, the country the CFA now thought China should copy. While he brought colour to the game and launched the career of a Chinese look-a-like who went by the name Little Schlappner, the big one was unable to make much progress on the pitch.

Having tried Hungarian and German coaches without success, at the start of 1998 the CFA turned to England, the mother of modern football, and appointed Bobby Houghton as head coach of the national team. He couldn't help either, but it wasn't really his fault. Like the others, he couldn't even talk to his players, and trying to get the CFA to change the system was impossible.

Despite the strong performances of cheap foreign imports in the league, it was still proving hard for China to attract big-name stars on their way to retirement as Japan was doing so successfully with its J-League. At the same time growth in China's export trade, while modest, started robbing the domestic league of its own best talent. It was a story common in developing football nations all over the world. Among the players to leave for Europe was Beijing's Yang Chen, who made his way to Eintracht Frankfurt in Germany. He was followed by Shanghai's Fan Zhiyi and Dalian's Sun Jihai, who both headed to Crystal Palace in England.

Excited by the news, I suggested to BTV Sports that we make a documentary on the players travelling to the UK: it would make fascinating viewing to see how China's stars, fêted by the fans at home, would adapt to fighting for places at a First Division club in south London. Unfortunately, I was not allowed to make the film. I was told that, as we would only be allowed to broadcast it if they succeeded in England, the risk of them failing was just too great. Documentary film-makers may cry at this point, and by the time we finally managed to track Fan down for a short feature, he was already in Dundee.

When new advertising restrictions finally killed the Marlboro man in China, the league changed into the colours of Pepsi. Locked in a bitter struggle in China with Coca-Cola, it was drawn in by the undeniable national 'potential' of Chinese football. Broadly in line with the roll-out of their manufacturing bases, the whole of China could be divided into Pepsi-blue cities and Coke-red cities. It was only in a few places, including Shanghai, that the two were fighting for dominance with huge marketing budgets.

Football was clearly Coke territory, and Pepsi and its eager agents never asked themselves why Mother Sponsorship herself had consistently turned down the chance to sponsor league football in China. Coke knew Chinese football did not connect with consumers in the ways Pepsi wanted to believe and Coke knew that football was detached from society, unlike almost every other market in the world. Coke was sponsor of the World Cup, and association with the Chinese league could only dilute and diminish that exalted position in the minds of the TV-addicted consumers.

By the tail end of the 1990s, the fizz was fading for Pepsi as standards of play in the professional league fell and rumours of corruption inside the game and gambling around it increased. Many Chinese people love to gamble, and, since it is illegal in mainland China, the state tried to capture these urges by launching state-owned welfare and, later, sports lotteries. The football lottery quickly became one of the most popular games, but nobody was naive enough to link it to Chinese matches; everyone knew they were too open to abuse. Rather, the coupon was made up of a selection of matches picked from such corruption-proof leagues as Italian Serie A.

As hundreds of millions of Chinese TV viewers settled down to watch the 1998 World Cup in France without China, the Chinese football league was witnessing open accounts about 'black whistles' (corrupted referees) and questionable performances from certain players and teams. As CCTV announced record advertising revenues from the World Cup, match attendance and TV audiences in China were in freefall.

In August 1998 one principled coach had finally had enough. At a press conference following the Division 'B' match between Yunnan Red Tower and Shanxi National Energy, the Shanxi head coach announced that certain members of his team had given a performance that was 'not normal'. It was a very brave move, and, a short time later, the club revealed further information about improper approaches made to the players before the match, even producing a tape recording to prove it.

The next month, during a Cup semi-final between local rivals Liaoning and Dalian Wanda, the Dalian team was so incensed at three separate penalty decisions that it walked from the field with the chairman shouting that the club would never come back. Once again, the situation had become so bad that teams were taking very public measures that threatened the authority of the CFA.

Dalian did return to competition, but, the following season, the problems continued with irregularities in the professional league, drawing more and more criticism. Since football had been allowed to leave state control, the state media faced far fewer restrictions in its reporting, and sports journalism became the frontline of oblique comments on the system itself. The farce reached its climax when Shenyang Sea Wolves and Chongqing turned out in a match that Shenyang had to win to avoid relegation. Many had predicted the result. Indeed, when Shenyang scored in the last minute, millions of fans and the media nodded their heads knowingly. This wasn't football, and the slogan 'Fake Ball' came into popular usage.

At the end of 1998, China's Olympic team made a fair showing at the Asian Games in Bangkok, coming third with a play-off victory against Thailand, having lost to eventual winners Iran. It made for lukewarm reading in the papers, but there was a long,

long way to go if China wanted its football team to bring it international honour.

Armed with this uncomfortable knowledge of how and, perhaps, why Chinese football had managed to continually beat itself up over fifty years of Communist and then capitalist madness, I convinced myself that the time for talking was over. Just like learning the Chinese language, the best way to approach China was to abandon all my preconceptions of logic and start again.

Deep inside, I felt I owed it to myself and to the Chinese people who had welcomed me to make contributions to follow my initial instincts: to travel back to the very beginning of modern football history and build a truly amateur football pitch. Only by proving it could be done with that symbolic act would I be able to 'speak with reason' about reconstructing football.

But before I did even that, I needed to learn to control myself, or things would get out of hand very quickly. The more passionate I get, the more excited I become, and there were delicate political implications of calling for sporting change in the system. Getting too excited is not necessarily the best thing when trying to get what you want in China; become too agitated or frustrated and your opposite number will just shut down. To better control and channel my well-intentioned, but increasingly impatient, urges to provoke change, I started taking kung-fu lessons.

16

Left Is Right, Right Is Left

Just as playing football had always been an important relaxation away from my media work, so martial arts became an activity away from worrying about football. My Master was a colourful character called Hog who came from Pingyao in Shanxi province, well known for its high-quality proponents of the martial arts. I was introduced to him along with a group of foreign friends who decided that years of living in China had been wasted simply as a result of laziness. The country was bursting with teachers able to impart the wisdom of the mysterious martial arts, and all we needed was to turn up and learn.

I first met the Master in the parking lot behind the Hilton Hotel in Beijing. That might make it sound seedy, but it was just a parking lot; he needed some space in which to show us his skills. These consisted mainly of being able to dodge our group's feeble attacks with just the slightest of movements and then, with a large amount of unknown force, throw the unfortunate attacker quite a few metres in a direction he had not expected. He also showed us some clever moves to thwart a range of attacks, and it all added up to be very impressive.

The Master was always smiling. In terms of close, unarmed combat, this was definitely an advantage as opponents recoiled from his breath. I tried to focus on his missing teeth when he spoke, but only as a way of trying not to register the state of the brown ones that still remained in his mouth. However, my mind was made up when he came marching across holding his index finger up and poked me with it. The pain went straight to the bone. It was like steel. 'Steel,' he smiled with mock surprise, repeating the procedure down the line of students to a series of similarly impressed 'ouches'. We agreed to meet weekly in Chaoyang Park.

At the start there were six or seven students, including two girls. The Master liked girls. He once boasted his *qi* was so strong that he could satisfy an entire village of women without breaking into a sweat. Since he would never find a village of women to agree, I doubted the veracity of this claim. As we stood around waiting for him, I lit a cigarette and was roundly chastised by one of the girls for doing so just before a martial arts lesson of all times. Just then the Master appeared with a cigarette wedged into one of his missing teeth. He proceeded to smoke his way through the entire lesson and assured me there was no danger.

Over the first weeks, there was no real progress as far as I was concerned. Very quickly, the Master had brutally divided us into different classes of student, ranging from 'dim and slow-witted' through to 'in his heart incompetent'. No matter how hard I tried, I couldn't find this damn thing he called *qi* and thus become the only 'model student'. Yes, I could tighten my muscles, but no, I couldn't make the 'feeling' move.

Throughout those early lessons, the steepest learning curve came in my new understanding of the various degrees of human pain. Apart from poking his steel fingers into different vulnerable parts of my body, the Master was fond of demonstrating the day's new moves on his students. I suppose it was necessary, but each new move could be mastered only after repeated punishment. And then slowly, after a few more weeks of pain and growing admiration for the science of human movement, something started to happen. It was physical, it was mental and it was spiritual, all at the same time. It totally shattered the distinctions between these fundamental human states that my western education led me to believe were separate.

Back home, my physical development was taken care of on the sports field. I sometimes exercised my brain in the classroom and I was meant to find spiritual enlightenment in church. I can't really remember many times when these three basic needs were presented together. Certainly, my football coach never explained there was a *yin yang* relationship between my foot and the ball or introduced the natural laws that defined the parameters of human capability. And yet here it was. Just as the Master suggested, it was possible to harness and marshal the physical strength within me, to express my intellectual understanding of space and time in new ways that defied my own western logic. He taught me that the process that led me inextricably from 'a' to 'b' to 'c' and then 'd' was taking me away from my starting position of balance. Life, he said, was circular. In Chinese there is no alphabet, no regimented order with beginning and end. To realize this, he told me, was to find the way to draw spiritual inspiration, even power, from such simple things as the earth and the sky. I also learned that Chinese martial arts draw heavily on the fighting skills and styles of animals. Not just the famous ones like the tiger, but many others including the chicken, whose quick darting movements teach important skills to those faced with a larger, but slower, opponent. I was never tempted to devote my life to the martial arts, but as I was a sports-loving, mentally inquisitive atheist, it blew my mind.

After some time, the number of students fell as work and other priorities took their toll. I was also finding it hard to make time to travel across town for the lessons, so I arranged with the Master to come and teach me at home. At that time, I was lucky enough to be living in a beautiful courtyard in west Beijing and here I learned much more about him, both his prowess at his beloved *xingyiquan* (sing yee chew-an) form and his general wisdom about so many matters of what was a form of common sense that I hadn't bothered to learn before.

The true value of the Master's skills was lost on most people I introduced. Having considered his slovenly appearance and atrociously massive and loud appetite at meal times, they dismissed him as a scrounger. For me, his little outlooks on life were priceless. One week, I received sample copies of a series on the best fights of Muhammad Ali. John and I were distributing the series to a TV station that had recently opened a new slot for boxing on its sports channel, and I took the time to look back at some of the great fights in which Ali had produced his magic.

When the Master arrived for my lesson, I loaded one of the tapes and asked him to tell me what he thought. As he stood there, smoking, he started tutting his disapproval and looked around for an ashtray, which was unusual, as he usually didn't bother. I let Ali demolish a few more opponents and then turned it off, as he seemed to be making the point that he had lost interest.

'You how think?' I said as we walked towards the door.

'We first eat food,' he replied, taking a left into the dining room. Once we had settled down, I asked him again what he thought of one of the greatest boxers of all time performing at the height of his powers.

'Too regretful,' he said, shaking his head, 'too regretful. They caught an extremely beautiful athlete, then teach him become handicapped! What disaster!'

'What meaning, what (is) called disaster?' I replied, frankly quite shocked. The Master grinned back at me and shovelled a few mouthfuls of food into his mouth. Not quite in between these impressive mouthfuls, he explained the reasons for his almost instant dismissal of the western world's fighting champion. He began by asking me how many eyes I had. 'Two,' I answered confidently, after blinking to check.

'You have how many ears?' he continued. 'Two,' I answered, using my two eyes to check left and right, which was obviously a very stupid reflex action. He grinned again.

'You have how many nostrils?' 'Still two,' I said, stopping myself from glancing down. I thought I was getting the picture. 'Arms?' he questioned. 'Two,' I replied. 'Legs? Feet?' he asked in quick succession. 'Two. Two.'

Seemingly satisfied with my answers, he returned to his meal. When he was full, which never happened before the maid's announcement that there was 'no more food left in Beijing' for the likes of him, he settled back and motioned for another cigarette.

'Speak,' I said, 'you what meaning, two, two, two?'

To cut his long story short, the Master suggested that, when he was born, Muhammad Ali was gifted with two good eyes to see with, two good ears to listen with, two good nostrils to breathe with, two good arms to punch with and excellent legs and feet to move with. He had a wonderful natural balance. For some reason that the Master could not understand, the people who had trained Ali had taught him to change this balance. He fought, the master said, like a man crippled down the left-hand side. There it was again – alternative logic. Whereas the western form teaches that, if you are right-handed, you lead with your left to set up for your strongest punch, the Master believed deeply that there is no left and right, or rather, as he told me with a huge grin, 'left is right, right is left'.

He found it very strange that, on discovering your left hand was weaker, your choice would be to twist your body to compensate. Surely, he informed me, you should be trying to bring the left side up to the same level of power and dexterity, trying to bring yourself back to the natural balance that you started with. I know that all sounds obvious to martial artists, but it was a revelation to me.

Ever since my teenage adventures in Brasil, I had always thought that a football was man's best friend. I told the Master about this theory and one week I tried a bit of ball juggling with him in the garden. Not surprisingly, he wasn't very good, but he did appreciate the coordination required.

The very next week he arrived with a larger grin on his face than normal carrying two sticks, a long bendy one and a shorter one. He said that football was fun, but there could be little doubt that a stick was man's best friend. With that, he handed me the shorter one and said it was time for me to find out why. Without further comment, he stepped back a few yards and started whipping his very long and flexible super-stick in impossibly rapid circular movements. The end that was hovering close to my head created a sound not dissimilar to a helicopter. Stepping back in automatic fear, I prepared to defend myself with what I felt was the short straw in my hand. Having missed fighting stick lessons at school, I clasped my weapon in the fashion of an early caveman, the baseball grip. As the Master frenetically increased the frequency of his stick's gyrations in tiny little concentric circles, it suddenly occurred to me that he might have lost face playing football and was going to prove a point by cutting my face open with a human-powered propeller. Thankfully, just as quickly as he had started, he withdrew the stick and did a short sequence of moves before bringing it back to its gentle resting position at his side. He looked contented, rather like an amateur footballer who has done 100 keepie-uppies in front of his envious mates.

Once we had stowed the big stick, in much more jovial fashion the Master demonstrated the many uses of the short stick, which he believed was the best representative for the 'man's best friend' competition. First, he showed me how ridiculous I looked holding it like a club by disarming me with embarrassing ease.

In his opening argument, he began by telling me that a man's fighting stick is an instrument to be cherished like a violin. Only the right piece of wood would do, with the right balance of flexibility, strength and smoothness. This appreciation itself was an important part of man's understanding and respect for nature and its laws.

For his first exhibit, he lifted the stick over his shoulder and, pretending to walk down the road and whistling, he told me that a stick was a friend to help you carry your belongings. Next, he pointed out a huge imaginary rock on the ground and made as if to wedge the stick underneath it. Levering it with all his theatrical might, he smiled and told me his stick was a friend who helped him move heavy objects. Then, he swivelled the stick around and dropped to his knee in a lightning movement. He was now holding the end of his stick like a hammer. As he started banging in imaginary nails, he turned to look at me. His broad, toothless grin told me that his stick was a tool that helped him build his home. As he stood up, the stick seemed to disappear and then it was there again in his other hand. He was now using it as a walking stick. Hunching over like an old man, he painted a picture of a long journey and said in a crackling voice, 'My heavens, if no stick, I for ever return not home.'

He had thought of a few more uses for his stick, including its role as an all-over massage tool and a back-scratcher for people like me who couldn't reach the bit in the middle. It was only then, after all these plausible and friendly uses, that he approached me with the stick in fighting mode. Without warning, he rapidly poked me twice very sharply in the solar plexus, with the second jab rising in a circular motion that clipped my jaw in the middle before retreating to within grabbing distance. Instinctively, I grabbed for the stick. It was the worst possible move, leading in milliseconds to excruciating pain and damaged wrists as he completed another little circle in totally the wrong dimension from my point of view. Rather triumphantly, he ignored my howls and ended his performance by spinning the stick into another position and doing a very reasonable impression of a snooker player taking a shot at the black.

'Fewest, (the) thirteen fist staff has eight uses. Your football has how many?'

Still nursing my injured hands, I told him rather curtly that the difference between a football and a stick is that my football sent a message of shared fun, while his stick gave the impression of impending violence that was particularly bloody painful for unarmed cavemen.

However, after a few lessons, the Master's magic sticks revealed to me their absolute brilliance when in the hands of even a relatively novice conductor. The computations involved when you add a stick into the martial arts equation are incredible. Extend your reach by thirteen fists of stout wood and you enter a new world of circular logic in which not only left and right are partners, but forward and back, up and down, top and bottom, inside and outside, under and over, soft and hard are all permutations you can control through your stick. Since your body may or may not be working with or against the motion of the stick at any given time, as soon as you start it moving, it becomes an evolving state of the above movements, limited only by your own speed and skill. I have to admit that, if a football doesn't work, a man's stick is his best friend.

Working with the Master gave me another fascinating insight into the relationships that Chinese people have with the world around them and how this understanding of universal balance is reflected in their interactions with each other. The martial arts not only brought me a form of enlightenment, they also totally cleared my body, mind and spirit for the football battles I was now ready to face.

Part Three

17

Education in the Countryside

In January 1999, my 'land for football' scout Professor Good came back to introduce a heavily bearded man I thought he called Mr Resourceful, who ran a company that built football pitches. His actual name turned out to sound like *chai*, the character for 'demolish', which seemed ironic at the time as it is painted on every condemned building in China. There were only about thirty football pitches in the whole city, so Mr Demolish was in a lonely profession, although my sympathy for him quickly turned to admiration as he told me he was able to win steady work from local governments and universities upgrading their stadia around the country.

Inspired by my plan to encourage millions of people to start playing the game, thus triggering the need for more pitches, Mr Demolish kindly offered to build my first pitch at cost and to advise on the thousand issues that I simply didn't know at the beginning. For a start, I grew up in England before the effects of global warming became apparent, and it was a muddy and pleasant land, a place where grass grew even if you didn't want it. Much of northern China, on the other hand, was a desert even before global warming, a place where very little grew without some artificial help and where water was in critically short supply. In such conditions, football pitches require an incredible number of tons of water, and this didn't sit well with the environmental discipline I also wanted to project.

In line with the environmental impact study I didn't have money to complete, I was sure my evolving idea that would provide entertainment for thousands of people and use only tiny pieces of waste land had to be better than the only other grass-based sport that was getting land at the time, golf. If you calculate the efficiency of various sports according to the number of participants per square metre of land used, football does quite well. Golf is totally ridiculous.

As the year sped past in a steep but absorbing learning curve, I also discovered that you couldn't just use any type of grass, but had to compromise between durability and duration. One type was very durable, but would only grow in May and die by the end of October, the other deteriorated more quickly with heavy use, but allowed play from April to late November. Great choice.

Still, the arrival of Mr Demolish on the scene gave me some hope again as, like Professor Good, he proved there were people in China who shared my vision and who were able to help it become reality as best they could. I knew I could trust Mr Demolish because his lush facial growth was very unusual in China, and it made him a deliberately distinctive and independent character. That said, I suppose, if he were ever to shave, nobody would ever find him.

Bearing in mind my friends' qualified advice, there was no point trying to launch the venture as a proper company; I would have to build the pitch and hope they would come. Like the other businesses I was advancing at that time in the even more tightly controlled media sector, if the football pitch was ever to be built, I had to accept the first rule of Chinese business planning: 'First do, later say.'

Just to be sure Demolish was playing it straight, through other contacts I got quotes from two companies capable of building a football pitch and then went back to see him. True to his word, his quote was about half that of the others, and he promised to give it his personal attention. He introduced the various stages that go into building a football pitch and guided me with helpful suggestions about the best time to complete each bit of the work given the harsh winter. Armed with this information and confident that I could at least fill in the fish ponds from my own savings, I went to see the State Farm. Big Plum, the Liverpool-loving leader, was delighted to see me again and cheerfully waved his hand to indicate full agreement to his assembled team.

'I like you, I like football,' he told me. 'You willing build a football pitch, introduce foreign friends come Dongbeiwang, that piece land, I give you use.'

'Give me, Teacher Plum? Extreme emotional thanks!'

Such an endorsement from the boss man is as good as a green light and signalled clearly to the other officials in the room that this was a project that was going to go ahead. Small Plum smiled and nodded his agreement. I wouldn't have time to complete the project that year, but there was now a real possibility that I would be playing on my own ground by the start of the new millennium. Big Plum's endorsement was most timely, and he showed me just how easy things could be if the right person in the right position said the right thing at the right time.

Over at BTV, my commentaries on the English football show were going well, and I even convinced the boss, Old Field, to let a crew including Song and me travel to England to commentate live from the 1999 FA Cup final. Since there was healthy sponsorship for the series that year, I also convinced him that we should take a studio at Wembley so we could deliver a live video feed for the first time. It was all going fine, until a bombshell. Literally. American-led forces bombed the Chinese embassy in Belgrade. Suddenly, the underlying anger that China has towards the outside world, which had been directed almost exclusively at the Japanese for years, was turned on foreigners of the Caucasian variety, especially ones who spoke English, though not exclusively. While angry students were being shipped to the diplomatic district to protest outside the American and British embassies on the other side of town, my maid was admitting that she had faced some pressure not to come to work that day. As I had known her for several years, it was a rude awakening and it left both of us feeling embarrassed. I also got a call from a friend at Beijing TV, telling me that I didn't need to come in for a couple of days. Apart from avoiding unnecessary comments, he told me that my well-advanced plan to take our coverage of the FA Cup final to a new level was also in jeopardy. They were expecting an order to cancel all media trips to UK and USA, and we might not even be allowed to broadcast the match. Even the imposition of martial law in 1989 hadn't stopped the FA Cup final.

True enough, BTV was told the expanded coverage and first ever Wembley studio was off the table, although the match could be broadcast. It was only when I pleaded that we risked losing a lot of goodwill by not sending anyone at all that Old Field reluctantly gave me the clearance to go myself and do an audio link with the Beijing studio at half-time.

'Only one thing,' the producer told me before I left, 'definitely not want speak politics or military affairs subjects, OK?'

I dismissed this as highly unlikely, given the nature of the chat at half-time in a football match. My disappointment at not achieving the type of coverage that many stations took for granted was more than balanced by the knowledge that I was going to attend the FA Cup final with childhood football heroes who were now employed by various media organizations. I had been in the ridiculous old gantry lift at Wembley before, but the FA Cup final brings out the world of football like no other event, and it was a veritable who's who of the English game all squeezed in on the way up. They all wore suits and had grey hair, which only added to the sense of historic occasion.

Just as air travellers dread the thought of sitting next to someone who talks all the time, so football commentators pray that they will not be sitting next to someone who talks very loudly. The South Americans are best for that. Luckily for the people either side of me, I was the quietest commentator they had ever seen. When they saw that I was not going to do any commentary at all, they looked at me strangely. 'Half-time interview,' I said, settling back to watch and smiling to myself at the strange route I had taken to get my first FA Cup final ticket.

When the game got underway, it was clear that Manchester United were stronger than Newcastle. Even an early injury to captain Roy Keane didn't seem to matter, and his replacement, Teddy Sheringham, put United into the lead. As the half came to a close, I picked up the line to Beijing and had a brief chat with the control room, where I knew that the producer, a Man United fan, would be in happy mood. He told me they would come to me a couple of minutes into the studio break, and I would have to keep going for six or seven minutes once we went live. I cleared my throat and repeated down the mike, 'Wei. Yi, er, san, san – er – yi, Luo Wen lai le Wen Bu Li.' I suppose the best translation would be, 'Hello. Three, two, one, one, two, three, Rowan's made it to Wemberlee!'

As the line went live, I was happy to chat about the first half and to concur with the studio guests in Beijing that it would be difficult for Newcastle to find a way back into the game. Song then opened up the questioning to get a bit of colour. 'Now half-time rest,' he asked, 'people all doing what?'

'Ai ya,' I laughed, 'Graceful United fans all leave seats, down go buy beer, prepare become FA Cup champions. Cow Card fans stay in seats, talk talk second half, they how can play match.'

'Two teams rest time, have what entertainment?'

It was a simple question. The teams are resting at half-time, what entertainment is there? I knew the answer, I could see and hear it in front of me, but I paused, not sure what to do. To answer truthfully, I had to break the only rule I had been given. I gulped and went for the truth.

'Er, FA Cup tradition invite army band play, everyone all listening to military music.'

Oh shit. It was there now, and I could only carry on as if I hadn't just provided the most damning evidence of the inextricable links between football and the armed forces that had helped bomb Chinese sovereign territory. I feared I was heading for a self-criticism on my return, but nothing was ever said. As it was, the whole embassy bombing affair got smoothed over very quickly as the Chinese people realized that their government might well have been providing some help to the regime of Milošević. Foreigners were once again friends, and my maid came to work with her old smile. It was like everything went back to normal.

Armed with Big Plum's magnanimous offer of land for my pitch, subject only to the small matter of a gentlemen's agreement, and with a lot riding on Mr Demolish, I went to see the head of BTV Sports once we got back from England. As his name was Old Field and the character for field looks like four little football pitches, I was confident of a warm reception for my grassroots plan.

I suggested that, as we were making fairly good advertising and sponsorship revenue from our broadcasts of English football, it might be a good idea to invest some more of that back into grassroots sport. Old Field had convinced me to support the establishment of BTV Sangao Academy, China's first junior football education academy, some years earlier, so I argued that now it was time to encourage participation among the adult population. He agreed to invest a small percentage of the profits from sponsorship around the English football live shows, and this was enough for me to get construction underway. Old Field is another true champion, a man who voluntarily took money from the top of the game and put it back in at the bottom. At the same time as allowing me to start reclaiming the site from the fish ponds and to evict the resident pigs, the official support of BTV and my football-led public profile were hugely important as a protection against any number of things that can go wrong in a 'first do, later say' project.

Despite seeing in the new millennium in a rainy Trafalgar Square with a BTV crew, as the world celebrated the realization there was no computer bug after all, I felt that we might all well be on the cusp of a new beginning. I didn't feel or look as old as I thought I would in the year 2000 and so I started the year with a spring in my step and feeling positive about life and the challenges ahead.

The Chinese national football team also started off the new millennium in fine fashion, beating New Zealand in a warm-up friendly and launching its assault on the Asian Cup with an 8-0 victory over the Philippines and a 19-0 destruction of part-timers Guam. A 2-0 away win against Vietnam also felt very good to the fans, who were once again getting a feel for this football business.

Out in the countryside, Mr Demolish was holding out the prospect of playing football on my own ground in just a few months. At his suggestion, I plumped for his special mixture of grass that happened to be similar to that which he wanted to use in another job, so he gave me an even bigger discount. This mix, he explained, was the best of both worlds, durable and dead for only a few months a year.

Next in the list of problems was the people needed to build a football pitch. To save money and promote the idea of urban money going to rural workers, I naively decided to employ locals with no specific experience. My mistake was to engage them through the tenant of the land bordering our plot, Manager Ticket. The diminutive Ticket was always out to gain a petty *renminbi* and he started trying to make a little bit of money out of filling in the fish ponds. He continued to do so at every stage of the project, even down to the dodgy basins and showers in the clubhouse. Although he knew about football from the television, I don't think he ever understood what I was trying to do, and I calculated his little extras into my budget.

With Beijing full of construction sites, disposing of displaced earth was a major problem, and people with holes to fill could charge to accept the dirt. According to Mr Demolish, only the top layers of earth needed to be high quality, so Ticket took that as licence to allow all sorts of rubbish to be tipped in and pocketed the proceeds. This included a pile of massive rocks, the perfect objects if you want your second season to be remembered for goals scored from the 'corner with a crater in it'.

As I could not afford the time to manage the project, Professor Good took control and, together with Ticket, muddled sideways and then forward, stepping over and round the most difficult problems for later. Progress was slower than expected and revealed how clear important instructions had to be. It seemed a simple thing to say, but it was, and still is, impossible to plan for every eventuality.

Thankfully, the levelling of the ground made my vision much easier for others to see, and several Chinese and foreign friends became enthusiastic as well. By early 2000, the pitch was taking shape as drainage channels went in, and I commissioned Professor Good to find someone to make iron grates. It all looked good until Mr Demolish dropped his own bombshell. Even if he went ahead with the spring planting on schedule, I would not be able to play on the pitch this year, as the grass would need more time to take root. He said spring 2001 was the new target for actually using it. Since this meant another year to wait, he convinced me to delay the planting altogether until late into the summer.

In the meantime, despite my previous military outburst, I managed to convince Old Field at BTV Sports to let me go back to London for the FA Cup final again. It was the last one to be played at the old Wembley Stadium before it also had a controversial refurbishment that would go over time and budget. This time Song went with me to deliver the full match commentary with our producer, Wang Qi, but the idea of having our own TV studio like the grown-up broadcasters had gone away. Still, it was a historic occasion, and to convey at least some of the excitement I felt at being present, when the Chinese viewers rejoined our commentary for the second half, I shouted, 'Stroooolllleeeeerrrs!' to my teammates, who I knew would be watching back in Beijing. Song was not amused and found it necessary to explain to the audience in some detail that I was upset at Wembley closing and should be excused this strange outburst.

Autumn offers the best weather in Beijing's otherwise windy, cold or hot annual cycle, and it was early September 2000 when Mr Demolish finally gave his men the OK to sow his special mixture of seeds. Like an expectant father, I watched nervously over the next couple of weeks until small blades of grass nervously poked their heads through the soil. After a month, the whole pitch was a riot of joyous young blades fighting to reach the sun, and at last it was time to take the final step. With Mr Demolish's agreement, I gave the signal for the groundsmen to cut my grass to regulation length.

This was an agonizing experience for two reasons. First, we had only a normal garden lawnmower, which broke several times before the job was completed over a couple of days. Second, when it was all finished, I could see and touch the finished product but, on strictest instructions from Mr Demolish, I wasn't allowed to play on it. It was beautiful – a massive wedge of green grass in the middle of a football desert. My first attempt to start a football revolution in China with one of the world's smallest regulation-sized football grounds had finally appeared out of the fish ponds. The addition of ceremonial corner flags completed the picture. Now, armed with a football pitch, albeit one I could not play on, I felt it was the right time to revisit the idea of football as a business with the core group of people who were now forming around that vision.

One of the first to join Mr Demolish and my Chinese supporters like Old Field, Professors Good and Fruit and Big Plum was Shani, a British-Iranian midfielder for Peking Strollers, who was running his own catering business in Beijing. His kitchen was operated from a hotel run by my old friend Mr Find from the Poachers Inn. Since Mr Find also had a bar/restaurant in the hotel that he was not really using, it was natural to merge the football pitch, the bar/restaurant and the kitchen to create the core elements of a good amateur football club. The only problem was that they were forty miles apart. It was impossible to find land for a pitch in the city proper, and there was no point having a bar in the middle of the countryside.

Andy, the wonderfully combative lawyer who was a partner at my media investment company, was also itching to challenge Chinese law by applying for an amateur football club licence. As far as he knew, none had ever before been granted, at least not on the terms he wanted to prosecute. Also back on the scene was Keith Bradbury, the enterprising student midfielder who had played football with the two Trevors when England visited in 1996. He had since graduated and become a member of a team of equally enterprising foreigners, including Strollers left back Mark, who built zhaopin.com, one of China's biggest recruitment websites.

Alongside their support, my Chinese backers continued to prefer playing advisory roles, telling me it was better to first create a foreign company outside mainland China, as I had done with my media services company, CMM-I. It was not that they were reluctant to provide me with public support, but rather that none felt as confident as I did in tackling the issues around sport and they all saw my passion as a foreigner as my best weapon.

In October 2000, Andy led us into incorporation of an offshore football investment venture that I named Amateur Football Holdings, or AFH. I became chairman and brought my football pitch to the party. Shani brought his experience in events and restaurants and his kitchen, while Keith agreed to join as the general manager once we were established. It was Andy's job to achieve the China trading licence we would need, and I used my joint-venture investment consulting company to incubate the project.

While we happily plotted away, Chinese attention was on the national team as it once again attempted to win the Asian Cup, the major regional trophy. It was an adventure that usually ended in heartache, and this time the finals were to be held in Lebanon. In a repeat of the 1992 competition, China made it into the semi-finals, where it faced Japan. Just as in 1992, the Japanese emerged 3-2 winners. This time, the Chinese team had led 2-0 before they collapsed, and I could feel the collective pain.

As winter approached, I went regularly to check on the pitch and found that Manager Ticket, whose antics were continually amusing, had been letting the local police in to play. There were also local children jumping over the fence in the evenings, and the delicate grass was showing signs of anguish around the goalposts. When I told Ticket he should refuse them entry, he just said, 'No way, police,' and shrugged his shoulders. By now, I knew the way it worked. As it was the local police, not the mafia, I knew who to go to for protection – the local police themselves. After establishing that I was the rightful user of the land and chairman of a club that represented many foreign friends of Beijing, I said how happy I was to find that the local police liked playing football.

'Welcome you come our club kick football,' I told them, 'but hope you possible wait next year, now grass just just start growing, very easy ruined.'

The police agreed with my offer of setting a regular time for one game each week the following season and even promised to tell the local kids not to go in while we waited. In return, they informed me about the regulations for holding matches and the need to gain their approval for any public activities involving over 100 people. Things had certainly improved since my university days, when the limit was ten, but was the Party ten times more open or ten times more confident?

In the end, I couldn't resist the temptation of the grass and authorized a couple of games without the police or Mr Demolish knowing. The first match at the ground, originally christened 'Beijing Number One Amateur Football Factory' in deference to the creativity of Chinese work unit names, was Beijing Strollers v. Beijing TV. As had become usual in such games, I played one half for each team. The first ever goal scored was a beautiful drive by John, a hard-tackling Scottish defender. Bastard, I was meant to get the first one.

Soon after this inaugural game, I was contacted by the organizers of the World Football Expo scheduled to take place in Cannes in January 2001. Delighted that I had now played on the pitch resurrected from waste land, I saw the Expo as an excellent opportunity to introduce AFH to the outside football industry and a personal chance to record my vision of how China might learn to love football. I knew the way trade shows operated, so I agreed a barter deal with the organizers which resulted in AFH getting a complimentary exhibition booth in Cannes. Separately, I managed to get myself on the conference programme as a speaker.

As it turned out, the organizers were delighted because Shani, Keith, myself and our friend Phil were the only representatives from a Chinese club at the whole event. It seemed amazing to me that not a single Chinese professional football club bothered to attend, and that it was left to a bunch of foreigners with a recently converted pig sty on a Beijing farm to fly the flag for the game. Nevertheless, there was considerable interest in the fact that China was attending at all, and we warmly accepted the accolades, receiving several famous visitors at our little stand, including Sepp Blatter, who kindly signed our football.

At the Expo conference, I introduced my vision of grassroots football and the establishment of AFH as the first company to focus on this level of the game in China. Among those who later expressed interest was the compiler of the football report released annually by Deloitte. He said he liked the idea but didn't like the name, it was too amateur. That was the whole point. To understand Chinese football, you have to forget all assumptions and clear your mind of the belief that football has always been there.

While I was in Europe trying to explain that football in China was different and needed specialist remedial care, a couple of Iranian players in the Strollers team had established friendly relations with the authorities in Tianjin as part of their import-export business. It had come to their attention that one of the police chiefs was a keen footballer. In fact, he had created his own team of semi-pros in their twenties, which had already beaten all local opposition. They suggested that we bring an international select team of foreigners to play a friendly game against them. True to his word, the police chief organized everything, and we made our way to Tianjin in a specially laid-on bus and played the game in front of several thousand fans in one of the local stadia. It was the first time I had played in front of such a big crowd, but we were no match for the police chief's team and went down 2-0 with no real chances to score.

A couple of months later, we were contacted again. The police chief had scheduled a match against the China youth team for the main stadium in Tianjin in a match to be covered live on local TV. However, the China youth team had cancelled at the last minute and we were invited to fill in. This time, we would get a police escort all the way from just outside Beijing to Tianjin and would be put up for the night at a top hotel. Remembering the tricks played in Guangzhou at the Women's World Cup, I made doubly sure to confirm they would provide take-away meals to eat when the bus set off, a good five hours before the match. They agreed, but when the bus turned up there was no food, and everyone was starving by the time we arrived in Tianjin.

On entering the stadium complex, there were large crowds cheering loudly, and we all forgot about our hunger and became excited at the impending chance to play to a full house in a public stadium with potentially millions watching on TV. Inside the stadium we were shown to our changing room and we slipped out on to the pitch to take in the atmosphere. It seemed incredible that so many would turn up to watch us play, but then again the police chief was an important man and, if he sent you an invitation, who were you to decline?

After changing, we headed out to the pitch for a warm-up and for the first time felt the pressure of a really large crowd. Whenever a less-gifted player fumbled the ball or sliced a pass, the whole crowd laughed at him. At the same time, all one had to do was jog over to the stands and wave at the crowd and they would all cheer back. We had brought a few footballs to give away, but when we kicked them into the stands, they were thrown back again. After several attempts, they got the message and more cheering resulted.

Back in the changing room, we gathered for a team talk, which was immediately disrupted when a few volunteers suddenly arrived. They were carrying large boxes that they proceeded to deposit in the middle of our changing room. It was the stacks of piping-hot Kentucky Fried Chicken we were meant to have received in Beijing. There were just thirty minutes to kick-off, but the smell alone had caused uncomfortable rumblings in my stomach within seconds. As a few players moved to explore the boxes, Scottish John shouted a prophetic warning, 'Don't eat it, it's a trick!'

It was too late. Seeing others groaning with pleasure as they tucked into the overdue chicken, I could resist no longer and tricked myself into believing it would be all right if I just had one spicy chicken burger. Of course, it wasn't all right, and several players had stitches before the game started. While we were eating, the stadium management was watering the pitch, completely changing the conditions from just a few minutes earlier. Since I was wearing my dry grass boots with no studs, I was effectively out of the game before it started on two counts.

We had put together a good team by our standards, but the police chief's team was better in every single position except his own. Even one of our Chinese forwards, Jimmy, who could break twelve seconds in the 100 metres, was outpaced by his opposite number. The police chief himself was not a bad player, and all free kicks and corners were left to him. He was protected on either side by two brilliant midfielders who won back the ball when he lost it and gave it to him to try again. They were so superior they could afford to work a series of small passes with him as they brought the ball out of defence, giving him several touches before they even reached the half-way line, then holding the ball until he caught up again.

With a chicken-filled belly and a pair of ice skates on my feet, I was worse than useless and I could see others in the team struggling around me. At half-time I decided that proper boots the wrong size would be preferable and I borrowed our goalkeeper's spare pair, which were two sizes too big. In addition to the embarrassment unfolding on TV, the stadium crowd was also being entertained by the public address system through which a couple of commentators were describing the action as the police chief's team cruised into a three-goal lead without a single dangerous shot from our side.

Although I wasn't slipping so much, the large-sized boots meant that, whenever I moved to prod the ball forward, I found I had already done so. It was also hard to chase the ball without catching the edges of my boots on the grass with each step. At one point, one of our team hoofed a long ball over my head, and I charged down the pitch with a good few yards on the nearest defender. As I reached the ball skidding away ahead of me, I could hear the excited commentator speaking very fast through the loudspeakers: 'You see, you see, our player runs, with foreigner compared, very fast! Now very easily overtaking him, collecting ball, now passing give his teammate. Beautiful.' As I glanced to my left, I saw that very same defender hurtling past at twice my speed and doing exactly as the commentator suggested with an easy smile on his face. The crowd roared their approval as I despondently trailed the redundant sweeper back to the half-way line.

With fifteen minutes still to go our team was completely knackered, while the police chief's team remained fresh and ready to play another three halves at the fastest pace we could offer. It seemed impossible that we would ever score, but we would try our best to the end. Suddenly, I found myself strangely unmarked as a through ball reached me deep into the opposition half. Turning towards goal, I expected tackles to come in from all angles, but only the goalkeeper stood in front of me, while two of my teammates appeared on either side. As we homed in on the penalty area, I saw the goalkeeper moving, not towards me, but sideways, out of the way.

It is normal for teams to lay off the pressure when a game is one-sided, but never before had I seen a superior team actually stop in the middle of the game to allow the opposition to score a soft goal. As I approached the penalty spot, I glanced back, and the police chief's team was, to a man, standing with hands on hips. How could I accept this gift? It made a mockery of the game and would be the ultimate loss of my sporting dignity. At the same time, if I did smash the ball into the net, I knew the Chinese crowd would be delighted, and the police chief would truly feel that he had given our team face. All the sporting contradictions between western and eastern culture that I had been grappling with became concentrated into that one single, highly public moment. To save sporting face, I had to lose Chinese face or vice versa.

Not sure what to do, I stopped the ball on the line and thought about this question as the stadium waited. To give the goalkeeper the chance to at least make a symbolic effort, I walked the ball along the line and started kicking it gently against the opposite goalpost. There was still no reaction, so I finally put the ball over the line for a goal kick. A good ten minutes early, the referee blew the final whistle, and it was all over. Some in the VIP sectiond may have found my action ungrateful, but I will never score such a goal. It would have to be much more subtle than that.

Later that evening at the official team hotel, we prepared for a night out on the town, but the police chief had anticipated this potential danger and was already several steps ahead. When I went down to reception to ask one of our kindly appointed police guides the best place to go, he said simply, 'You special guests, no have good place. You stay at hotel.'

Although I knew where he was coming from – he had instructions – there was no way the international football team was going to spend its Saturday night in the hotel and so we dismissed his pleas and headed out to the street to catch cabs to a bar that one of the team had heard about. Amazingly, when I flagged down a free cab, he asked, 'You are (or) are not special invited football team?'

I hadn't expected the match would make us so famous in Tianjin, but it augured well and I proudly told him that we were indeed that team and started opening the door to get in. 'No good, no good,' he said reaching across to close the door again. 'Special police instructions, not take team anywhere. You return hotel!'

In the end, the only thing we could do was split up into small groups and pick up taxis from a few blocks away where we might easily be mistaken for ordinary foreigners who were allowed out at weekends. In the end, we all managed to turn up at the bar we were aiming for. After a single beer, it closed. Jumping into taxis again, we went to another place. Sorry, they told us, just closing. And so it was everywhere we went until we ended up back at the hotel.

As the weather warmed up again in summer 2001, China started practising holding its breath for the result of the IOC's final announcement of the city to host the 2008 Olympic Games. This time around, Beijing was in the final hat with Toronto, Istanbul, Osaka and Paris, but was widely believed to be the favourite. Given China's progress since the last attempt and its increasing status in a post-Cold War world, surely the IOC representatives could not deny the Chinese people again. As in 1993, I was involved in the media side of Beijing's official campaign and I celebrated with the rest of my colleagues when the news came through on BTV's live feed. I felt particularly proud as it was my first ever co-presenter, the graceful Saucy Flower, who reported the news as part of the team sent to Moscow for the 13 July event.

The hundreds of thousands who poured out into the Beijing streets that night were not part of a staged government rally. Although there were some of those too, it was a true outpouring of emotion fuelled by the huge value attached to the Olympic Games as a symbol of China's re-emergence, every single Chinese citizen's re-emergence, into the international community of nations.

I rejoiced with my Chinese friends and took excited phone calls from friends and family in Europe and America, but I also knew China had just signed up to the biggest challenge since Deng Xiaoping embarked on his opening policy. This time, it would be international rules inside China, and there would be a vast number of requirements that would challenge the government from the Ministry of Foreign Affairs through to the Environmental Protection Agency.

The principles and ethics of the Olympic movement would provide a platform for all those tricky issues, not so much the three sensitive 'Ts' – Tiananmen, Tibet and Taiwan – but the 'ABCs' – Asset-stripping, Bribery and Corruption – and human rights, the environment, health and safety, religious freedom, press freedom and many others. While other people would argue about all these matters, it was football and the true values of sport that I hoped could become an inspiration to the Chinese nation.

Sadly, the one area that was likely to remain immune to criticism and closed to change would be the sports system itself. Over at the glorious Sports Ministry, officials were already being tasked with making sure China won as many gold medals as possible in as many Olympic sports as possible. The first order from the top was to: CONCENTRATE ON THE ELITE. Now that the PRC had won the right to host the Olympics, it had to win them. As the government ticked off the sports, it was only football that caused a major problem, some officials even suggesting it might be better to concentrate elsewhere.

Fresh from my awkward experience in Tianjin, my wider concerns about what the Olympic spirit meant to the Chinese leadership and, to a large extent, the people only served to drive me forward. At the small converted plot in the farmland near Beijing, I finally moved to pre-operation stage with my new amateur football sanctuary, a place where there were no such things as teams stopping in the middle of a match and where the 'strenuous, rigorous, competitive training' advocated by the CFA was a relative term for minimum Sunday league fitness.

Beijing can be made green in summer, and I was desperate that the site include as much plant life surrounding it as possible. Establishing a small budget for the beautification project with plenty of time, Professor Good, at the very last minute, finally introduced his friend, an elderly professor of landscape gardening. It was a comical disaster: 90 per cent of the trees and plants, specifically chosen for their suitability, were dead when I turned up to check. Bearing small tags with Chinese names that I had never seen before, they had been delivered late at night on a Monday, when 'nobody was there'.

According to Ticket, this missing link meant that clarifying exactly when, where and how they died and who was responsible could never become more than a matter of intense dispute. He personally blamed the old professor for picking scientifically inaccurate plants that he said he could have got much cheaper. His manager, meanwhile, poured scorn on the truck drivers who fled the scene having dumped their load, shaking his head and repeating, 'Dead on arrival, dead on arrival,' again and again. I was not going to track the truckers back into Hebei for an explanation, so I could only give up and take the hit.

Thankfully, most of the site was lined with mature trees and various plants described to me as 'weeds' started sprouting up along the boundary walls far more effectively than the dead plants I had bought. Ticket, who was still saying he could get some 'grow fast trees' at half price from nearby, was perplexed to see me informing his work team not to touch the pesky weeds he had told them to remove. 'If green,' I told them, 'don't kill, add water.'

Together with the blooming expanse of football grass in the middle, the overall impression was certainly green enough for anyone living in Beijing. Mr Demolish had warned me that water supply would be an issue once we started using it regularly, so I entered into early discussions with the salad cream factory next door to see whether I might use the waste water produced in their manufacturing process to feed the pitch. By chance, China was instituting new rules about waste management and, as always, the first enterprises targeted in the campaign were Sino-foreign joint-ventures. Japanese-invested ventures were at the top of the hit list. While the grass kept growing inside the compound, a brand new waste-water treatment plant sprang up just over the back wall. The only question was whether the treated water was all right for the pitch.

Mr Demolish suggested that, in principle, if you could drink it, it was OK, so Ticket offered to hire somebody to try. I didn't think that was the best idea, and the factory clarified that, while within legal limits, the water was not for human consumption. Neither could it be relied on to cover our needs during the scorching summer months when we most needed water; the salad cream was already in the shops by then, so production was down. In the end, I followed local convention and allowed Ticket to drop an unregistered well hidden in a small building with an 'observation post' on the top.

Back in town, our new rickety old wooden football bar started receiving customers with a Shani-inspired menu that included such favourites as shepherd's pie, English breakfast and the highly regarded beef stroganoff. These dishes are seldom seen on Chinese tables, but the mix of western specials attracted eclectic groups, including football-loving members of a new generation of Chinese white-collar fans who had grown up with McDonald's and Pizza Hut on every corner.

Although I had established an offshore football company, it was still not legally operating in China, so while the principle of 'first do, later say' had succeeded in enabling me to get going, it was a precarious position once my partners and I started trading, as the value of any assets could not be protected.

From the time AFH was established as the holding company, it took lawyer Andy and our local agents nearly a year to achieve the next step, which was to establish a joint-venture in China with Mr Demolish's pitch-building company. It was much harder than I had thought, but only because it had never been done before. The type of venture we wanted could normally be approved at a district level in Beijing, but the local administration of industry and commerce was worried that the sports sector was still restricted for foreign investment and required a letter of support from the Beijing Football Association.

I knew the BFA president, Zhang Heng, another great servant of the Chinese game as a player and official, and the BFA was willing to help, but the rules forbade foreign companies from buying or operating football clubs. This was a rule set up to protect professional clubs for some reason, but I wanted an amateur club licence. I told Mr Zhang I specifically did not want a professional club licence.

Officially, the BFA was delighted that somebody wanted to invest in a sector that it did not, but, as such a venture had never before been suggested, it was felt more prudent to refer the matter to the China Football Association. There, the response was basically the same. Unofficially, the CFA thought I was mad, but as long as I wanted no part of its professional league or elite Olympic structure, it could see no official reason to refuse. However, to be doubly safe, it was felt prudent to secure the blessing of the central sports administration first.

While the administration remained faceless to me, somebody nodded agreement, and the correct letters were finally provided. It was official: I had full government permission for the first joint-venture amateur football club in Beijing and, as far as I knew, mainland China. In Chinese, courtesy of a brainstorming session with Professor Fruit, the name was officially certified as 'Beijing Ten Thousand Countries Mass Stars Football Club Limited Company'.

I had already decided the English name, it was something I said all the time. 'What China needs,' I would tell people repeatedly, 'is proper club football.' I could think of no words that better reflected my central idea about the need for amateur clubs or more succinctly expressed my aim to build a club of such clubs, so I just stuck them together to create ClubFootball. From a copywriting perspective, it was generic and inclusive and indicated a claim to the central space created by China's missing consumer football market. Even better, the words 'football' and 'club' were widely known by millions of English speakers of all levels across the country, so if they could just learn to put their club first, it shouldn't be too hard to get my message across.

Although the authorities still couldn't see it, my undertaking was horizontal, not vertical. I did not want to win the Chinese FA Cup, but organize millions of people with no more personal ambition than to enjoy the game at the same level that I did. That is why they thought I was mad, but I saw it as proof I was still sane. I truly believed that building from the grassroots was the only way China would ever achieve its dream to reach even the final stages of the World Cup.

Because the process had taken so long, no champagne was uncorked when the papers were finally received. It was only as I presented my new ClubFootball name card to my Chinese friends and colleagues that it finally sank in. They all joked that I was now a big businessman with the title of 'Football Club Chairman'. If it says so on your name card, they said, it must be true.

After a decade of playing, talking, reporting, thinking and dreaming about football in China, a Deng-inspired leap of revolutionary faith while nursing my testicle had set me on a path that led to a group of Chinese and foreign people who shared my hopes. With their support, I had reached an important new milestone. I was no longer just the foreigner who talked about football on TV, I was the chairman and legal guardian of a fully licensed football venture. We were located just a long throw-in from the Workers Stadium, the heart of Chinese football, and it was the heart of the game that I wanted to revive.

18

The Liverpool Stories

Even as I was happily getting started with my hugely ambitious but focused bottom-up plan of attack through the new ClubFootball joint-venture, some of the big European and South American clubs were looking beyond the idea of TV rights and summer exhibition matches and addressing the potential for extracting further revenue from consumers in booming China.

Back in 2000, the issue of club ownership had come into sharp focus in England when Rupert Murdoch's Sky TV made what was then considered an audacious pitch to take control of Manchester United. Scrambling to get a piece of the action, ITV player Granada had also sought to invest, this time in two top clubs, Liverpool and Arsenal. However, the British government had intervened, and both media organizations were restricted to purchasing a maximum of 9.9 per cent in each club and establishing subsidiaries to exploit opportunities in new media, including broadband TV.

Driven by efforts to build a value-added relationship with Liverpool, Granada decided that China was a suitable market in which to test the merger of football and media interests. In these two respects, at least, it was the right place to start, and I was engaged to advise on the project. China's football crisis is so huge and fundamental that the best efforts and biggest budgets can disappear into the country without providing sustainable results, and it was going to be the same with Liverpool. For this reason, at the very outset, the initial investment into 'Liverpool in China' was limited to the level of a modest PR project and focused on media applications.

When I first arrived in China in the late 1980s, the great Liverpool teams of the era were revered. The club was at its peak just as the country was opening its doors, creating something approaching an emotional attachment and even hinting at some chance of loyalty among fans over thirty-five (an unchartered demographic, as most brands focused on advertising at younger people). Among the great players in those Liverpool teams, the Welsh goal machine Ian Rush stood out in Chinese minds as one of the best players who, like China, had never played in the World Cup finals. Given that Ian was considerably less expensive (and more available) than the club's then striker Michael Owen, we invited him into the project, and Old Field at Beijing TV agreed to come on board as the first broadcast partner.

I started by travelling to Liverpool to file a series of short reports introduced by Ian, including a guided tour of the club. From the moment he arrived at my hotel, it was obvious that Ian had the freedom of the city; the people's passion for football reflected back on one of its star players long after he had retired. Everyone, from the doorman to other drivers on the road, waved and shouted greetings everywhere we went. It was just like being a foreigner in a provincial town in China.

At the training ground, we wandered in past the Japanese fans at the gate to watch Gérard Houllier take charge of a full training session and chatted with a couple of the players. At the end of the session, we set up in one of the buildings to record the signing of the shirts that would form the centrepiece of our 'Liverpool in China' prize competition. With many people in China increasingly sceptical about 'authentic' signed shirts finding their way into prize competitions, this was a process I wanted to film – to show Owen,

Gerrard and the others sign our shirts. It was amusing to watch the players' reactions as I introduced them using my own interpretations of their likely Chinese names.

'Ai ya, everyone look, he is Ga Li Ma Ka Li Se Te!'

Signing shirts is an integral part of a professional footballer's life, so it makes perfect sense to regulate the process by fixing regular times, such as after training, to grab a few signatures. As with all important football memorabilia that came in my direction, at least one of these shirts made its way back to the wall of the Club-Football Centre. Since the Liverpool team signing that day had five cups to their name in a single season, it remains one of the more valuable items.

After failing to get an interview with Michael Owen because he was upset about being dropped (and, as Ian kept pointing out, I was still interviewing the groundsman), we headed off to the Liverpool FC Academy to meet Steve Heighway and learn about the youth development system that had brought through Owen, Gerrard and Jamie Carragher. Like the elite facilities in China, it was a wonderful centre with indoor and outdoor pitches, training rooms and classrooms – the top of the junior elite pyramid.

In England, Liverpool are restricted to scouting for young players living within a certain distance of the club and, like their rivals, Everton, and all other clubs in Britain, it has well-established links with schools and amateur clubs in its catchment zone. It is a great honour for the red side of the city to play in the famous shirts, but the programmes went far beyond the depth strictly necessary to catch emerging talent as in China. The Liverpool Academy and the club itself played an active role in popularizing the sport throughout the community, providing the right social conditions for talent to emerge.

Back at Anfield, we stood by the Shankly Gates, and Ian talked to camera about the pressure the opposition felt as they went through them on match day. We paused by the Hillsborough memorial, and he took the time to explain to Chinese viewers how that disaster and the earlier calamity in Belgium had affected the whole city and the club, but also revealed their great community strengths.

After seeing the changing rooms, we touched the famous 'This is Anfield' sign in the tunnel and emerged into the stadium just as a group of museum visitors were coming past. Suddenly there was a scream as one of the group saw Ian and rushed towards him. She was a fanatic Liverpool fan from Wales, and Ian Rush was her all-time hero. Her husband had given her this trip to Anfield as a birthday present, and she almost fainted when she saw him standing in front of her.

With the utmost grace, Ian signed autographs for the whole group and posed for a series of photos with the excited woman standing in front of the Kop. As our camera rolled, I knew that he would enjoy China. After they had gone, we wandered up into the famous stand, and he told me how the crowd could virtually suck the ball over the line. For Chinese fans used to watching matches in cold government stadia, this feeling would be very hard to imagine and was impossible to convey on television.

The next stage of the 'Liverpool in China' project involved collecting a selection of great matches from the club's illustrious history that had never been seen in China before and presenting them as a TV series called *The Liverpool Story*. Although it proved hard to get the rights cleared, we ended with a series sponsored by Virgin Atlantic that included an in-depth documentary and a selection of classic matches, including the great European Cup quarter-final second-leg win over St Etienne in 1977. Having packaged the series in Beijing, we welcomed Ian to make a tour of China to promote the club and *The Liverpool Story*.

We started off in Chengdu, where the Chinese TV industry was again gathering for the biannual Sichuan TV Festival. Outside the exhibition hall, there were several hundred local people hoping to catch a glimpse of their favourite TV drama stars. Even the odd foreigner, working for a distribution company, elicited some excitement. With Ian Rush's arrival timed to coincide with a small function for *The Liverpool Story*, I travelled ahead of Mark, Adrian and George from Granada to make sure everything was in order.

Since the objective was to make a splash, I took time to pick out a single hopeful youngster wearing a football shirt and whispered to him that Ian Rush, the top goal-scorer of all time for Liverpool, would be arriving soon, and I would get him an autographed T-shirt. A few other people had seen me talking to him and, as I moved on, they eagerly surrounded him to ask what the foreigner had said. When I came back out of the building a few minutes later, there was an expectant gasp, and the eyes of the crowd followed me as I made the short walk across to the car park opposite the exhibition hall. Before he got out of the car, I warned Ian he might have to sign a few autographs on the way in. 'No problem,' he said.

The 100-metre walk to the exhibition took us nearly ten minutes as thousands clamoured round for Ian Rush's autograph. He did his best to scribble as many as he could, but, rather than diminishing, the jovial crowd just got bigger and bigger, until we were lost in the middle, moving backwards and forwards with each new surge. Quickly, it became ridiculous, and I doubted we would ever make it inside. This was even better than I had expected.

With a lot of laughing and shouting 'Protect (the) famous person!', which was a deliberately mixed message, we inched our way towards the doors and nearer to the security guards, who were standing by equally powerless until we got closer. As we squeezed through the barriers in front of the doors, I saw the boy whom I had whispered to, hanging on with both hands. I turned back and shouted to him, 'I not able forget you. Wait fifteen minutes, I back come.'

Inside the hall, conditions were calmer, although Ian spent more than the allotted time being photographed and signing *Liverpool in China* T-shirts for TV station executives from across the country. As soon as I could, I asked him to sign one for me and went outside. The crowd was gone, but the boy was there and beamed as I handed it over.

Having been to every major TV festival in China since 1990 and attempted organizing several functions of my own, I knew it was extremely hard to create the right atmosphere at a networking party for both international and Chinese guests. *The Liverpool Story* party held in one of Chengdu's hottest new pubs did just that. With live music and Liverpool prizes drawn by Ian Rush, it is still remembered in TV circles as a legendary event that ran into the next day.

The Chinese media is usually focused on the latest matches, so when the series finally started broadcasting, it caused consternation among the fans. Viewers were totally unprepared for the sudden appearance of goalkeepers with offensive sideburns who repeatedly and brazenly picked up the ball from obvious back passes without the incompetent referees issuing a single yellow card. To limit the phone calls and letters, each time the keeper picked up the ball, the commentators had to chuckle and explain that the game came from the 1970s.

After visiting the local pro club in Chengdu, we headed back bleary-eyed to Beijing so that one of the all-time stars from one of the world's biggest clubs could lend his support to one of the newest and smallest clubs in the world. After dumping stuff at the hotel, we headed straight out to Beijing's first amateur football pitch for the official opening of ClubFootball, which had been rearranged to take advantage of the legend's appearance.

Despite being the worse for wear, Ian slogged it out up front for the first half of the IFFC Division One match, Beijing Strollers against BTS Korea 94. A true sportsman, he refused to leave it at that and boldly came out for a further twenty minutes in the second half. Receiving a warm round of applause from the crowd, he finally made way for Grasshead, who was warming the sub's bench. Within minutes of coming on, Grasshead had scored two and brought the Strollers level at 3-3, bagging a great story for himself in the meantime. Meanwhile, poor Ian made for the changing room and the showers. Typically, Ticket had failed to hook up the hot water, and it was freezing cold, so Ian had to make do with a nice cup of Chinese tea. Later that evening, back at the ClubFootball Centre, Ian once again proved his consummate professionalism, posing for photos with everybody and his dog and signing hundreds of autographs for various ClubFootball supporters.

The schedule did not let up, and the next morning we were at the BTV studios to record a special edition of *The Liverpool Story*, an in-depth interview about Ian's career and playing for Liverpool. It was conducted, with dodgy simultaneous translation, by BTV's two Liverpool-supporting presenters, Little Tummy and Porridge Wind. As far as Porridge was concerned, Ian Rush was the biggest star to come to China since Pelé in 1977. Tummy argued that point, but Porridge was adamant. Pelé's subsequent visits didn't count since he was promoting MasterCard, while Maradona had not behaved like a gentleman. Even Bobby Charlton, he said, had been on British government business when he last came. No, as far as Porridge was concerned, Ian Rush was the first star to come simply to promote his old club and he would hear about nothing else for weeks.

Following the studio show, I took Ian to visit the Beijing Guoan FC Academy, where China's system of junior development met the ambitions of one of China's most well-established professional clubs. At a facility equal to that in Liverpool, he worked with the club's most talented group of sixteen-year-olds and was then asked by the attendant Chinese press what he thought of the level of players compared to the Liverpool Academy. His answer did not surprise me, but it did give me hope that things could be improved. He said the technical and physical levels of the players were every bit as good as the lads he watched at the Academy in Liverpool, there was only one difference. Even during the brief goal-scoring routines he set up, he could see they were used to training according to robotic formulas. Some might argue that this is a facet of training that they share with Britain, but the need to encourage individual skills and creativity was a point very well made.

It was important to me that Ian's schedule included an introduction to all aspects of urban football in China, and there was still time for him to visit to BTV Sangao Academy. Formed by Beijing TV's Old Field with money made from English football and the middle school attached to the prestigious People's University, BTV Sangao was the first elite academy that put education at the centre of its programmes for budding footballers.

Since the vast majority of protégés would fail to make the football grade during his or her school years, a second stream was set up so that a full education to university level was still available. To complete this hopeful picture, we invited children from international schools to join Ian and their Chinese friends at the Academy. Ever the professional, Ian signed the shirt of every single child who participated, missing his tea and cakes. All too soon, the 'Liverpool in China' tour with Ian Rush finished with a rowdy expat game in Shanghai courtesy of Virgin Atlantic, and Granada never spent any more on the project. Ian, however, returns to China from time to time and always takes off an evening to visit us at ClubFootball.

Apart from Liverpool at the top end and ClubFootball at the

very bottom end, a number of middle-sized clubs also were looking for elusive China solutions, primarily the opportunity to uncover a young prospect. One of these was Stockport County, still in English Division One when it first arrived in 1999. Living in the shadow of bigger clubs in the UK, rather than try and compete in major cities along China's coast, it took the logical step of trying to build relationships in smaller cities in the vast interior.

Unfortunately, despite the success of several exchanges based on sincere investment into support at community levels, the bottomless hole that is Chinese football easily swallowed up the club's best efforts and its development budget without getting indigestion and with no impact on the underlying system. Stockport later purchased 50 per cent of a Chinese team, but no Chinese star has yet emerged through their efforts, and the club does not have a massive fan base of active consumers in China's vast hinterland. It certainly has a few good stories to tell, but, in England, the club has been relegated more than once, and the story-tellers have left, making it even harder to maintain a foothold in China.

Indeed, the experiences of all the various clubs that have invested in China without appreciable commercial returns all point to one of the great problems facing the game of football in the 'emerging market' of China, where there is no history of community participation in the game and fierce competition from basketball in the shape of the mighty NBA.

When I was learning to be a tennis teacher as a young man, the senior coach explained that my job, working with kids from the age of four, was to make tennis as fun as possible, specifically more fun than all the other naughty sports that were also trying to grab their attention. If I failed, and my kids decided to play cricket the following summer, the game of tennis might never see them again.

In terms of competition for the hearts and minds of Chinese youth, the NBA is the deadly enemy of football, hell bent on converting Chinese youngsters to its game and not ours. The single NBA brand controls the best competition, the best teams, the best players and all the associated TV, marketing and merchandising rights in one of the most popular team sports. What it takes out of China in TV and merchandising revenues it invests back in China through a slick marketing operation that integrates multi-media applications with genuine nationwide grassroots activities. It has a huge star in the shape of Yao Ming and a growing rosta of major sponsors unheard of in domestic Chinese sport.

By comparison, football is in total disarray – less represented as an international sport in China even than minority pursuits such as American football and baseball, both of which have established advance offices here. Apart from football's various international governing bodies, national associations and domestic leagues all fighting their own corners and taking as much as they can in TV money out of China, all the major football clubs are competing religions, leaving very little genuine cooperation between them.

Despite the experiences of various football entrants into the mythical China market, each league and club has ignored the reality and tried to go it alone. None of their ideas, however brilliant, could really succeed simply because sports brands, just like other products, have to work very, very hard to secure customer loyalty, and China has very little of that. The brand equity the clubs considered so valuable was so highly diminished in China that the sale was all about catching fast-moving fashion, not harnessing lifelong passion.

My best advice to the premier leaguers that came around from time to time was that, unless football clubs could lose the ego and work together 'for the real good of the game' by supporting the grassroots over the long term, they should limit the damage by spending as little money and resources on China as possible. That made me very sad, but the truth is that the foreign clubs which had yet to invest in China at the turn of the twenty-first century were well ahead of the game; they had not yet made any mistakes. Inside China, some of the biggest mistakes were yet to come.

At the end of 2001, I went to the UK on another football filming mission with BTV, and this trip also provided a quiet time to look back at something of an international festival year for China and look forward to the next stage of my efforts to build ClubFootball. By establishing the club and becoming its chairman, I had ended the formal separation between football and business in my life. As in my media enterprises, I needed to recruit more people with the same level of dedication, people like young Keith Bradbury, who was now working full-time in a small office above our football bar.

The next person to commit his life and soul to ClubFootball was David Niven, a quiet gentleman from Scotland, who joined Keith in the office. Uncle Dave was not only a weekend league mid-field general, but a dedicated and selfless partner who would help us turn vague football ideas into real football business. Along the way, he has become the world's living expert on the logistics of running amateur football activities in China, acutely aware of a thousand potential pitfalls, but also the incredible joy of watching children of all ages getting involved in the game.

China was exploding firecrackers at the end of 2001 because Beijing had won the right to host the 2008 Olympics that July, China had finally smoothed out the final obstacles to its entry into the WTO and, with wins against Oman, Qatar and Uzbekistan, the Chinese national men's football team had qualified for the 2002 World Cup finals for the first time in forty-four years. They had finally done it; China had won its invitation to the biggest football party on earth.

Given the automatic qualification of the joint hosts, South

Korea and Japan, for China not to be represented would have been the ultimate loss of face. In its effort to qualify, the CFA had been forced into making the most inspired coaching appointment in Chinese history, fear alone encouraging it to go for a strong and unpredictable character with a track record of taking small teams to the finals. For once, the central leaders were in agreement and, in early 2000, maverick Yugoslavian coach Bora Milutinović, or 'Mi Lu' (Me Loo), was unveiled to his instant legions of Chinese fans. He proved a success in the national hot seat and got the team through a depleted group to South Korea . . . just.

Alongside all this distraction, the China 'A' League at the top of the regular Chinese football system was crumbling before the nation's eyes and ears through the media. Between October and November 2001, the football-loving public was rocked by further bribery and corruption scandals, finally broadcast in a programme shown on CCTV. The stories first broke when the presidents of Geely FC in Guangzhou and Lucheng FC in Zhejiang both admitted they had paid bribes to referees and were ready to be punished. Soon after the first Geely announcement claimed money changed hands in 70–80 per cent of all professional matches, a penitent referee in Guangzhou delivered a public letter of self-criticism to the club along with RMB 40,000 (£2,500) in an envelope.

Meanwhile in Zhejiang, along with the crusading director of his local Sports Bureau, the Lucheng FC chairman announced he had evidence that at least seven top flight referees were involved in bribe-taking. He told CCTV that he was required to hand over six-figure sums to secure the right result in a top game. The revelations caused a massive national debate about how criminal laws might adequately protect football against such activities. Many commentators shared my view that the system was the real reason for the crisis, and that these issues in football reflected deeper moral challenges facing Chinese society.

At the National People's Congress, delegates called for legal action to be taken and, in March 2002, the Supreme People's Court issued a notice saying that referees could be prosecuted under the charge of accepting bribes as staff members of a corporation according to Article 163 of the Criminal Code. New legislation was good, but it could only be a minor improvement to what one delegate called a market of 'hooligans, cheats and blackmailers'.

Despite this ruling, the CFA admitted that referees who owned up to their immoral activities would not be named publicly and would be allowed to continue their careers, while those later found guilty would be severely punished. The scandal was brought to an unsatisfactory conclusion with the arrest of one guilty referee who was later sentenced to ten years in prison. The CFA went on to reveal a list of clubs implicated in the outrage but it issued only fines, allowing all the clubs to continue in the league.

Even the football fever that broke out when the World Cup kicked off ended up turning people away from playing the game. Mistakenly seen by the foreign media as sporting passion, the bubble deflated quickly when China returned home having recorded three straight losses. Even worse, the scorelines were widely predicted and had a sense of inevitability about them; 2-0 to the weak Costa Rica team, 3-0 to the fancied Turkey team and 4-0 to the mighty Brasil.

Despite the massive hype, the huge advertising and sponsorship revenues and festival atmosphere during the World Cup, China's international efforts failed to persuade many youngsters to go out and play. All the money that had been generated disappeared from the game, leaving little sign of its existence. The only person smiling was the coach Mi Lu, and he wasn't here any more. He had done his job and made a *renminbi* fortune by endorsing what seemed like hundreds of local products during the lead-up to the World Cup, so many that the CFA had to step in to remind him of his contractual obligations.

I was also smiling, but not because I had predicted before the tournament that England would be knocked out due to a Seaman goalkeeping error. Hundreds of so-called 'World Cup bars' had appeared in Beijing, but the little ClubFootball Centre was the only authentic place for true fans. From this perspective, the World Cup had been a great success, with packed houses and daily visits from international and local media looking for, and finding, painted faces and real football passion.

The World Cup also provided a platform to build ClubFootball's name and reputation in the minds of many more people, including the millions who watched famous CCTV presenter Crumbly Forever; the Chinese equivalent of Jonathan Ross. When Crumbly, an ardent football fan, decided to hold a special World Cup edition of his highly rated national chat show, *Real Words, Real Talk*, his producers turned to ClubFootball to provide the Chinese-speaking foreign guests and most of the studio audience. As one of the guests, I was asked to take along an item of football memorabilia that symbolized my hopes for England in the World Cup. When I revealed that my special item was David Beckham's football boot signed by the player himself, Crumbly became very excited and asked repeatedly to hold it. After showing the audience, he asked me if he could have it and, without waiting for my answer, jokingly put it down carefully next to his chair. Later in the show, he went into the audience to get some comments, and I took the chance to quietly retrieve the boot. I only had one of them, and he would have to do a lot more than host a cheeky football show to get his hands on it.

In an effort to promote ClubFootball, Keith and I also appeared on other CCTV shows during the World Cup, including the *Fans World Cup* in which we performed a hastily written song as the

England supporters club, accompanied by my old friend Under-pants on his harmonica. 'Denmark Bye Bye' would never make the charts, but it did at least accurately predict England's victory over its northern European opponents that night.

I even managed to convince BTV International to produce a daily World Cup chat show at the ClubFootball Centre. The back bar was converted into a makeshift studio and we interviewed hundreds of our foreign members from around the world as they went through the highs and then lows of elimination. The audience was fascinated and saw, perhaps for the first time, that people from all walks of life and from all over the world all share a passion for football that includes playing the game at least once a week.

19

A Game of Two SARS

In late 2002, news started emerging in the overseas press about a new, deadly form of the flu that had emerged in southern China and Hong Kong. It was called SARS, which for some time I thought had been deliberately named to stand for Special Administrative Region Sickness. Typically, the Chinese government sought to cover it up as much as possible to avoid panic, and the situation was under-reported or not reported for a number of months before news started reaching people through the internet, and outside medical teams forced China to face up to the facts.

As the crisis grew, my partners at CMM-I, Anke, Kristian and Tammy, worried that our plans to take China's largest ever delegation of TV executives to the world's biggest TV content market, MIPTV in Cannes, would be in jeopardy. We had only recently won the agency contract for the event, and the last thing Europe wanted was a planeload of Chinese people from all over the SARS-infested country. In the end, we managed to get them in and back out again before the growing number of deaths in China instigated full panic among the international community.

Just like in 1989, it took only days before Beijing was drained of its international community, as embassies and companies opted to evacuate families and move to skeleton operations. With factories closed as soon as someone sneezed, badly exposed doctors and nurses were among those dying in the largest numbers as they fought to contain an enemy they did not understand. I made no secret of the fact that I was routinely reserving seats out of the country on various airlines – I was worried that, if the whole country was quarantined, it could last for months, and we would not have a single person outside the zone. In Beijing, the whole city was mobilized in defence, including the propaganda units like Beijing TV. When I spoke to Mr Tiger and said I was considering leaving for Europe, he said simply and sternly, 'If you now leave, not able come back.'

I knew exactly what he meant. If I didn't stand together with the rest of my colleagues at this, the most critical, time it would forever call into question my dedication to China, the Chinese people, the city in which I lived and all the friends that I had made. This was not a political crisis but a medical crisis, albeit with deep political overtones. I called a meeting with my other foreign partners, and we all decided to stay and contribute as best we could. Our lives were all invested in China, and BTV even came over to film us, saying 'We stay here, with Beijing people together fight SARS.'

As I had established a number of businesses, it was mesmerizing as well as frightening to experience the fluctuating impact that a deadly disease has on trade. For Jeff at Chinalive, our production services company, it meant the cancellation of every single production project. But then, slowly, foreign clients started ringing up to say they didn't want to come themselves, but perhaps we might film the story for them, a more lucrative business.

Having successfully got the Chinese TV delegation into and out of Cannes, CMM-I faced the decimation of its exhibitions business in the other direction as the Shanghai TV Festival was cancelled. Then, a case of SARS at the State Administration of Radio, Film and TV led to its complete closure, effectively stalling all media exchange activities. The China Environmental TV Awards I had created for the British government's Think UK project was one of the projects severely delayed. Conversely, foreign companies could not afford to ignore China completely, and budgets earmarked for Chinese events were redirected into advertising in our Chinese trade publications.

The biggest change, however, came in my consulting contract at Beijing TV, which underwent 'emergency adaptation' to reflect the urgent need to produce daily news and public information in English for the international community. Many others had decided to stick it out, some having nowhere else to go and others staying with local family members and their China-based businesses.

I had been involved in the launch phases of English News at CCTV and BTV in the 1980s and 1990s, but *SARS English News* beat them all. If there was an award for 'Most Pointless TV News Show', this would be the winner. Created solely using BTV's official Chinese-language materials, it regurgitated the best of the day's lies, misconceptions, misunderstandings and crossed messages, as various authorities tried to get control of the situation.

With every programme department across BTV's channels ordered to produce SARS specials, the volume of confused content was remarkable, and our summary lasted a ridiculous fifty minutes a day. If pre-plasma viewers ever wondered what a TV vacuum looked like, they needed to look no further. There was no way I could survive the ordeal alone, so I recruited Keith's old mate Jonathan as an English editor. We were the first people who saw the whole picture of the day's events, and it was obvious when figures didn't add up or advice led to contradictory messages. It was leading to public confusion, and people were dying as a result.

Contradictions or not, we were instructed always to go with the information provided in the report that came higher in the news order and so involved higher leaders. As the weeks dragged on at red-alert status, I suggested it was time for *SARS English News* to get out of the studio and do some first-hand reporting. Mr Tiger finally agreed, and I was dispatched with a producer and cameraman to front a report from the Beijing United Hospital, the first joint-venture hospital in Beijing, and one of the designated reception centres for foreigners suffering from flu-like ailments.

Having interviewed the Canadian hospital director, herself a long-term Beijing resident, and filmed the isolation unit, I headed over to the patient reception area to be kitted out in regulation head-to-toe protective gear. Beijing was a surreal ghost town and, with a little less gravity, I could have been on the moon. A few days later, I suggested to Mr Tiger that we produce a series of reports on international residents who had not fled in the face of SARS, but who were risking their lives by continuing to operate in their chosen fields. Again, clearance was granted, and crews were dispatched to meet many people who were doing just that. Despite these rare moments of interest, the work became more and more mind-numbing.

Once news controls had been re-established, no programme departments were allowed to do any SARS specials without central clearance. Despite the immediate disappearance of lots of dodgy SARS shows, which was a blessing for the public, we were instructed to continue cobbling together a fifty-minute show. It was weeks before they reduced the sentence to thirty minutes a day.

Among all the tedium, there was only one thing to do: play football. The evacuation of the international community decimated ClubFootball's core customer base at that time, but then a strange thing happened. The foreigners who decided to stay in Beijing and the locals who played with us needed two things that we could offer. The first was exercise. Despite various orders to 'stay indoors', then 'go outside' then 'stay indoors' again, the international community, for the most part, preferred to get its information from independent sources rather than BTV, and we knew all along that taking fresh air and exercise was a most excellent idea. On one SARS weekend, we arranged some matches at Laiguanying, the biggest football pitch centre in Beijing.

I invited BTV along, and, as we drove into the complex, the whole place was completely empty. Not a single local team was taking the opportunity of the enforced holiday to play football. Right at the far back corner, we could see some small dots running around, 'mad' ClubFootball members every one. Incredible as it may seem, the Chinese tendency to keep one's head down had gripped the city, and BTV reported that the ClubFootball members that day were the only people to be found outside playing an organized sport in the whole city.

The second SARS-related effect on ClubFootball was very closely linked to the ways in which the disease could be contracted. Basically, if you came into close proximity with an infected person, you could catch it. Most of the various face masks being airlifted into Beijing were deemed by professionals to be little more than useless. Thus, it was widely acknowledged that, apart from taking exercise, it was best to stay at home and avoid places with lots of people. That is fine for a few days, even a few weeks in pirate DVD China, but longer than that and the need for human interaction becomes overwhelming. Consequently, more and more people started asking themselves, 'If I was to go out, where would I go and who would I go with?' The answer, of course, was based partly on emotion, not science. They would go to places they trusted and with people they knew. The biggest winner in those crazy SARS times was a bar called the Tree Lounge run by Jack and his girlfriend, Cloud Clearance, an old friend from early Poachers days. The little ClubFootball Centre was also on the 'trusted' list, and business in the kitchen and bar was constant.

•

One afternoon at BTV, I was particularly bored to tears and started thinking about ways of connecting the emerging truth about the benefits of exercise and the fine example of community strength being shown by foreign residents into some kind of statement. After mulling it over, I found the solution I wanted. It wasn't Master Hog's fighting stick, it was still football.

SARS was a war that we were all waging together, so what better way to celebrate final victory than hosting a symbolic friendly football match? I decided that if the international community was to be properly recognized for its contributions as citizens, I might as well lead from the front with ClubFootball. We already had members from over forty countries and were unofficially the only organization using sport to fight SARS.

In the following days, I put together the rough plan for an event that would see a ClubFootball All-stars team (comprising foreign nationals who had remained in Beijing throughout the SARS crisis) invite a Capital Health XI (comprising brave doctors and medical staff who had led the fight from the frontline) to play in a friendly match to celebrate the end of SARS. I added that the match should take place at the Workers Stadium and be broadcast live on Beijing TV, with the same level of media build-up that you would expect for the visit of a European super club, a team such as Real Madrid, which was, at that very moment, waiting for a decision on its own tour match later that summer.

I was also negotiating for ClubFootball to build an amateur football centre in the grounds of the Workers Stadium, so I decided the whole SARS football project should be devoted to achieving exactly that, the establishment of a lasting and highly practical showcase venue for amateur sports. I thought it was such a good idea that I wrote to the mayor. I never received a formal reply, but the letter did make its way up the chain of command to the highest level, thanks to the support of Madame Net, the strong chief spokesperson for the Beijing government. I had worked with her for years at Beijing TV and knew her capabilities. Once control over the SARS crisis was reasserted, she became a well-known face, making daily appearances at press briefings.

As Madame Net carried my letter and idea upwards, so it gained momentum. In the end, the project was given the big green light. The 'SARS Victory Cup' football match would lead off a series of public events to welcome back normal life just as soon as the target for the continuous period of time with no new leaked infections was achieved. Immediately, all the difficulties of organizing such an event started to melt away, and, one by one, I was introduced to the very friendly leaders of the departments required to deliver a mayor-backed government drive.

Coordinating from the Information Office was Madame Net, and first on my target list were the Workers Stadium and Beijing TV. They both signed off, agreeing to provide full support at way below cost. They were followed immediately by all Beijing's other official media, including the big four newspapers and the official government website. By the time I arrived at the BFA to get permission to hold the match, President Zhang and Mr Open had already rubberstamped it.

I met the jolly folks over at the Spiritual Civilization Department, who are responsible for mobilizing large numbers of people. Best of all, I met the Health Department, the people who deserved the big day out that we were going to give them. Our group discussion about the match was passionate and full of excited laughing and joking about how we could further improve it. It was the first time for many months that I had seen people smiling and I quickly became caught up in the whole event. Even better for the smooth operation of the event, one of the vice ministers was a keen player in his youth.

To help the Capital Health players, who had not played for

many months and never together, I recruited two big-time football celebrity coaches for them. The first was Coach Deep, a well-regarded international player and now coach of the national Olympic team, and the second was Coach Sole, a former goalkeeper with the Beijing team and co-presenter with Song and me on early editions of the English Premier League shows. He was one of the most naturally positive and upbeat men I had met in Chinese football and was now deputy general manager of Beijing Guoan FC, the main professional club in Beijing. He also played China's Uncle Football as a chuckling pundit on CCTV's Italian Serie A and World Cup shows and so was well known to football audiences all over the country.

Over in the ClubFootball camp, I picked Shani to coach the team, and we agreed to try and get people from as many different countries as possible into our allotted squad of twenty-two. He did an incredible job to locate sixteen nationalities, ranging from players barely out of their teens to medical sector executive Rob, who denied he was in his fifties.

To make the most of the occasion, I even suggested that Song, the bespectacled voice of English football in Beijing, should be dragged out of his comfortable place in the studio and made to referee the match, with Little Tummy taking over his commentary position. Let's see how Song would perform in the role that he was so quick to criticize whenever there was a slow-motion replay.

Song's beaming linesmen, Petros and Mamadu, came from Eritrea and Mali respectively and both were studying to be referees at the Beijing Sports University. Given the state of Chinese refereeing, it was surely one of the most bizarre exchange programmes in world football, but they had won their places in our game by bravely sneaking out of their quarantined compound during the SARS crisis to officiate at our matches. The fourth official was the pitch manager of the Workers Stadium, equally delighted at this chance to get involved. All of them were football people through and through and they loved the chance to get involved at this level. It was shaping up to be a great day out for people normally found working behind the scenes or sitting in the stands.

Just as I had suggested, the official media were instructed to cover the match exactly as if it were a professional match. This was to be the first day for People's Football that I could ever remember in China, and entrance would be free. In a series of warm-up features, BTV's cameras and reporters travelled out to my little pitch in the countryside to watch both teams train. The vice minister himself turned out to take a few practice touches. Despite lacking in height, he still had good feet, and I was actually quite impressed.

With just a week to go, the Capital Health team mysteriously disappeared. Finally, I managed to extract some information. As agreed, Coaches Deep and Sole were invited to see the ClubFootball team train and they had quickly determined that part-time preparation would not be enough for their team of flying doctors. In an effort to mould a cohesive unit from a bunch of physicians who didn't know each other and were still recovering from the toughest ordeal of their lives, once the early trials had revealed the best players, Mr Deep took the squad to a closed retreat at Beijing Guoan's dedicated football training centre outside Beijing. There, they worked on ways to stem the tide of what they feared might become a repeat of England's visit in 1996.

Over at the ClubFootball Centre, our disparate group of equally out-of-kilter players from all over the world were fighting for their places by claiming bloodlines to nations that were not already represented. It was sure to be a game of two halves, and Shani was confident that, like any well-formed club with a selection of players of various abilities, his two teams were ready – one stronger and one weaker, to cover any eventuality. Since the game allowed unlimited substitutes, and players could rotate as much as they liked, he could mix them as well. I told him to do whatever necessary to avoid a situation where one team had to stop playing completely and gift a free goal.

A few days before the match, I arranged final warm-up sessions at the Workers Stadium for both teams, and the media were there in numbers. Both squads had portrait shots filmed so that BTV could create player graphics for use in their lead-in. This time, I noticed the diminutive vice minister was in goal, saving penalties. Surely they wouldn't risk him in the match? Later that evening, we all travelled across to the International Hotel, where the Beijing government had laid on an official presentation and a chance for the two teams to get to know each other.

The whole thing had taken less than two weeks to organize and was now a bona fide historic occasion, but there was still no commercial sponsor, and the government was grumbling at the mounting cost, especially once it decided that medical workers were to get free *yiwu* (voluntary-compulsory) tickets, transport and water. The logistics became considerably more complex again once it became known that the most senior leaders in Beijing might make an appearance at the match.

Finally, I made a breakthrough when the Ford Motor Company, one of the biggest supporters of football in Europe, agreed to put a small budget towards the event. Although I had completed a major report and proposal on the opportunities for Ford as a sponsor of grassroots football in China a few months before, disastrous sales results in the US had scuppered any chance that it would apply its considerable muscle to football in China. If it did so properly, it might sell some cars here too.

Unlike many US companies, Ford had decided that its senior executives should remain in China through the SARS crisis along with their local employees. Now that the crisis was over, it was looking for ways to tell people that it had stayed. I cannot reveal the amount Ford paid for the whole event to be renamed and rebranded the Ford Cup, but I can guarantee it was the most cost-effective sponsorship deal ever signed in Chinese football.

Although the government grumbled at the amount, it did bring a big-name foreign company, which couldn't hurt much, as the underlying message was 'Beijing – open for business'. They should both have been happy, and even though ClubFootball made nothing either for a huge amount of effort, so was I. For the first time I believed that combining my work in media and football made sense and felt that I was finally making a significant contribution as a respected member of the community.

With Shani set to pit his tactical brain against China's top football minds from the coaching bench and Uncle Dave tipped to lead the ClubFootball Allstars out as captain, poor old Keith, as a Chinese speaker, was assigned to put his suit on and sit in the VIP box to network with the leaders. He loved it really and was fast becoming an expert at dealing with the Chinese establishment.

Madame Net had different plans for me. At the rehearsal, I was introduced to the famous radio commentator with whom I would broadcast the match across the stadium sound system. Despite simplifying his vocabulary to take account of the fact his audience could see the ball, he spoke so fast and with such wonderfully descriptive characters that I barely understood him at all. TV is so easy by comparison.

On the day of the big match, I arrived early at the Workers Stadium to find BTV's outside broadcast truck in position and my colleagues busying themselves with cables. After covering so many foreign games with BTV, it was great to think that all the work was for a match between a bunch of my foreign friends and some doctors. The atmosphere was good-humoured as they cursed me for getting them out of bed.

When the ClubFootball team arrived, the first thing the players wanted to do was wander around the pitch. Very few had been in China long enough to remember earlier days when the Workers Stadium hosted a number of amateur friendlies, and none had ever dreamed of participating in a televised match like this. Since this was the first game for many months, the grass was just about perfect.

Given the heat, we were scheduled for an early-evening kick-off with the full match broadcast delayed until the 8 p.m. prime-time slot. In line with the promotional plan, all Beijing's official media organizations turned up, including photographers with massive sports lenses who set up beside the goals, just as you would expect at a full international.

Soon, the medical crowd starting arriving, thousands of them in buses carrying huge banners that proclaimed the hospital's name and their happiness at the victory over SARS. Joining them was the Beijing Guoan FC supporters club (on particularly good behaviour that day) and a group of foreign guests, mostly friends and relatives of the players. We were hardly going to fill the stadium, but as kick-off approached there were nearly 10,000 spread along the stands on both sides. When they started cheering and blowing their horns, I knew this was not going to be your average amateur league match.

Madame Net was in control of the protocol, and when the leaders' delegation arrived I saw that Mr Dragon, the former president of BTV, was among them. Now heading the Beijing government's propaganda department, he was flanked by other senior leaders who had decided, or been instructed, to have a day out at the football. While I was responsible for the ClubFootball team, the government was responsible for inviting foreign VIPs, including embassies. The formal introductions revealed that the ambassador of France and an Australian attaché were both in attendance. I checked the team sheet and saw that neither country was represented in our team, but there was nobody to worry about that.

After introducing the various leaders, Madame Net invited them to leave the VIP stand and shake hands with the teams. Down on the pitch, Dave and his medical counterpart walked them along the lines, introducing each player and announcing his profession. Although it was a formal occasion, there was no doubting that everyone was very happy to be outside. According to the schedule I had developed with Madame Net, after a group photo with the leaders the teams would take up their positions on the pitch, and the captains were meant to accompany the most important leader to the centre for a symbolic kick-off. The leader and Chinese captain waited on the touchline, but I noticed immediately that Dave was absent without leave.

Taking over the stadium mike from my co-commentator, I boomed out his name, 'David Niven'. As the sound reverberated around the entire stadium, I could see Uncle Dave standing in the middle of the pitch looking confused. 'David Niven,' I shouted again, finding it hard not to laugh as he looked around for a voice that completely surrounded him, 'please return to the touchline immediately, you are meant to walk out with the leader!'

When the game finally started, both teams were a little over-excited, and a series of simple errors revealed to me up in the commentary box that anybody can spot a bunch of amateurs even if you dress them up and put them in a stadium. As my co-commentator continued to wax lyrical, I interjected some disparaging facts about the players on our team.

'Ah, now control ball is Lu Ke. He before was very good player, but now made rich, we call him Big Fat Lu Ke. Ay yah, such long hair, he forever never score goal.'

With the score still 0-0, Capital Health finally made some progress, and their striker found himself in the ClubFootball area. As he darted forward, it looked very much as if Turkish Tim, our symbolic Welsh defender, had taken his legs from under him. The crowd roared for a penalty, and I immediately looked for Song in the middle. It was his first test, and he took a good look, before waving play on. Hah, he was so worried about being accused of helping the Chinese team, he had bottled it in our favour!

ClubFootball went in leading 1-0 at half-time, and I handed over my position in the commentary post and sped off to the dressing room to kit up for the second half. Out on the pitch, the vice minister was entertaining the crowd. I had originally hoped to have a junior ClubFootball XI play a game against Sons of Doctors, but there weren't enough small foreigners in town, so the government took charge of this section of the proceedings. The highlight was the post-SARS penalty shoot-out. It featured two vice ministers of health, led by my chubby friend, donning goalkeeping gear and facing a series of penalties. The penalties were taken by the real celebrities, a group of recovered SARS patients. The next day, the newspapers carried a picture of the vice minister in a full-length dive as the match dominated the local news.

As agreed before, Shani had a balanced team tactic, and in the second half a couple of the faster players were replaced with slower ones. Despite our changes, the doctors were struggling with their own problems. Coaches Deep and Sole had been banking on their first XI to at least get on the score sheet in the first half. With no anesthetists capable of turning the game for them, one of our forwards, Jan from Germany, set off on a run that ended with beautiful looping chip from the edge of the area. Highly appreciated by the crowd, it earned him the best player award and put ClubFootball into a seemingly unassailable 2-0 lead.

Shani had warned the team at half-time not to punish the doctors too much, and now he did his best to limit our increasing dominance by throwing on the old codgers and semi-injured, including Chris, our reserve goalkeeper. In the heat of the moment and playing in the game of their lives, none of the ClubFootball players were capable of doing anything other than their very best, and it would have been wrong to expect any different. Finally, Shani turned to me. I was his last chance of Capital Health getting back into the game, so he sent me on at my most hated position, right half. Bastard. As it was, I forgot everything about tact and diplomacy and played as well as I could. Win, lose or draw, there really wasn't any other option with the ball at my feet. After a smart interchange of passes, the ball fell to Scottish Kenny, who fired it into the net to put ClubFootball further ahead.

Stuck out on the right with large acres of green in front of me and only a couple of flagging pediatricians to keep an eye on, I missed the action on the other touchline, where Coach Sole walked across to confront Shani. He wasn't chuckling any more and told him simply, 'Please you not again score goal.'

He need not have worried, because Coach Deep had a final tactic up his sleeve. With fifteen minutes to go, he reintroduced some of the better doctors from the first half, and soon it was Club-Football under real pressure. As the doctors pushed on, our reserve keeper, Chris, became involved in a terrible collision in which a hero doctor was flattened. While it was a brave and legal challenge, he was clearly outside his area at the horrible point of impact and was mortified at having crippled a hero in front of the whole city in his first international. Subsequently, he was a little disoriented when one of the star doctors floated in a ball from the right that was heading for the far post. Somehow, it kept on drifting and, when it ended up in the back of the net, there was real football justice in the world.

3-1 was a fair result of a magical game that was played in the best spirit I have ever seen in China. At the end of the match, the two teams met again with the leaders to receive the impressive Cups for the winners and losers and best players. Faced with an array of cheap plastic models in Beijing, Madame Net agreed we should import all of the main cups from Britain, giving us authentic football trophies for an authentic football occasion.

Madame Net had also fallen in love with a crystal angel statue that was in the catalogue, and this became the special trophy that I presented to the vice minister as a symbol of our thanks for their efforts in the SARS crisis and our solidarity as citizens of Beijing. As the teams ran across to applaud the crowd a last time, Beijing's hospital workers rose to salute both teams, and I was filled with pride.

After the prize-giving, the ClubFootball team and supporters returned to our bar for well-earned beers and to prepare for the broadcast of the match on BTV. I was invited to the Capital Health celebrations and found myself watching the match with a large group of over-excited doctors and nurses. They did not care about winning or losing, they were just delighted with the whole experience. Every time the camera focused in on one player, the whole room went wild. If a player wasted a pass, everyone laughed at him; when someone did something a bit special, everyone clapped.

When the game finished, BTV kept on filming, and a huge cheer went up as the large screen showed me and one of the vice ministers swapping shirts. There it was, larger than my life, my stomach – the ultimate betrayal of my amateur status. Despite my embarrassment, this was what football was all about, finally! Coaches Deep and Sole could feel it and so could the vice minister.

At the end of the party, he addressed the assembled crowd, reminding everyone about the battle that had been won and congratulating the team on their spirited performance. Indeed, he was so moved that he went on to announce that a new fund would be created to ensure that the Capital Health team could continue to play football regularly. That got the biggest cheer of the night and rounded off by far my best ever football day in China.

By accepting me as a representative of Beijing's international community and by embracing a public-spirited event that I had conceived, developed and delivered as a trusted partner, I gained the most important thing in China, a combination of political and public legitimacy. This special status would become more and more important as the Olympics approached and it proved yet again that, with the right support, anything can be achieved in China.

20

Smack the Royal Horse's Bottom

If the success of the 'SARS Victory Cup' in 2003 helped create the conditions for a full return to normal life in Beijing after months of crisis and etched 'Luo Wen' and ClubFootball into the minds of the city, the visit of Real Madrid a couple of weeks later had much larger political and social importance.

Unbeknown to the club called 'Royal Horse' in Chinese, even as it prepared to travel, the government was scheming to use the tour to release months of pent-up energy that had been building through the SARS crisis; it was to become the occasion for a huge collective sigh of relief, the perfect sporting celebration finally to put the SARS story to bed. Not only would it show the whole world that China had recovered, there would be even more media focus as Real Madrid fielded its latest superstar for the first time: an Englishman called David Beckham. In Chinese, it is possible to make several interpretations of the characters used to create his name, but my pet version is '(The) Shell (who) overcame (a) Chinese wet nurse', or 'Little Shell' for short.

Although I hoped ClubFootball could ride the bandwagon, and we became one of the official ticketing sub-agents in Beijing, I had no direct links to the club in Spain at that time. The political hype building around the event had served to make the local promoters, Great Gate, wary of any and all approaches for association with the tour. They were understandably keen to jealously guard their red-hot property, but it meant attention was diverted away from the international press interest that Little Shell's visit to post-SARS China was starting to create. They were unable to deal with the flood of requests, and soon frantic news desks in London were trawling the internet for any companies that might be able to help them out in Beijing. The little ClubFootball office, which usually dealt with requests from amateur teams looking to book a pitch or someone needing a pair of boots, started getting urgent calls from *The Times*, the *Daily Mail* and other national newspapers and broadcasters in the UK. They demanded journalist accreditation and wanted press tickets yesterday, sounding a little pissed off that we were unable to answer immediately.

We did our best to facilitate their communications and felt more than justified in charging for that work. Jonathan, partially freed from his deathly work on the *SARS English News*, became the *Daily Mail*'s special reporter in Beijing, and we filed a brilliant piece about Beckham's iconic status among China's gay community. Within all this press interest, I spotted an opportunity, but there was not much time. Although I would have preferred to work directly with Real Madrid to maximize the social benefits of the tour, I could still engage the media and build some more valuable relationships for ClubFootball there.

I put in a call to football-loving Mr Hemp, the chairman of Beijing All Media and Culture Group (BAMC). At that time BAMC had control over all Beijing's important radio and TV assets, and I was advising Mr Hemp about Beijing's new push to cooperate with foreign media. I explained to him that, building on my experiences of the 1991 Women's World Cup, the 1996 visit of England and the recent SARS Victory Cup, I had identified that BAMC had an opportunity to mark the historic visit of Real Madrid by sponsoring an international press tournament at which journalist teams from Spain and England would compete against foreign journalists living in Beijing and BAMC's own journalists, led by Beijing

TV. Mr Hemp loved the idea and gave me the go-ahead, but for everyone at ClubFootball I had simply created another massive logistical headache that they really didn't need. For a start, the Real Madrid match organizing committee was swamped with work, so the Spanish journalists didn't hear about it until it was too late. Then, the UK journalists who had scrambled to find a way to China announced they would only be coming for the match itself. For once, only the Chinese side was up for a game.

This problem (no travelling Spanish or British journalists at all) could have been solved simply by inviting other journalists who looked Spanish or British and who would agree to wear the right shirts, but there was another problem. In creating the Club-Football squad for the SARS Victory Cup, we had already searched through all the potential players in Beijing, and there were hardly any lazy foreign journalists among them at all.

In the end, we managed to cobble together three teams of people who did not look Chinese and occasionally read news-papers, including a couple who were at least suspected by the attendant reporters as having come from Spain. To manage even that, ClubFootball employees were recruiting among foreigners shopping nearby right up to kick-off. Fortunately, the assembled Chinese press was government-controlled, and no reporter was moved to expose the breach of purpose.

After some comical performances from people with no boots, the BAMC team emerged as the winners, and the captain was delighted to receive the International Press Cup from his big boss, Mr Hemp. As I applauded him for spending some money on foot-ball, I decided not to dwell on the fact that the core members of the BAMC team had been banned just weeks before for outrageous on-pitch violence. If they were prepared not to mention the fact that the foreign teams included no proper journalists, who was I to take back the Cup because they fielded banned players? We had all got away with it by the skin of our teeth, and BTV reported with a long lens on the happy Spanish journalists who had taken part in all the fun.

The experience taught me an important lesson about expecting too much of my fragile network, and my partners saw for the first time that, as far as the state-owned system was concerned, there was no difference between artificially manufacturing the illusion of community exchange like this event and the real thing like the SARS Victory Cup.

Real Madrid were also struggling to distinguish between cosmetic adulation and true love as they finally arrived to a welcome more in line with returning world champions than a club on a commercial summer tour. The club management knew that Beckham was an important factor, but they misinterpreted the crazy scenes that followed them throughout their visit, believing it was China recognizing Real's elevated position in football's pantheon. Beckham aside, several European super clubs would have received a similar welcome at that time and no doubt would be welcomed in any country where the people had been starved of human contact with each other and the outside world for months.

Real Madrid were set to play a Dragon XI team made up of players from four First Division clubs, but the Chinese players seemed more interested in having their pictures taken with the big stars than winning the game. Led by Zidane, Figo and Beckham, Real Madrid dispatched the Dragons 4-0. The heady days of 'Unbeatable at the Workers' were long forgotten as the crowd gave in to the spectacle.

After the Spanish team left, the auction of Little Shell's hotel room fittings, including his sheets, seemed to symbolize the ridiculous level of the success of the whole tour. It was said Real had earned €4.5 million for their troubles, more than the combined revenue of the Chinese First Division that year. Immediately, Real started planning their next moves in China, but, as I looked back at the whole saga, it was clear it was again a matter of fashion, not passion. The Real Madrid tour was a massive, short-term, unsustainable, legacy-free exercise that was dismissed by most fans in China along with their newspapers. Like the many tours before it, none of the energy of that one glittering night flowed into the roots of Chinese football. Real Madrid left China believing they were something special but missing the real opportunity to promote the game itself.

At least they came and gave everyone an evening of entertainment and a Beckham experience to remember. Liverpool, on the other hand, decided the risk of the players catching SARS was too great and cancelled their tour to Shanghai, Liverpool's twin city in China. Since the match was scheduled after Real Madrid had successfully visited SARS central in Beijing without loss of life, the Shanghai media was understandably incensed at the decision. When it emerged that Liverpool had, while cancelling Shanghai, agreed to play in Hong Kong, many in the new centre of China trade wondered what message the club was trying to send. Everyone in Shanghai knew that the only place with more SARS than Beijing was Hong Kong. For Liverpool, it was also an opportunity lost.

By the autumn, SARS was history, and bird flu was starting its silent spread; things were again returning to what already seemed almost entirely normal to me. The Chinese football lottery continued with the appointment of the next foreign coach. As Hungarian, German, English and Yugoslavian coaches had all been tried before, these nationalities were out, and the CFA and its superiors spun the wheel again. They picked Dutchman Arie Haan as the man to lead China to regional success and ultimately a berth at the 2006 World Cup.

Away from the press hype that always follows the arrival of a new manager, there was just one outstanding matter from the anti-SARS campaign that continued to cause me trouble. My negotiations on building a new five-a-side football centre inside the grounds of the Workers Stadium had stalled with a change of director, and it became clear that certain people favoured an alternative proposal from a company that wanted to develop a golf driving range. Keith and Dave were so angry that this rare space at an Olympic venue and the only practice pitch at the symbolic home of Chinese football was, like many before it, going to be turned over to a non-Olympic elitist sport that they convinced me to write another open letter to the mayor, this time with a copy to the Olympic Games Inspection and Disciplinary Commission.

The news of the golf project came despite ClubFootball's efforts to mobilize hundreds of foreign embassies, business and cultural associations, companies, media organs and schools to contribute to building new amateur football pitches there, so I felt there were strong grounds for protest. Our plan was to convert a small part of the space into a venue capable of welcoming 150,000 amateur footballers of all ages to play at the historic venue each year, so I appealed to Beijing's hopes for a People's Olympics. Although my letter was well crafted, this time there was no reply at all, and one should never be expected from an open letter of complaint like that in China. I may have helped kill the golf project, but I also killed my own project. Nobody in the government was prepared to stick their neck out and help when the disciplinary commission was watching with interest.

Instead of pushing the matter further, I focused more on the success of the SARS Victory Cup and started broaching the subject of organizing similar events in other cities with local TV stations I met as the international adviser to the City TV Stations Association. This group has 227 TV station members, and their leaders meet regularly through the year in one exotic city or another. Although I have been invited to tour all the cities, if I visited just one every month, it would take me twenty years to complete the task. As it is, many of my best travel experiences in China have come on these trips organized by a hilarious man called Mr Butter, including my best attempts to keep up with the drunken banter that is such an important part of Chinese professional networking.

I was the first and only foreign member of the City TV Association, so a simple polite toast with the rest of my table at dinner often turned into a marathon with up to eighty different TV stations queuing up to give me the chance to exchange honorary toasts. Getting drunk on Chinese *baijiu* (buy joo) is very hard for someone who does not drink any spirits, and I incredibly managed to avoid the pain for many years by lying that my father forbade all drinking in our family. Although it normally takes three refusals before you are allowed to pass on a Chinese toast, the revelation of this excuse seemed to work first time if illustrated by a lowering of the head and disapproving tutting at the guilty drinkers.

I will always remember the time I finally succumbed in quantity. It started at 7 p.m. on 12 November 1996, at an internal TV industry dinner in Shanghai. Lifting my head from an innocent bowl of soup, I was faced by the combined senior leadership of the Ministry of Radio, Film and TV, headed by a vice minister known to me as 'Fluent in Spanish'. He was standing in front of me and demanding with ministerial confidence that I accept his thanks by downing a white one.

I knew it was a rhetorical question, and I looked at all the other people around him, each silently willing me to drink and not upset the vice minister. I did the honourable thing and swallowed his welcome in one. That first taste was pure paint stripper, but as I fought back the urge to retch, the vice minister proffered a cigarette, and I gladly accepted. After that it was easy. The glasses are only small, and, chased with beer, I discovered that subsequent glasses became briefly harder and then easier and easier to knock back. My growing familiarity with the warm feeling led inevitably to self-erosion of my non-drinking excuse about family abstinence. As my tolerance increased, there was also a marked improvement in the quality of my networking, even if sometimes it did get out of control, and Mr Butter had to bail me out.

During my visits around China with my TV colleagues, the combined influence of alcohol and rowdy peer pressure led to 'Luo Wen' making many indiscretions, including stripping to the waist after a dinner in Changchun, dancing madly around a fire with a Kazak TV presenter on a mountain in northern Xinjiang and, finally, skinny dipping in front of the whole delegation in a Guizhou lake. In my defence, I was blind drunk, it was very dark, the cool water was irresistible, and I was forced to take desperate measures when my underpants, drying from an earlier swim, were stolen. I never found out who took them, but I have my suspicions that it was the foxy lady from a small TV station in Inner Mongolia.

These executive retreats sometimes felt more like a football tour, but we did do some work as well as make friends. A number of years before, I had organized China's first city-level Environmental TV Awards, and that had sparked several groups with an interest in this crucial subject to meet and exchange ideas as well as celebrate achievements. Now I looked for interest in the idea of the ClubFootball All-stars uniting the cities through football. Through such projects, I could provide the TV stations with original and interesting 'international' content at a fraction of the price of Real Madrid, and we could spread the message that people should play football at the same time.

The opportunities to combine the antics of foreigners with

football particularly appealed to Mr Wang, the president of Jinan TV, the local broadcaster in the capital of prosperous Shandong province in the east of China. We discussed the project for many hours while bouncing along in a bus heading to the Changbaishan Mountains on the Korean border. He agreed that we should aim to beat the standards offered by the police chief in Tianjin by having a fair match whatever the score and by ensuring everybody was fed at the right time. In return, Jinan TV would get 120 minutes of live football action, and there would be no appearance fees.

Mr Wang was so delighted to have the chance to encourage the citizens of Jinan to play football that, instead of taking us directly to the post-match banquet, he invited the whole team to become the subject of Jinan TV's Saturday-night prime-time chat show. I compèred with the sharp-witted host and only managed to drag her out of her comfort zone once, when I compromised her coiffure by teaching her to head the ball.

Despite accepting the warm hospitality of President Wang and successfully delivering a ClubFootball group message to the good people of Jinan, I knew, as we headed back to Beijing, that this type of event did not change the cash flow situation, and that it was still hard to see how ClubFootball could grow its business. Like big club tours, occasional messages delivered through the media did not mean much without the infrastructure and the systems to manage the people's interest, and I was losing money every day.

Towards the end of 2003, Shani, one of the first foreign friends to join my football revolution, whose moral support I had relied on and whose menu had been satisfying our staff and members for years, announced that he and his wife Penny were leaving China for Canada, in no small measure to protect the health of their three young children. Compared to the pollution enveloping Beijing on more and more days each year, the green forests and cool lakes of Canada sounded wonderful.

21

More Football Noodles Anybody?

While my dream of bringing proper club football to China was buffeted sideways and then forwards with the support of Beijing's alien community and the recognition of parts of the government, that same government was collectively dealing with the challenges of delivering the first of its pre-Olympic spectaculars just weeks after the end of the SARS crisis – the grand unveiling of the 2008 Beijing Olympic logo.

Building on the success of the SARS Victory Cup, I was officially invited to organize representatives of the international community to attend the majestic logo event, which was to be held at the Temple of Heaven and choreographed by famous film director Zhang Yimou. The performance would feature thousands of athletes, and so I asked whether there shouldn't also be some foreign athletes in the impressive procession.

The SARS crisis meant there was still a distinct shortage of foreigners in Beijing, so the Organizing Committee gave me two specific jobs. First, I was instructed to establish two football teams, which would sit in the VIP sections to make the event look more international. That was easy, and most foreigners have been upgraded to first class at official events when there is no appropriately ranked foreigner. I have won several prestigious awards at the Shanghai and other Chinese TV Festivals in that way.

Unusually, just a few minutes into the performance, we had to slip out from our seats and change into special imperial red and yellow football kits. Taking up well-rehearsed positions just behind China's stars of TV and film, Keith and I then had to lead the teams in a sprint past the TV cameras, waving at the bright lights. After that, we had to quickly change back into our formal wear and take our seats in time to clap the end of our own performance. The whole thing was surreal and will never be forgotten by those who took part.

During the hours spent waiting during the rehearsals, I managed to convince several senior officials and stars to sign our football, including Mr Jiang Xiaoyu, the vice-president of the Games Organizing Committee, and Director Zhang Yimou himself. For our efforts, I was issued with a smart official certificate that made clear that my club and its members were a valued part of Beijing's Olympic family. Just as during the SARS Victory Cup, I felt that the Chinese establishment was truly recognizing my role, not only as a foreigner, but also as a friend.

A couple of weeks later, I received another call. This time it was the China Football Association. China had already won the right to host the 2004 Asian Cup, the equivalent of the European Championships or Copa América and, since the Women's World Cup had been one of the sporting casualties of SARS, the Asian Cup had to be a success. It was an order from the top. To celebrate the one-year countdown, I was invited by the CFA to arrange for Club-Football to lay on, at our own expense, some football games for hundreds of children gathered at the Temple of Heaven. I felt some duty to help, and the kids enjoyed the games, but by the time the Asian Cup started the following year, the CFA and everyone else in power had forgotten about our little contribution. That amateur football clubs receive no support from the CFA is bad enough, but it was another thing to be running further into debt to make them look good and then paying them for the privilege. I was subsidizing ClubFootball operations and calculated we had spent over

RMB 20,000 organizing that event alone so I declared that I would not pay the RMB 10,000 annual CFA registration fee levied on all football clubs for at least two years. It is testament to the BFA's ambivalence that they have never even asked for it since then.

In a somewhat combative mood, I took my grassroots message to the 2003 Shanghai Football Forum, arguing that thousands of little pieces of waste land around cities should be turned immediately into what the Chinese press called 'lawns to play football on'. It can be done, I told them, proudly showing pictures of my pitch with Ian Rush on it.

At the Shanghai event, Keith and I met Madame Study, a newly appointed CFA official who had been brought in from outside the football system, a closed group in any country. She was a former athlete and considerably younger than many of her colleagues and she was charged with trying to effect change. However, as an English-speaker, she was quickly pushed sideways into taking charge of women's football and talking to various foreigners who needed to be placated from time to time. From that position, I knew she would find it hard to effect any real change inside the domestic system that cared little for foreigners unless they were famous, but it was encouraging to meet a senior official who was so positive to learn about the true potential of the game.

Meanwhile, under Arie Haan, the China national team's preparations for its own Asian Cup was filling the CFA with dread. With the central leadership demanding the same level of success on the field as off it, the team stumbled forward with losses to South Korea and Japan at the East Asian Championships. It was lucky China was hosting the Asian Cup or it might not be there at all.

When the Asian Cup finally got underway in June 2004 and the competition progressed, Chinese fans once again grasped the opportunity to wave the national flag, as China won its way through the early rounds. Their interest was piqued only after the entire Chinese nation united to complain bitterly at the comments of AFC Secretary-General Peter Velappan, who suggested that Beijing was not yet ready to host the Olympics. His reasons were that Chinese fans had booed the opening speeches and that the Workers Stadium was only half full for the opening match. Believing it would help solve the problem, the Organizing Committee announced the booing was not directed at Sepp Blatter and the AFC, but some members of the CFA who were standing with them. So that's all right then.

Despite the differing views about the launch of the event, everyone knew that a Japan–China final would be the ultimate test of Chinese fans' ability to swallow nationalist sentiment and embrace the sporting occasion. So, when those two teams did make it to the final, the *People's Daily* laid out a plea to unruly fans. It included the following passage from a lengthy editorial published just before the game.

> Sports competition [also] values friendship, civility and politeness. Vying in the field and shaking hands outside, this agrees with the Olympic spirit and also represents the lofty sports morality. Foreign friends have given positive comments on the hotness and order in the Asian Cup held in China. There have been some overacting fans occasionally in major international games, who, however, are not what we want to copy.
>
> Chinese people are traditionally warm-hearted and hospitable. We, of course, will hail all out for the Chinese team, as well as pay respect to our rivals. Any match has judges, to whom we should also pay respect. No dizziness with success, no discouragement with failure. What we want to see is, besides a progressing national team, enhanced exchange in sports and friendship with all the nations worldwide.

Crowd trouble is by no means just a Chinese problem, but the attitude of the crowd towards the Japanese team that (very controversially) beat China 3-1 on the night, and the ugly scenes outside the ground afterwards, could leave no doubt that football was not being used to promote enhanced exchanges in sports and friendship. The few fans who remained in the stand for the prize ceremony booed the Chinese team as it collected the runners-up trophy, its best ever international performance.

When football is making the front pages in China, I am often called to CCTV's *Dialogue* current affairs show, and the subject of the anti-Japanese 'feelings' expressed by Chinese fans at the Asian Cup was the most sensitive subject I had yet touched. It was also a freak football clash that the draw often throws up in competitions around the world. In a list of great historical grudge matches, China versus Japan in Beijing in the final of a major competition would definitely make the top ten. The fact was that China would be very unlikely to meet Japan in the final of a football competition held in either country unless there was a major upset at the 2008 Olympics. After that, the best bet would be the 2018 World Cup, and that was an opium pipe dream.

The day after the ill-tempered Asian Cup final, the AFC announced the event a huge success and went back to Malaysia. Then, with the best of timing, Spanish giants Barcelona turned up to play their first friendly in China against Shanghai United. It thought it was going to get a Real Madrid-style SARS welcome, but it got a lower crowd than the one that had turned out for the SARS Victory Cup. The single loss to Japan in the crunch match of the Asian Cup was enough to make China go totally cold on football all over again.

Despite these powerful signals of the deeper malaise, China's good run in the Asian Cup provided some impressive TV and spectator numbers, and these were enough to tempt Siemens, the next lamb to be fattened for slaughter on the altar of top-down football in the PRC. In 2004, the German powerhouse decided, logically from a western standpoint, that professional football was the only possible vehicle for its national campaign to win the mobile phone wars in China within three years. Once again, it aligned with a leading international sports marketing agency, Octagon, and set about helping the widely discredited but untouchable CFA create a China Super League from the ashes of the 'A' league.

Unlike Marlboro and Pepsi, Siemens did not even get any good seasons out of its sponsorship, as the new league launched to the same old criticisms from fans. Adding to the problem, the Shanghai Media Group, headed by a new western-educated management team, outbid CCTV for the rights to the new league, the first time that a regional station had gone head-to-head with its political big brother. Even with its own satellite channel and multiple regional broadcast deals with other local stations, the league's broadcast footprint, and hence its national impact on the psyche of the nation, was limited by the Shanghai deal.

The lack of consistent national coverage also served to move the fan base away from general spectators and towards small groups of ultra football supporters who had come to see the matches as places to let off steam. They also realized that, if they shouted loud enough, their obscenities could be heard on the TV. This led to the upgrading of artificial crowd noise machines in all football stadia, but nothing could disguise the ugly scenes as brawls broke out in Sichuan, Tianjin and other cities.

Amidst the general depression following the Asian Cup loss to Japan, the league finally collapsed, with players walking off the pitch and stories of large cash exchanges in the referee's room before and even during the games. The scandals were revealed by a domestic state media hungry for scapegoats after years of World and Asian Cup disappointment and eager to bite the feet that could no longer feed it with back-page drama. In the northern province of Liaoning, the Sports Bureau announced the suspension of one professional goalkeeper after he was spotted driving around town in a brand new Volvo SUV.

Throughout this mad experiment, still nobody in a position of real power stopped to look at the reasons why an instant super league was not sustainable and still nobody bothered to examine the fundamental problem of trying to impose football reforms from the top when there were no foundations at the bottom. The professional club chairmen, led by Dalian, kicked up quite a fuss about the state of the game, and, through a flamboyant football agent called Louis Liu, I was invited to advise the so called G7 group on the grassroots programme of its threatened breakaway league. Every one of them ended up avoiding the real issues as their actions started to ruffle comfortable business relationships with the government. They might all have professed to love the game, but this dedication only went so deep, and not as deep as the dedication to the Party, making money and short-term success did.

In January 2005, Siemens realized its grave mistake and used exit clauses to pull out from its contract, in particular citing a number of games which failed to finish due to pitch walk-offs. From its peak of 500 million TV viewers in 1995, the Chinese league now attracted only 120 million. Crowd levels fell below 10,000 for the first time, less than half the level of those first years of Marlboro-induced remission. Far from boost sales of its mobile phones, the association with Chinese professional football led to widespread consumer shunning of Siemens products, and it would exit the whole mobile phone handset sector worldwide within a couple of years. As the shiny surface presented by the CFA wore away to reveal the lack of substance underneath, millions of Euros were lost and another player went away tail between legs.

Faced with the disaster of losing its big, fat German sponsor, the CFA went scrambling for money, but 'domestic' and 'football' were dirty words in the same sentence. Amazingly, in the whole of China it could not find one company, Chinese or foreign, interested in taking on the title sponsorship of the national professional league. Imagine the Bundesliga offering naming sponsorship rights at cost and still failing to find a taker.

Finally, agents affiliated with the CFA secured support for the next season from Iphox, a start-up internet phone company based in the UK. Although it had no operating licence in China, the sponsorship went ahead at the very last minute. Unusually for a commercial sponsorship, there was very limited information about the company or its product to be found. As I wrote in an editorial in the *China Media Monitor*, China Telecom was far from amused with the idea of free phone calls and reminded the CFA that no VOIP licences were likely to be issued for a number of years.

This led Iphox to invoke its own sensible exit clause, and the season carried on without a major sponsor again. Not for the first time, China's league troubles were mirrored internationally and, much as predicted, China missed out on the 2006 World Cup finals after a series of humiliating performances against generally weak opposition. Once again, the football public cursed and kept their backs turned.

The Chinese media were so bored they turned their attention elsewhere to find salacious football copy with any relevance to China. When Big Ron Atkinson, the controversial manager who had led West Bromwich Albion to China back in 1978, allegedly insulted 1.3 billion Chinese people by calling Chinese women ugly at an event in Sheffield, the Chinese media pounced. According to the social commentary site danwei.org, one Chinese blogger responded, 'We should forgive Big Mouth [Big Ron]. A male baboon on heat will of course think that no woman in the world could be as pretty as a female baboon.' Ouch!

China's elimination from the 2006 World Cup in the qualifiers provided time for several home and away friendly games, a chance for the team to recover its composure. By the time the finals started in Germany, China's record in friendly matches consisted of losses against Spain, Ireland, Germany, Serbia and Montenegro, Honduras, Switzerland and France. There was a single friendly win against Costa Rica, but the fans had given up all pretence of deeper interest in the World Cup. After a brief respite in 2002, it was back to the foreign entertainment product again.

Amidst all this depression, I found increasing emotional refuge in the lonely football pitch I had created on a couple of fishponds in northern Beijing and the little bar near the centre of town. While the rest of the country grumbled, the strange concept of people actually organizing football for themselves was still alive. But, even working on the principle of 'if it can go wrong, it will go badly wrong', pitch management continued to throw up unforeseen expenses that conspired to keep the venture in the red. I was subsidizing the 24/7 upkeep costs of a grass football pitch that the club could only use a fraction of the time, basically at weekends.

If it rained, it couldn't be used for two or three days for fear of ruining the grass. If it didn't rain and lots of football was played, the grass deteriorated even faster. If there is one thing that amateur footballers of all nationalities are quick to complain about, it is paying premium rates for a mediocre pitch. It was a lose-lose situation. When the grass went down with a herbal version of SARS, I had to pay for emergency medical treatment.

I looked at the numbers with Keith, and it was the same with the bar. We could pack the place out during exciting matches, but the rest of the week it was hard to attract customers. Who wants to go to a football bar on a Friday night when there is nothing on? Friends of Manchester United spent millions learning the same lessons when they launched 'Red Cafés' in China. While United remains incredibly popular among Chinese fans in surveys, all of the Red Cafés here have now closed.

The occasionally wonderful grass and quiet surroundings still made 'Rowan Park', as it had been dubbed by my teammates, a great place to play, but it was also a long, long way away from the centre of town: over forty minutes by speeding car for the teams that travelled from the east of the city. With costs exceeding even optimum revenue projections, it was with a mixture of relief and sadness that I took a call in autumn 2004; it was the authorities of the Dongbeiwang State Farm. The new leader had just realized that Big Plum, now retired and therefore respected but irrelevant, had handed over for free a piece of land that was now valuable as Beijing expanded north. His sidekicks told me they were going to start charging RMB 120,000 per year rent. Even if there were no other costs (and there were many), ClubFootball would have to host 120 games a year at the full rate to pay off the rent alone. With nearly half the year frozen, a few weekends lost to rain and grass that could only take a certain number of games when it wasn't sick, it made even less sense with rent. Without cheap or free land, the grassroots amateur club football model I had originally proposed just didn't work, and I had to wave goodbye to my little oasis. Like many grounds before it around the world, it was swept aside by the industrial revolution – a briefly sighted romantic vision from a hundred years ago.

Losing my revolutionary base forced me to rethink the next moves in what increasingly felt like a football insurgency in which I was surrounded by encircling forces. I wrote to our members to tell them that, very regretfully, I had decided not to extend the lease and that all matches would transfer to other locations immediately.

It was emotional thanking everyone who had been involved in creating China's first working example of how football had taken root around the world. The grounds keeper was devastated when I informed him, since he lived with his wife and child next to the pitch in one of the club buildings. On the day before the eviction, he called to say there was still some petrol in the shed and to request permission, bless him, to scorch the grass he had lovingly tended as a final protest.

Despite its commercial failure, this smallest of club grounds had achieved one of my first objectives, adding colour to China's empty local football landscape and hosting hundreds of senior and junior events, competitions and amateur games that people would always remember. I had also welcomed many special guests to this little piece of England, from the opening with Ian Rush to the SARS-fighting doctors and nurses. In abandoning the pitch and Manager Ticket to their fates, I also recognized that the intangible bond it had helped create was hard for many other people to let go of. Those who had complained most vociferously when playing there about this and that problem were now harping on about how it was the soul of the club that could not be replaced.

Notwithstanding my mixed emotions, the whole affair did have wider implications for grassroots sports in China and only strengthened my determination to lobby for the interests of the amateur game. I had learned a lot from the process, and it was time for a radical change in direction. In terms of football facilities, the future was artificial turf. I was sad to part company with the small plant on which all my football memories stood, but there was no choice. Beijing's elite might be flocking to the city's first floodlit golf course but, to build grassroots football, grass itself must be consigned to football history.

·

The closure of the pitch also represented a symbolic end to my football world before the reality of ClubFootball life set in, the idealistic period when everything seemed possible and little was defined. To mark the closure, a limited number of prints of the photograph of Ian Rush playing at the official opening in 2001 were offered to members, but I was starting to get angry that the system was conspiring against my efforts, and that meant calming myself down by pulling out the Master's stick and thrashing a small padded tree in my garden.

Although the club spirit had been wounded by the loss of its little temple, Keith and Dave were busy refining the ClubFootball business around three key themes – learn, play, live – that still put club spirit at the heart of the operation, but that could actually work in China. At the end of the 1990s, I had set out with AFH to look at all possible revenue streams from the Chinese football consumer and, after Dave joined the business, I started to see the real importance of structure and organization behind even small networks. It would take generations for football to take off in China at the rate we were going, but we were racing up a steep learning curve that took us into unchartered territory, where knowledge is at a premium.

Kids are the biggest challenge in Chinese football apart from everyone else and one of the obvious sectors to explore was junior coaching. In line with the explosion in learning English, nobody could fail to notice more and more young native English speakers from Britain, America and other regions coming to China to teach at the thousands of private English schools springing up to meet demand. Naturally, a fair number of these young teachers played football and it did not take long for them to find ClubFootball and get involved in one of the teams competing in heavy metal Robert's International Friendship Football League. Among these new recruits were two likeable young British lads, Adam and Keef, whose registration forms revealed they also had football coaching qualifications.

As a young tennis coach in the UK, I had seen how kids have the capability to study several things while learning a sport and even taught several classes to speak simple French by association with the games we were playing. It didn't take much to see that working with football and discussions with Keith and Dave led to a new proposition that we all felt had merit. ClubFootball would employ these young coaches as football qualified English teachers and have them deliver 'English through Football' lessons. Not only was it a service badly needed by schools that did not have professional staff, it would be much more interesting for the teachers than being stuck in the classroom. The ClubFootball coaching programme subsequently launched at the International School of Beijing and it is now the biggest example of its kind in Beijing. Those first two cheeky young coaches are now employed there full-time.

As ClubFootball moved forward in this different and exciting direction without the burden of having to pay for its own temperamental football pitch, the big foreign clubs were still searching for ways to move forward in China by trying to kill each other. Soon after Manchester United announced it would visit Beijing in summer 2005 in a tour organized by international giants IMG, Real Madrid made the imperial announcement that it would also visit Beijing in the summer of 2005 in the 'Great Return Tour', once again organized by its local promoter. It would play just four days earlier than its English rivals.

Real Madrid's management believed that, as on its visit in 2003, the club would enjoy another hugely successful tour. They were wrong. There was no SARS, and it was no longer the first time Beckham had come to China. The sentiment of the media and Chinese fans towards commercial tours had turned sour, and a series of silly errors with schedules and player appearances set off vitriolic attacks in the state-owned press. By not realizing the underlying reasons for the success of their SARS tour and contractually unable to deliver the sincere interest of their bored superstars, Real Madrid failed to fill the Workers Stadium and turned off millions of floating fans who just two years earlier had been screaming at the *galácticos*.

Manchester United was said by some commentators to have pounced on the opportunity by behaving with polite respect, but it also failed to sell out. The club's best genuine effort to make a difference was down to Keith, who convinced MasterCard to team up with the MUFC charity, United for UNICEF. The project was part of the MasterCard Community Campaign, which Keith had built into the biggest sports-based charity project in the city. The original Beijing Community Cup was established by a couple of British players to raise money for the Huiling charity managed by my old girlfriend Jane, and, as the event grew, ClubFootball took over the management.

As in the SARS Victory Cup, the community spirit shown by every person involved was a shining example to everyone in Beijing, and I was immensely proud we were able to raise money for charity by giving people a great day of fun. Even Mr Sole, who gamely turned up to support, felt embarrassed that his own professional club, Beijing Guoan, was unable to raise as many funds for charity as we did. Indeed, he told me with some relief that he had finally managed to get rid of the club's official supporters club, which was nothing but trouble. Not only did the members not purchase much merchandise, they gathered before the matches and shouted obscenities, which got him into trouble with the authorities. The fan club was, he chuckled, now being managed by the Party's Spiritual Civilization Department and was off his hands. Despite freeing the club of its own fans, he was very positive about my efforts and turned up at our press conference to scold all the lazy journalists who he said were 'writing too much about Beckham's haircut'.

The 2005 MasterCard Community Cup competition that he visited was played inside the Workers Stadium, where the original athletics track had been replaced by artificial grass five-a-side football pitches. It was a great idea and lasted less than a year before the Workers Stadium closed for Olympic refurbishment.

Dipping its toes into the community through support for our charity campaign and broadcasting a video address presented by Ryan Giggs before the game was a start, but if Manchester United really wanted to get one over on Real Madrid, they should have arranged for all the players to come out onto the pitch and join ClubFootball volunteers in kicking 2,008 MUFC souvenir footballs into the crowd. Uncle Dave could have sourced them for two quid each, and it would have led every sports news around the world. Instead, I picked my way through hundreds of *hutong* traders selling poor-quality fake merchandise off the floor. It is common to see fake goods near stadiums all over the world, but this unofficial market was operating inside the stadium complex in full view of everyone, including the bemused assistants manning the one official outlet.

When young Portuguese star Ronaldo appeared for a warm-up at half-time to a huge reception, he couldn't even manage a wave to the crowd. If he had just jogged his way around the stadium waving, or, heaven forbid, done a bit of juggling, millions of Beckham fans watching on TV could have been converted, and his agent would have been delighted. There is still time. As it was, Manchester United won the game easily and then went home again.

There was at least some good news for Chinese fans that summer. In August, China finally won its first ever international tournament, holding Japan and South Korea to creditable draws and beating North Korea 2-0 to squeeze out victory in the East Asian Cup. It was a small victory for what had shown itself time and again to be a nation of fickle fans, but, as every fan in the world agrees, they all count.

In January 2006, English club Sheffield United went a step further than even Stockport County and did what only regional Chinese entrepreneurs with money to burn had done before – it bought a Chinese professional football club. The Chengdu Blades, playing out of the capital city in Sichuan province, promised to instil the English model into its operations, a bold move given the wider Chinese football world in which the club has to live. Indeed, the notion of marrying a club with more than a century of football tradition and a club formed in 1996 playing in a bankrupt league is likely to lead to confusion. This was confirmed by the club's English website, which is not meant to read like my conversations:

> Chengdu Blades FC is the first Chinese football club controls by someone who comes from out of China that was the big shake to millions and millions Chinese football fans when the contract had been done . . . Blades also wants to give young lads opportunities to take the challenge and test themselves as possible as the club can, that is unique in China.

Although the Sheffield involvement created important links that enable Chinese young professionals to benefit from UK expertise and experience and other players to gain experience in China, as long as the initiative remains an isolated drop of development in a sea of unchange, the football potential of the venture (as opposed to the real estate) might boil down to whether it is lucky enough to find an outstanding player. Fingers crossed.

The 2006 World Cup in Germany should have been the time that millions of Chinese fans heard the message that the true joy of football was playing it. But, having been involved in several World Cups with the regional TV networks (who licensed matches from CCTV), and having experienced the temporary retail impact before, I knew that all the media content, advertising, sponsorship and hospitality around the event would not result in money flowing into the game.

Since it was to be the Germany World Cup, I took on Jochen, a young German midfielder playing for my new team, Forbidden City FC, to coordinate my activities across media and football. Fluent in Chinese, he had done his graduation thesis on football in China and was enthusiastic about the prospects. We reasonably concluded that the World Cup would be the perfect opportunity for German companies to promote themselves to millions of fans in China and, at the invitation of the Chamber of Commerce and the German embassy, we created several creative proposals for 'Germany' World Cup projects ranging from €1m down to RMB 5,000.

At the top end, I dusted off the *Soccastars* project we had been developing for Siemens when they decided to escape. *World Cup Soccastars* would offer tens of thousands of kids in twelve Chinese cities the chance to have their football skills tested by German coaches, with the best winning the opportunity to travel to the twelve host cities in Germany. Anybody interested, we asked the German business community. 'Nein,' they replied.

To take advantage of the media build-up, I went as far as purchasing the rights to a TV series produced by Deutsche Welle, the German government broadcaster. It introduced all the cities hosting the World Cup, including the new stadia and other places that it would be hard to get access to before the event. To make the stories more football-relevant, each episode featured interviews with the stars playing for clubs in the major cities. With CCTV controlling the official competition rights, it was a sure-fire series for wide syndication across regional networks in China ahead of the finals. With the help of a local agent, it was placed on several stations before the series finished shooting. We asked over 1,000 German companies if they wanted to put their brand in front of 20 million viewers for less than a return airfare to Germany, and they replied, 'Nein.'

We proposed several other ideas, each of which was turned down. These included a commemorative photographic history of Germany's proud football culture with Chinese captions and a foreword from Mr Beckenbauer. As gifts for Chinese clients in World Cup year, it would have been the perfect solution. We also proposed a Junior World Cup in Beijing, a charity auction of German football memorabilia, an SMS prize competition and even building football pitches as legacy projects.

The result of all our work, all Jochen's meetings and national questionnaires to thousands of German companies was that none of our 'promote Germany through the Germany World Cup' projects secured any support at all. First it was too early, then it was too late. The big players like adidas and Lufthansa had their own plans and most other German companies had no clue at all. China wasn't even in the World Cup, and the motto 'A Time to Make New Friends' seemed rather hollow in Beijing, as the German embassy went ahead with its invitation-only opening party.

The German embassy did commission ClubFootball to deliver a one-day World Cup football competition, featuring German company teams, old friends of Germany and official Chinese media. This made Jochen feel even worse, as he watched his countrymen kicking balls at each other while the best opportunity they had ever had to make a cultural and sporting impact in China disappeared for ever.

Apart from the continuation of the MasterCard Community Campaign, the unexpected surge in ClubFootball business did not materialize despite continued enthusiasm from everyone I met. The club was still too small to register in the plans of the major advertisers and sponsors, and it was little consolation that nobody else seemed able to convert the commercial frenzy into sustainable development projects either. At the same time, the schedule of the World Cup matches, mostly in the evenings or early mornings, played right into the hands of all the bars and clubs that once again turned into 'football bars' for the duration. There were tens of thousands of white-collar Beijingers hoping to spend the World Cup with their friends, but young trendy people didn't want to be in our cosy wooden bar, but sitting in huge gardens watching big screens and drinking cocktails. I knew it would happen, but, with resources already stretched to the limit, there was nothing we could do in response.

At least the media was still focused on ClubFootball as the centre of true fan passion, and I agreed with CCTV to record a World Cup Special show involving a studio audience of over fifty ClubFootball members from China and around the world. The moment of the show came when the Chinese wife of an unsuspecting American announced to the nation that she had never liked football before meeting her husband but that, since their marriage, he had forced her not only to watch the games, but also to fill in his World Cup wall chart because he was too drunk to do it himself. As the camera turned to him, he was left red-faced and speechless. I had rarely seen a Chinese person deliver such a wicked practical joke on her partner, especially on national TV, and it was worthy of great admiration. In fact, it was such a classic that I put it on YouTube for them.

The biggest star of the 2006 World Cup in China was Yellow Arrowthinker, the Italian-loving CCTV commentator who became the focus of national attention when he lost the plot completely at the end of Italy's match against Australia. Unable to control his ecstasy at the Italian victory, Arrowthinker had screamed louder and longer than any South American commentator, wildly castigating the Australian team and shrieking that the Italians would live 10,000 years. His outburst was repeated ad infinitum on the internet, as people debated why he was so delirious, some asking if he had money on the game. His eruption even became a popular ringtone, but it also put his employers, CCTV, in a difficult position. TV presenters in China used to be known as 'teachers', and the government still frequently issues notices on the proper decorum. Arrowthinker resigned, but soon reappeared with his own daily show on Phoenix TV, a Hong Kong-based channel seen widely on the mainland. In an excellent example of wry Chinese humour, he was also fronting a TV ad campaign for zhaopin.com, the professional recruitment site.

The Olympic countdown clock was getting louder, and I knew I was in a unique position with ClubFootball, but I was also praying that the build-up to 2008 would finally act as the catalyst to connect the various pockets of support I had built into a meaningful campaign. At last, I could present a strategy based on real experience in Beijing and, when asked awkward questions, I could answer with practical solutions. I had consolidated ClubFootball's symbolic position as international sports representatives in Beijing, and groups of our members from around the world were permanent fixtures at every major Olympic warm-up event, including the unveiling of the Paralympic logo, where once again we created the international images for the hungry TV cameras.

And yet, even though I was also being called regularly to the Beijing Organizing Committee of the Olympic Games (BOCOG) to advise on various issues as a trusted expert, there was always a niggling concern that people from all walks of life who did not have high-level connections would be forgotten when the circus finally came to town. This became clear as BOCOG started formally appointing foreigners to positions within its organization, including some I knew had limited experience or credentials. I have known various BOCOG directors for many years, so I asked an official high in the broadcasting division why, for example, highly experienced producers who spoke Chinese and understood the challenges were not being invited to join the Olympic broadcast project in senior positions.

'We of course not invite you (plural), this type of foreigner,' he told me quite openly, 'you understand too much, give me carry bring very big trouble. You ask too many questions. No, we relatively like not too understand China foreigners.'

Thinking about it from his official position, I could see the logic behind this strategy, but the knowledge that China was fulfilling its IOC obligations by employing foreigners who may well be good at their professions but specifically did not know too much about the ways things operate in China was uncomfortably typical. It did not escape me that the IOC also welcomed this policy; the Olympic TV production bonanza has long been a job for the boys, although Beijing TV and Australia's Network Seven have successfully negotiated a piece of pie for the 2008 edition through an innovative joint-venture.

The policy of being 'careful' with foreign staff appointments did, however, make more sense of the advice I received from my Chinese advisers when first launching a media company and then a football club. They told me that working as a foreigner directly for the system could open up many doors, but that over time I would be changed by the experience more than the system. It was best to start with an independent foundation that could not easily be uprooted if the political winds changed.

22

Learn, Play, Live Football (and Repeat)

On the day I first crossed the line from being an amateur footballer into a life obsessed with trying to prove football could be as powerful in China as it is in Brasil, I found myself investing much more than was emotionally or financially comfortable. I now know that this is the lot of chairmen all over the world. But, whereas most clubs know how far they can go, I was building into a hurricane-scale cultural wind. I was used to sailing the trade winds, but it is never easy playing football in those conditions.

Despite the fact that ClubFootball was still not breaking even and so draining cash reserves earned from my small media businesses, the shortfalls were getting smaller as we improved our models and tapped into subtle changes starting to emerge in Chinese society. For the first time, responsible Chinese parents and energetic kids were joining the foreign kids at our after-school and weekend courses. From our start in just one international school, we were now operating at several and launching courses direct to the community in public parks. The Chinese kids were having fun they did not know was possible and they were taking the message back to their friends. Apart from Uncles Keith and Dave, nobody was prouder to see kids wearing their ClubFootball tops even when they weren't playing.

Individual breakthroughs and word-of-mouth referrals make for slow progress, and we still could not break into the Chinese school system. The Ministry of Education has tried many times to popularize sports, but the ways in which most Chinese headmasters responded to Dave's approaches were totally the opposite from their foreign counterparts. For the international schools, contracting ClubFootball to deliver its football courses was seen as having several benefits and was something of a 'no-brainer'. It meant that the school's expensive sports facilities were used more, rather than lying idle. It meant that kids in the school were given the opportunity to have professional coaching at a level that was hard for all but the richest schools to justify as an in-house service.

In addition, our policy of running courses open to all kids, not just those studying at that school, played an important part in convincing international schools to join the ClubFootball network. Not only was this seen as an important community service, it provided new cross-cultural experiences for the kids. As the number of schools increased, our mini-clubs started competing in well-matched inter-academy leagues. I almost cried at the beauty and simplicity of Uncle Dave's model, but the Chinese headmasters who really needed to come on board often took a very different view.

First, they brilliantly argued that using their sports facilities more would increase the costs of repairing them. Second, given the focus on academic achievement, they doubted that many parents would see optional after-school football lessons as a benefit. Third, in response to our ridiculous idea of opening the facilities and courses to all children, they said this was impossible from a 'public safety' perspective. Finally, schools saw themselves as being in the special position of having fulfilled all their responsibilities to the wider community by being, er, schools.

While this was frustrating to say the least, the logic behind Chinese school policy actually reflected the view of most Chinese parents. Allowed only one child, all of your efforts too would go into ensuring that he or she succeeded in line with the academic and career standards set by wider society. Given one lifetime chance to get it right, would you risk letting little BaoBei play rough-and-tumble football unless there was a real chance of her turning professional one day? Many people around the world would shout, 'Yes,' it is even more important that BaoBei is allowed to play football if she wants to. If the whole family expects to rely on BaoBei later, she had better know what life is really about now. Chinese parents often cry back that if BaoBei falls over, she might miss her piano lesson. I completely understood the logic, but, if it is professionally organized, the physical, intellectual and even spiritual benefits of sport must outweigh the risks of falling over for most children. At younger ages, parents have to make the call, and that means letting their children decide.

Taking all these factors into consideration, we reworked our model for Chinese schools, and Dave's team went around trying again. Unlike the international schools that provided the facilities for free, ClubFootball offered to pay rent for the use of Chinese school pitches. Instead of asking for help in promoting the courses to kids and parents, we offered to pay each sports department a commission for each child properly enrolled on a course. While these payments cut into our margins, the rental and registration procedures also addressed access and public-safety issues.

Whereas international schools needed no convincing that football contributed to their educational vision, we offered to send our English FA-qualified coaches into Chinese schools to provide free taster sessions. Regardless of all these efforts to meet their concerns and real evidence of increasing numbers of Chinese kids travelling to our open courses elsewhere, we still could not get a single Chinese normal school to sign up. When a Chinese school did finally join our network and establish regular football courses, it was Li Mai, a newly established private boarding school, that paved the way forward.

Liberated from the loss-making grass pitch, our efforts to organize competitions for free-range adults also evolved according to market conditions. It is very hard to encourage any group of unorganized people to form into a traditional eleven-a-side amateur team capable of turning out a full squad on a weekly basis. This was even harder in China, where very few groups had the necessary levels of voluntary-compulsory commitment unless somebody else was paying. The trick was to make it as easy as possible, and that meant five-a-side.

Over recent years, the small-sided game has exploded in several traditional football markets and for very good reasons that all apply to China. Even in Britain, the bastion of the traditional amateur club, the numbers involved in five-a-side now exceed those in the time-honoured one. A decent five-a-side team requires three times fewer people to function properly and plays in more, shorter, games; it is a format that looks very efficient compared to the cumbersome 'home and away' model involving hours of travel and wildly varying surfaces, shower and bar facilities. Five-a-side also delivers much more 'individual ball-time' than the full-sized game, a huge advantage when the target market is white-collar workers who have never reserved time for organized football.

By the end of 2006, the main ClubFootball five-a-side league had sixty teams involved in weekly competitions at two sites in eastern Beijing. It was tiny by European standards but it was already the biggest regular league structure in Beijing, and I was proud to claim that we booked more play time than any other group in the Olympic city. The bottom line was that ClubFootball bookings were keeping the two main facilities we rented alive. Our model was sustainable, even profitable, once the scale made it more attractive to sponsors and the maturity of the leagues enabled all the teams to find their natural levels.

Nearly ten years after I first hypothesized about building nineteenth-century-style football pitches for a country yet to start its football revolution, a big circle had been completed. We were now looking at building and operating state-of-the-art twenty-first-century artificial turf facilities, not for some mythical teams that I hoped may emerge one day, but to house the amateur leagues and coaching courses that our club was already operating. Like everyone in China, I took the liberty of jumping over 100 years of development in just four years. To build football in China, it was necessary to dump the eleven-a-side game into the rubbish bin along with real grass. We would have to come back to it later.

Mr Demolish, who had also gone artificial, agreed with this approach, and so did Keith, who had become an expert in turf matters through work with various manufacturers, including the world leader FieldTurf. With Uncle Dave's adult and junior teams dreaming of a new home, we came back round to that most basic of problems – finding land. In the intervening years, land had certainly not got any cheaper, and the Olympics were fuelling prices in the wrong direction from the point of view of community sports. Just as I had done a decade before, Keith and his team went off scouting for locations.

Away from the playing side, China's leisure and entertainment industries were expanding fast in two international-style directions. On one side, western brands like Starbucks were standardizing coffee culture where for millennia it had been time for tea, but, on the other, Chinese restaurants, night-clubs and leisure retreats were taking deliberately ostentatious European characteristics and embellishing them with outrageous Elton John flourishes of their own. Watching live football on TV with a beer was the poor relation, finding neither cultural nor commercial space in the new flashy entertainment pie. And the 2006 World Cup had shown how painful football can be for all those involved in selling it to a sceptical Chinese public the rest of the time.

Rather than try to get members to all come to one place, there was much more scope in leveraging the value of ClubFootball's active membership in other retail outlets that matched their lifestyles all through the week. The Beijing entertainment sector was cut-throat, with an impossible number of new openings and franchise expansions on a weekly basis, and everyone was always looking for an advantage. This encouraged us to launch the Club-Football membership card, a rudimentary loyalty programme that bridged the gap between the white-collar 'early adopters' who were starting to play football and all the sexy businesses looking to attract them.

At the same time as these positive measures made incremental contributions towards growing the numbers of kids in our academies, adults in our leagues and partners in our retail programme, I was also tired of endlessly peddling a message that too few yet knew how to support and that we could still only promote on a shoestring budget. I loved what we were trying to do and I never once doubted that football would win in the end but, as I turned up for endless interviews with Chinese reporters who skirted around the subject, I realized that what had once sounded fresh and inspiring was sometimes like a broken record in the Chinese-language part of my head. 'Learn Football, Play Football, Live Football!' I repeated at the speed of the slowest student.

I always keep my eyes open to all opportunities around the game but, given the state of the Chinese Super League, I didn't have very high expectations when Keith and I were invited to visit Beijing Hongdeng (hong dung) FC, the capital's only representative club in the Chinese Second Division. To give us another perspective, we invited a director of Scunthorpe United, who was working in

China at the time. When we arrived at the Hongdeng offices, it was clear the smiling chairman was prepared to invest in the club, and that the seasoned coach and club manager were both committed to building the playing side. This was encouraging, but my concerns were more focused on the world outside their little office and the football system into which their hopes fitted.

At the ground, a rather run-down government-owned stadium in the far west of Beijing, the crowd numbered 250 at most, and I knew that none had paid for their tickets. As we settled into our seats, my old friend, the BFA's Mr Open, arrived as the official guest of honour, and many pleasantries were exchanged. For Hongdeng's sake, I was pleased to see that at least the TV cameras were there. I knew the commentator and the producer had been in the Beijing TV team with which I had won the Bureau Cup a decade earlier. After catching up with them, I asked how the TV coverage worked and was shocked to learn that Hongdeng FC was paying for it. He confessed that viewers were mostly annoyed at having their European football repeats delayed by the live broadcast, but there was some government pressure to promote the local game, and BTV had agreed a price that the clubs had to pay for the privilege.

As the game wore on, I looked around and calculated the various revenues and costs involved. The chairman had told us that, not only did Hongdeng have a full squad of first-team players, including a couple of foreigners, the league rules also demanded a second/youth team be established. This group was housed at facilities outside Beijing, which could not be cheap to maintain.

On the revenue side, TV rights were another cost. On the far side of the pitch, I could see old and battered permanent billboards. They were dominated by squeezed-up Chinese characters rather than consumer-friendly messages, which clearly revealed them to be promoting local companies. If there was any revenue, it would go to the stadium. In the absence of any ticket sales, I wondered who covered the costs of the security, which was, as always, present and reasonably correct. The shirt sponsor was the chairman's own company, so it was hard to distinguish that as a club revenue stream at all. There was no match-day programme or club merchandise available, so even if all the supporters were gathered into one group you still wouldn't know which team they supported, and I seriously wondered whether they would.

By my calculation, the chairman had bought a club that had no revenue streams at all. With the possible exception of player sales, itself a total lottery in China, it just didn't add up. Now why would he do that? Maybe, I thought as I stole another look at him sitting at the back of the stand, he is really passionate about football. Maybe he just loves the game.

After the match ended in a 1-0 win for the 'home' team, we made our way back to the VIP room for a nice cup of green tea and some more chat about possible cooperation. When I pointed out some of my observations, he nodded his head and, straight-faced, agreed fully that these various income streams didn't exist. Quite unmoved, he told me that, far from what I had thought, not only was he not passionate about football, he didn't even like it very much! The whole thing was just about business and his efforts to win important contracts in Beijing. Completely deadpan, he explained how it had been suggested to him that investing in the capital's second football club would be an excellent way to show the government his company's credentials as a potential contractor. As we drove away, I speculated how many other chairmen around the world would be so honest and reflected on the irony that the government had to provide business incentives to get investors involved in football at all.

Seeing the sorry plight of the second elite level of Chinese football just reinforced my resolve to concentrate my own club's efforts far lower down the football pyramid, but I couldn't get the question of what could be done with the Chinese Second Division out of my head. I again got in touch with Madame Study, the senior official at the Chinese Football Association whom I had first met in Shanghai. She was still trying her best to effect changes, but it was very hard.

Among the ideas I presented was one of simplest contributions that could be made to the Chinese Second Division and the regional divisions below that. It is really very simple. In England, there is a team called the National Game XI (now England 'C'). It is a full national team organized by the FA and represents the best players from outside the Football League. Originally known as a semi-pro team, it is principally comprised of players from the Nationwide Conference (the fifth league in English football). The National Game XI plays international matches against similar national teams in countries such as Italy, Holland and the USA as well as important international exchange friendlies against national and Olympic teams from smaller football nations. The idea of providing players lower down the system with the chance to represent their nation is not just a fantastic idea, it is essential. Especially in China, where the idea of wearing the national team shirt is an ambition treasured only by the elite of the elite, such an initiative would be a landmark move back down the system. I envisioned the creation of a China National Game XI, featuring professional and semi-professional players who were specifically not playing in the China Super League or involved in the Olympic programme. Having their own national team would have a very profound effect on clubs, players and fans who could see little hope or ambition in front of them each week. It wouldn't even cost very much. At my meeting with the CFA, Madame Study and the other officials at first expressed their surprise at such a team being common in Europe and then became excited at the possibility that the same thing could be done in China. They promised to look into the matter and asked if the England National Game XI would come to China for a tour.

This was very promising news, and so I made contact with the English FA. The FA is no stranger to promoting football with friendly matches all over the world and it agreed to consider the National Game XI playing a historic match in Beijing one year before the Olympics. Even better, it proposed to work on a recip-rocal basis, inviting the new Chinese national team across to the UK in 2009 with the possibility of a bi-annual tournament includ-ing a number of countries at this level. The CFA would only need to pay for the China costs of the England team, always easier than trying to find foreign currency.

After a number of exchanges, it really looked as if the idea might work, and I started wondering if this could be a major breakthrough in thinking at the national level. At that very moment, the pace of exchange dropped on the Chinese side as Madame Study met opposition – or was it just apathy? – in vari-ous departments. I regretted my confidence and, as the English FA's final deadline for an official invitation approached, I was informed by the CFA that, while it was a good idea, the regulators, clubs and players of the Second Division were too busy to consider playing internationals. I was totally stunned.

Despite complaints from the clubs, the world's top players all find space in their busy calendars to play internationals, while every league I have ever known jumps at the chance to form a representative XI to test its best players against well-matched opposition. It was strange, no, it was incredible, but I was no longer surprised. Throwing away the promise of a historic encounter with England at the Workers Stadium in Beijing one year before the Olympics, the CFA and the Chinese Second Division were too busy. I marvelled at what the hell were they too busy doing and apologized to England, who went to Finland instead.

While I was at the CFA, I also updated Madame Study on Club-Football's development, explaining that we were now the largest junior and amateur football network in the capital city with over 60,000 registered e-mail fans, thousands of active adult players in affiliated leagues and open-to-the-public junior clubs at ten locations. In line with these contributions to football in Beijing, I was concerned that I still had no official voice in, or support from, any government departments, sports or educational associations. Madame Study sympathized with my position but, as the CFA does not even have a department for amateur football, she could only give me moral support.

Even as I completed another circle of making official suggestions, hearing official excuses and continuing by myself as before, the reality of my situation was now having an impact on the way I played the game. No longer did I protest at teams avoiding charity tournaments unless everything was paid for and there were fancy prizes. Instead, ClubFootball specifically concentrated on building in special rewards and awards to encourage teams to take part and maintain an interest once knocked out of competitions. Perhaps worst of all, I had come to accept that, in special cases, rather than try to defend the principles and spirit of the game, it is often better to orchestrate the match entirely to suit the occasion, if you know what I mean – especially in official Olympic warm-up events.

A case in point was the Yanjing Beer Cup, a November 2005 ClubFootball production for the Beijing government and the Olympic Games Organizing Committee. On that occasion, the reason for all the fuss was the unveiling of the 2008 Olympic mascots, five cartoon characters whose child-like names spell out the words 'BeiBei JingJing WelWel ComesComes YouYou' in Chinese.

Having again represented the 'rest of the world' in the glamorous unveiling celebrations at the Workers Gymnasium, a ClubFootball All-stars team, this time comprising players from the seventeen countries that have previously hosted the summer Olympic Games, was bussed out to the Yanjing beer factory to face a ringer-strengthened team representing the Organizing Committee. The beer was kept back until after the match, but there were certainly echoes of the Women's World Cup friendly back in 1991. For a start, thousands of cheering beer workers gathered to watch. Like the SARS Victory Cup, I was asked by Madame Net to work the stadium sound system, and the same radio commentator soon appeared along with his tricky vocabulary.

This time both teams were primed to perfection. Neither could be fooled into winning too easily or outflanked by cheap tricks, but there was no subtlety about it. ClubFootball coach Steve was fully briefed about the importance of a diplomatic result, and so it was with some concern that I watched as the ClubFootball Olympic All-stars rushed into a 4-0 lead before the first half was finished. The second half was a different story, as the Olympic Games XI introduced their ringers, a core group of ex-professionals who were a league apart from even our stronger players. The game finished correctly 5-4 to the Olympic Committee, with Jenne, one of our veteran German players, missing the penalty that would have forced a final shoot-out, his effort ricocheting off the bar. He was later found to be working for an official Olympic sponsor, but fiercely denied any suggestion of improper conduct. I've known him for years, and he certainly couldn't hit the bar if he tried.

The crowd enjoyed the free-scoring match and laughed as my co-commentator used the public address system to warn the

BOCOG team that one of our strikers was lurking unnoticed at the back post. The Yanjing Beer post-match party was a riot, but, beyond another good day out, it was just a media show. I felt I was coming up with my side of the bargain by organizing people sincerely passionate about sport, but everybody else was in it for the media spin. Just like Ford, Yanjing's support only lasted for the day.

Elsewhere, China's Olympic team was getting important practice at the Asian Games in Doha, where wins against Iraq, Malaysia and Oman saw it go through at the top of Group E. In the quarter-finals, China managed a 2-2 draw with Iran, but cruelly went out 7-8 on penalties. There was more heartache all round and more annoying grumbling from the Chinese football fans. At least this time I could sympathize as an England supporter.

As old father time sprinted into the last year before the Olympics, I increasingly saw ClubFootball's last chance ahead of me. It was my last chance too. I could continue to encourage football to grow organically at the grassroots, but if I couldn't grab the attention of those in power before the Olympics, the task of trying to encourage replication of our growing success in Beijing, forget nationwide, would be set back many years. If that happened, I did not know if I could face struggling another twenty years in Beijing. Added to this restlessness, two years earlier I had fallen stupidly in love with Helena, a Chinese woman who lived in England and who was now gently suggesting it might be time to give up my ridiculous efforts in China and come home.

While I mulled over these unusual 'you *can* leave China' thoughts, I got a surprise call from Mr Find, informing me he was selling the Red House Hotel, which housed the ClubFootball office and the ClubFootball Centre, to a group of rich farmers who wanted a slice of Beijing before the Olympics. He was cashing out of this particular business and, along with the other small businesses operating out of the hotel, we would have to clear our office by the end of the year.

After Josh's departure for Malaysia some years earlier, the final end of the Poachers Inn had come too, and Mr Find was now running the New Poachers in a different location on the same road. Just like the original, it served up cheap and cheerful entertainment and drinks accompanied by classic disco tracks, but now it was filled by people several years younger than Mr Find, his DJ Little White and the security team. Mr Find was lucky in that his shaved head and imposing, but silent, presence was still considered cool, and young foreigners and Chinese flocked to the New Poachers to freak out to the original dance tracks on wooden tables and chairs he made in his own factory out of town.

Mr Find loved the bar business and helped arrange a stay of execution that meant the ClubFootball Centre could continue to operate until the end of the European football season in May 2007. Like the decision to abandon my original grass pitch, the sale of his hotel prompted a review of the numbers and confirmed that the ClubFootball Centre, for all its authentic memorabilia and scarves donated by fans from around the world, had lost money every year since we opened it. Even considering its significant value as a venue for members and the savings to the club's sales and marketing expenses (particularly, inviting people to lunch), it didn't make sense as a business. I agreed with Keith that, when we finally closed, we would not reopen our own football bar again. No longer would the ClubFootball accounts be littered with invoices for uneaten German sausages. However, the club would need a new office, so ClubFootball set up temporarily in the pool and darts rooms of its own bar – even easier for anyone wanting a quick beer before handing in their match fees.

·

On my return to the UK for Christmas, discussions with Helena confirmed that she was committed to staying in the UK, and the Olympics was once again floated as an important marker, the point at which decisions about our long-distance relationship would have to be made. I wondered whether either of us could last so long seeing each other only once every few months, but the combination of business and personal pressure was positive, and I set targets for where I wanted to be by August 2008. Part of me wanted to be relaxing on a beach somewhere quiet with Helena, but, professionally, nothing had changed; I wanted to be at the heart of the action when the Olympics finally came face to face with China and I wasn't going to get out of the way.

It was essential for the Chinese government to make international friends in the Olympic lead-up, and so it was simultaneously horrifying and amusing when Chinese football finally received worldwide publicity in February 2007. It all kicked off when the Chinese Olympic team visited Britain at the invitation of headline-seeking Chelsea FC, an ambitious nouveau riche club that talked a good game about 'investing not harvesting' in China but was short on real impact on the ground.

The tourists' friendly match against Queen's Park Rangers reserves degenerated into a full-scale fight between British pros who knew every trick in the book and a group of shielded Chinese teenagers unprepared for international battle. The ugly brawls and outrageous high kicks were captured on video and posted on the internet. While the CFA often ignores or downplays similar incidents at home, higher levels of the government demanded swift action to deal with the international embarrassment brought to the country by the football team. The guilty Chinese players were sent home in disgrace as official apologies flew between London and Beijing.

This type of news did not help the Chinese government, but the main Olympic promotional plans were already in position and could not be changed. The sumptuous budgets offered by international organizations falling over themselves to get a piece of the action had been successfully diverted into the waiting government-run projects. All the official Olympic sponsors had been sucked into supporting government projects as well, leaving many non-aligned organizations uncomfortably on the sidelines.

By the start of 2007, the Olympic hopes of the fledgling independent sports sector in China were already focused on the bunch of 'guerilla' marketers now considering how best to undermine their competitors. Locked into rigid programmes, the official sponsors had declared their hands very early, giving the outsiders valuable time to create campaigns that chipped away at the exclusivity clauses without breaking them. MasterCard, alienated after FIFA cut a secret World Cup deal with its main competitor Visa, was ClubFootball's only major brand supporter. When it emerged that the game of football would have to pay MasterCard US\$ 90 million in compensation for FIFA's shenanigans, I prayed that some of it might come to China, where FIFA has been abrogating its responsibilities for decades.

To make the most of the glamorous Olympic platform, the government, sponsors and media were also signing up all kinds of celebrities to perform at thousands of official and unofficial hospitality and promotional events planned for the lead-in as well as the big month. Many would be promoting worthy charitable projects, but, while it was an outstanding opportunity for football to push its message, it was the NBA making all the right strategic moves again.

Bypassing normal sports procedures, it cut a deal direct with BOCOG and was appointed to help manage the presentation of the Olympic Games basketball competition. Behind the scenes, it also established a new management company with one of China's biggest quasi-private conglomerates. The NBA had a much bigger post-Olympic vision to take control of the game of basketball in China and it was already laying the pre-Olympic foundations. Once again, international football interests were conspicuous by their absence.

Even if sponsors and international celebrities could be found to help drive home football's message before the Olympics, to effect real lasting change no amount of international support could work without political standard bearers inside China – visionaries respected by the people who could 'speak with reason' about a healthy future for football in China. In the quest for inspiration more recent than that found in ancient China, I focused on one compelling candidate, a political giant loved by the people whose wise thoughts had already changed the nation once. He might have been dead ten years, but there was no doubt he loved his football.

23

Lord Ye Loves Dragons

Everybody in China knows that Deng Xiaoping was a football fan. According to leading professors of sports history and those who saw his passion first hand, the paramount leader not only loved the game, he was completely mad about it. Deng was born at the turn of the twentieth century, and his world view was shaped by those turbulent years in China's history. In his early teens, he spent time in Shanghai just as the foreign amateur leagues were growing, and I am not the first to speculate that he became enthused by the game at this point.

By the time he travelled to Europe to further his studies aged just sixteen, football was very much on his mind, despite the hardships he faced as a poor immigrant, working to cover the costs of his studies. After he landed in Marseilles in 1920, one often repeated legend tells that he was so determined to watch a game of football that he even sold his jacket to pay for a ticket. Of course, 'losing your shirt' to watch a game of football is normal for many fans of top European clubs today, but Deng's act of sacrifice back then is one of which every Chinese fan should be proud.

After the Communist liberation, Deng rose to a position of power in Mao's government, serving as the general secretary of the Party Central Committee. China managed to play many football friendlies throughout the 1950s and early 1960s, and, to a large extent, it was Deng who was behind China's football diplomacy;

he rarely travelled to a country before the football team had paved the way.

The Cultural Revolution was a terrible time for football's greatest supporter and, labelled China's 'Number Two Capitalist Roadster', Deng was twice discredited. So cruel were the Red Guards that they forced Deng's son into jumping from a window, confining him to a wheelchair to this day. Since that time, Deng Pufang has bravely dedicated his life to disability issues and is now a senior member of China's committee for the 2008 Paralympic Games. During his 'time away' from Beijing, his father continued to search out football matches to watch and would often turn up at a stadium in the west of the city. He didn't mind who was playing and happily watched amateur and junior games that were held there. When he was in power, he sat in the VIP seats, but if he didn't have a ticket in the box, he was just as happy on the terraces.

Even after his rehabilitation in 1972, the ascendancy of the Gang of Four spelled trouble for Deng. Alleging he played a role in anti-Gang chants at the funeral of Premier Zhou Enlai, they forced his removal from Party positions once again. Less than a year after the Gang of Four split up, Deng Xiaoping began his final rehabilitation. Very soon, China gained readmittance to the AFC and started welcoming foreign teams again. It was nation-builder Deng who was the inspiration for Pelé's New York Cosmos tour in 1977.

More significant than Pelé's visit, Deng chose the Beijing match at the Workers Stadium to appear in public for the first time since his last fall from grace, and the crowd went wild. According to the British ambassador, Deng also appeared in the same stadium in 1978, when West Bromwich Albion visited. The responsibility for the British side of that match lies with the London Export Company and the 48 Group of British traders with China. According to LEC's Stephen Perry, the tour was part of efforts to get China readmitted to FIFA. It was one of the key 'ice-breaker' matches that helped end the practical ban on competition that China's isolation technically demanded. In true spy thriller fashion, 'certain contacts' were arranged by senior officials at the English FA, and Stephen and his brother found themselves travelling to Birmingham for a meeting with an unknown club. Although there were three main choices, it was only when Big Ron Atkinson walked in that they realized the club ready to become the diplomatic ice-breaker was the Baggies.

The Chinese were also avid football tourists at the very end of the 1970s. Deng was kicking, and football was his way of sending a personal message of hope to his own people and to the outside world. In 1978, at his personal insistence, the final of the World Cup was broadcast in China for the first time. Back then, television was a community activity, and Deng ensured that football was there at the beginning of the home entertainment revolution. At the start of the 1980s, when he had consolidated his position as captain of China and was set to lead his billion-strong army in a very different economic direction, he took time to give the clearest possible directives to build a football nation from the grassroots.

Chinese leaders are well remembered for their little phrases – observations with the power to change the nation. Deng Xiaoping has his fair share, including 'To get rich is glorious' and 'It doesn't matter if the cat is black or white, as long as it catches mice.' He also made several insightful observations about football, which I have noted like commandments. As Party secretary in Chongqing before the Cultural Revolution, he arranged for the national team to train in the city, visiting them on a number of occasions and issuing several instructions before posing for team photos.

When the China women's volleyball team defeated arch enemy

Japan on its way to winning the World Championship in 1981, there were spontaneous outbursts of sporting pride at several universities in Beijing. An enthusiastic official is reported to have suggested to Deng that the wonderful day should be commemorated as the official 'Day of China's National Sport'. Considering the request for a few moments, Deng replied firmly, 'National game? Should be football!'

I added this classic line to my repertoire of helpful Deng truisms; it was the clearest indication of his sincere and long-held belief that only when China could stand with the great football nations of the world would it be possible to celebrate a Day for the National Sport. I am sure he meant no disrespect to volleyball or the Olympics.

It was under Deng's benevolent care that China launched its early-1980s grassroots campaign, again reflecting his deepest aspirations. The Hope, Sprout, Child and Baby Cups were built on his central ideas about 'from small babies grasp upwards', but his calls for Chinese football to turn its attention towards young children had been turned into a grotesque corruption that focused on the elite when it was clear he meant the whole nation.

Deng's opening and reform policies also encouraged China's shell-shocked amateur footballers to re-emerge from their dugouts. Unlike Mao, Deng was not interested in building a personality cult and, as he steadily handed the daily reins of power to others, it freed up more time for his favourite pastime. By the Mexico World Cup in 1986, he had retired completely and managed to watch every single match of the finals. According to the *Beijing Review*, his assistants were tasked with recording all the matches he could not watch live, and nobody was allowed to tell him the score.

I loved these stories and was surprised at how few Chinese people knew them. Deng continued to enjoy watching football on television through the 1990s, and I wondered whether, in his final years, he might once or twice have tuned in to BTV's live coverage of the FA Cup and noticed the strange foreigner from London making weird comments about the players' haircuts.

Knowing this colourful history was great, but more importantly it provided a form of political inspiration. After twenty years analysing Chinese media policies, it didn't really seem that hard in principle. If the country could unite behind Deng's thoughts on openness and reform of the economy, why not his thoughts about openness and reform of football? Everything works from the top down, so if the right leaders united behind a single vision, top-down support for bottom-up solutions could be achieved in world-record time. Given that my whole life was now totally sunk into this mission, and time was running out, there was very little to lose in testing this theory in practice.

The key was that Deng Xiaoping's understanding of the game was forged, not in China, but in France. At the very first match he attended there, it would have become clear to him that football was a game for the common workers and that it had an incredible ability to unite communities, while also providing them with entertainment. It was in this sense that football was socialist, and that is why he was happy to watch any level of the game and why he loved meeting with people who shared his passion.

If I was to invoke Deng, everything I had learned in China told me that this was not the time for sudden action, but quiet reflection on the nature of the challenge and analysis of the implications from every conceivable angle. Everything is linked to everything else, and taking this line would lead me into sensitive areas. Nobody could go around in public quoting Deng Xiaoping unless he was very sure of himself. Even my very limited knowledge of the martial arts had taught me that you should learn a defence for every possible attack and an attack against every possible defence. One of the best defences in the modern world is the legal one, so

I turned my scrutiny onto the international and national laws and regulations of football.

FIFA's statutes had first become a source of surprise to me during the Women's World Cup in 1991, and every time I read in *Titan Weekly*, China's leading sports paper, that FIFA had suspended Iran, Kenya, Poland or some other country because their governments had forced political appointees into FA positions 'in breach of Article 17', I wondered again how China, which had a totally government-organized sports system, was still a member of FIFA at all.

Article 17 states that, as a member of FIFA, the CFA's bodies must be elected or appointed by the CFA itself. This means that the stakeholders in the Association, usually including football clubs, should appoint the official bodies and not any outside organizations. The Article also states that the CFA's statutes must provide for a procedure that guarantees the complete independence of these elections. If these bodies have not been elected independently, even temporarily, the CFA shall not be recognized by FIFA. It even says that any football decisions passed by bodies that are not independent shall not be recognized by FIFA.

I am not a lawyer, but it should be very clear to everyone that China's national laws and regulations make it impossible for there to be independent election of sports bodies at any level because the state is responsible for all sports. The CFA is a national sports association under the direct control of the national General Sports Administration, which answers to the State Council. Not one senior official at any Football Association I have met in China has ever suggested that all the senior officials are not appointed by the Sports Bureau at the appropriate level.

Again, I am not a lawyer, but I am the chairman of a sports organization in China, and it is my duty to understand and accept that appointments to my direct regulator, the Beijing Football

Association, are not independent and do not involve any elections made by the stakeholders. Instead of procedures to ensure the independence of the CFA, there are procedures to ensure state control of it. This is the law, but it is also the opposite of FIFA Article 17. Just like the soft goal I was offered in Tianjin, there was a fundamental conflict that could not be ignored. To be loyal to the laws of China meant disregarding the laws of football. It could not be any clearer.

When I was applying for the trading licence for ClubFootball in 2001, I successfully invoked China's 1995 Sports Law with the final paragraph of Article 4. This states that the 'State promotes reform in the sports administration system. The State encourages enterprises, institutions, public organizations and citizens to run and support undertakings of physical culture and sports.' As I was a legal resident who had established an enterprise that promoted reform in the system through positive and practical action, I went back to the Sports Law again to clarify the role played by the state and to get legal support for the case that serious reforms should be introduced after the Olympics.

The PRC Sports Law is far more effective in defining China's official view of sports than any research into the history of football or all my combined experiences over many years. If there are people in other countries in doubt that sports are owned by the state in China (and not the people), the Sports Law puts everything neatly in order. Naturally, it is formulated in accordance with the Chinese Constitution, and Article 1 makes clear from the first whistle that sports exist, rather like media, as mechanisms for promoting socialist material, ideological and cultural development. As far as the Sports Law relates to FIFA Article 17, I would like to bring Sepp Blatter's attention to the first paragraph of Article 4, just above where it calls for reform and enterprises getting involved. It states that the 'administrative department for physical culture and sports under the State Council shall be in charge of the work of physical culture and sports throughout the country. Other relevant departments under the State Council shall administer the work of physical culture and sports within their respective functions and powers.'

In the English edition of the Law, the version most easily read at FIFA in Switzerland, the first fifteen Articles, dealing with responsibility for sports, begin with the words, 'the State' or 'local people's governments', 'state organs, enterprises and institutions', 'trade unions and other public organizations'. The first time that the 'whole of society' is mentioned as being responsible is in Article 16. It states that the whole society 'should be concerned about and support the aged and disabled people to participate in physical activities'. This is a fine aim, and, as I get older, I hope that society will continue to be concerned for these 'groups', but why does the Law not extend society's concern to the sports activities of everyone else?

The concentration on proclaiming the central position of the state becomes repetitive, but for every piece of power the state enshrines for itself in the Law, the greater the overall responsibility of the state to uphold that Law. In this respect, the Sports Law of China makes absolutely clear that the state is responsible for supporting the type of work that I felt unilaterally compelled to do out of sheer desperation at the failure of the system to do exactly that. The law states clearly that schools have to offer after-class sports activities and governments have to provide land that cannot be diverted for other uses. It even demands that society respect and properly remunerate professional coaches.

The combination of a real working example in ClubFootball, the inspiration of Deng Xiaoping and the laws and regulations of the game provided me with the ammunition to build a cohesive argument for change, and I received encouragement from Chinese friends when I informally presented my case, many pointing out that only a foreigner could attempt to effect change in China with such a strategy. Emboldened by these responses, but not yet ready to play my Deng card, I decided to take a risk and speak out more openly and directly about the real problems in Chinese sport at a public forum.

The platform I chose was the International Football Arena, a high-level think tank that brought together hundreds of football delegates from around the world in Beijing in May 2007. On the first day I argued that the Asian Football Confederation's Vision China project was another misguided attempt to build football from the top down. Indeed, the plan for fifteen cities to join Vision China was being quietly abandoned as only four local Football Associations had signed up. Many others told me the AFC did not invest any money in the programme but sent its experts from outside China to teach them how to run amateur leagues they had to pay for themselves. That was never going to work.

After many years operating amateur leagues in Beijing, it was clear that the Vision China strategy was based not on reality but on the vision of the AFC president, who tried to explain football with a childlike graph of eleven 'players', including 'men' and 'women'. The Beijing FA was one of those refusing to participate in these naive antics, and so the project offered no benefits on the ground. In my lecture on day two, I went much further, revealing a series of small pyramids to show what football should look like and what it actually looks like in China today.

Instead of the normal green pyramid that represents the growth of the game from the grassroots in strong football nations, my Chinese pyramid was bright Communist red and turned upside down. As some local members of the audience coughed in surprise, Chinese journalists quickly tried to copy down the sequence. Rather than further crucify the system, I explained briefly why Chinese football could never succeed with a top-down government system and then turned to a case study on ClubFootball, showing how we had developed a practical model that was now engaging thousands of people without any government support at all.

I received nods of approval from senior officials representing FIFA, the AFC and other international interests. The AFC quickly asked if it could use my presentation as a case study in the ongoing training of Chinese clubs, but I told the official that it was more important for the AFC to recognize the work being done by football organizations outside the government sector and help us do the job. I have continued to ask for that recognition, but the rules of football forbid the AFC, like FIFA, from doing anything in China except through the CFA. Since the CFA does not even recognize amateur football with its own department, it is difficult to see how official change can ever be introduced.

The verbal response from the international football community was encouraging, but it was the Chinese press who grabbed on to my message most enthusiastically. In a fierce editorial by a Xinhua News Agency journalist called Mr Anaesthetic, I was cast as a dragon coming in to save football in China, a role that set me directly against the representative of the CFA who had opened the conference. This is the opening part of the quick translation I made at the time:

British man grieves: Chinese people don't understand football, even don't respect football

During his opening remarks at the 'International Football Arena', China Football Association Deputy President Xie Yalong expressed his hope to learn from western football's 'leading technology' and 'latest theories' through this forum. Soon afterwards, a British person took a clear-cut stand, going straight to the heart of the matter and pointing out: Lord Ye loves dragons, that striving for the highest and most distant methods cannot rescue backward Chinese football, that the prescription for effecting a radical cure for the chronic and stubborn disease in Chinese football lies in 'grassroots football'.

This Briton's name is Luo Wen, Beijing Ten Thousand Countries Mass Stars FC chairman, he speaks fluent Chinese, ~~a middle aged man who~~, in moments of desperation, even uses Chinese to curse. During a speech entitled 'Plan for Chinese Football Grassroots Solutions', he said: 'Huge investment in Chinese football cannot create a successful men's national team . . . the top to bottom model cannot manufacture football world champions, and cannot cultivate loyal fan groups.'

The phrase 'Lord Ye loves dragons' was a new one on me, but the more I read the more I liked the way Anaesthetic had built his very political piece. This is the summary explanation of that phrase from *Telling Chinese Tales*:

> 'Lord Ye loves dragons,' the Chinese say
> When a man calls 'love', then runs away

It refers to the legend of old Lord Ye, who was so infatuated with dragons that he had thousands of them carved and painted in various materials throughout his palace. But when a real dragon decided to pay him a visit, he was scared witless and fled in fear. It meant that, although the CFA talked about 'adopting advanced western methods', when real ones actually arrived (in the form of an angry middle-aged man from Britain), it ran away. It was powerful political allegory, and Anaesthetic was only just getting started.

Having eulogized my efforts to encourage China to build a

pyramid system of organization, starting with amateur football, he dashed readers' hopes by reporting that nobody listened to me and I was forced to go it alone. The polemic he released with my support and using my voice described my deep hatred and resentment at the recent failure of Chinese football to progress, drawing direct comparisons with Britain, where Anaesthetic had studied and where he knew that football was the people's game. By attributing the fluent comments to me, he found a voice through which to express his own view that football was a government action, not a true sport.

Picking up the story about my visit to Hongdeng FC and the CFA's excuse that the Second Division was too busy to play internationals, he posed in public all my private questions, demanding to know how many amateur football clubs there are in China and repeating that I never really bothered the CFA or the BFA because they knew that ClubFootball did amateur work better than them. In his final summing-up, he revealed a view that I had always believed was shared by everyone who really cared about football in China, his more eloquent choice of Chinese words giving me a new sense of how I could best get my message across to more people.

> Chinese football professes to have realized its professionalized revolution and still sponsors the so-called Premier League but still ignores grassroots football construction. Losing this foundation, all the methods of chasing after 'leading technology' and 'latest theories' are harassing the people and wasting money, wasting physical strength nothing more.

The highly provocative article was widely syndicated across official newspapers and online, and the argument that football could not succeed under government control started to elicit responses from China's huge online blogging community. There was much more support for my ideas than I had thought, and, among several hundred online comments I read, only one was negative: asking whether a foreigner had the right to make comments about football in China. Anaesthetic's article also intrigued certain members of the administration. At the closing function for the IFA, the CFA's Madame Study came over to once again encourage me to keep up the good work. After a few drinks, I revealed to her that Deng Xiaoping had appeared to me in a dream and silently inspired me to work for a revolution in Chinese football.

By the end of the same week, I was invited to formally reveal this inspiration in a three-page feature in the Chinese current affairs magazine *Global*, also published by the official Xinhua News Agency. By speaking out directly, I had opened a new front in the battle and I was considerably heartened by the response of the state media and the online support from ordinary people. There was only one voice urging caution, but his advice meant more to me than any other.

Dr Man is a retired Chinese ministry official whom I first met as a young consultant during the tumultuous events of 1989, when he had led his department in support of the students in Tiananmen Square. While always outwardly conservative in line with his high position, over the years he had privately willed me to attempt stunts he said only I could conceive as a foreigner. I always kept him up to date with ClubFootball and, when I spilled out all my thoughts on Deng and FIFA and the law and the Olympics and the opportunity to engage in direct debate via the internet, he quickly calmed me down. He warned me in hushed tones that I was no longer dabbling but talking about making big political statements. He told me that if this was really the direction I wanted to take, I had better make sure it didn't go wrong. If I misjudged the government's mood or upset its Olympic rhythm just before its big party, the charmed existence I had enjoyed for far too many years might be in jeopardy. I took his advice seriously, but the Olympics had to be the right platform. The very laws of China made clear that to change the sports system, some conflict with the government's ingrained interests was inevitable.

'Man teacher,' I said to him, 'I must out come say these things Olympics before. If wait Olympics after, nobody consider sport, no leaders encourage grassroots football. I wait twenty years, now is my speak out these things time. If you tell me I speak with no reason, I forever again not speak. If I speak (with) reason, why not use biggest voice speak out?'

Dr Man did not disagree, and his eyes were alive, but again he warned that my freedom to run around largely unmuzzled inside the state-controlled media was based on a long-held understanding that 'Luo Wen' posed no threat to anything other than the quality of TV football commentary. Never losing his grave expression, he leaned in closer and went on to explain exactly what I had to do to make the maximum impact and minimize the risks.

'First, I already told you don't with Communist Party play. Your plan definitely must include Communist Party, take advantage of Communist Party principles, give government possible (to) breathe space. If government not support you, you finished. If Communist Party still stay your supporter, you can do very many things.'

He told me that, although I had worked deeper inside the TV system than any other foreigner, I had failed to garner support at the levels that could make national policy. As a foreigner, I entered society with 'special' status but could never rise through the system, and that was why I was still so far away from achieving my football dreams. However, by combining my advantages as a foreigner who understood China well, he told me I had done enough to finally bring the issue into the national arena and allow Chinese people to make their own judgements. He suggested I think about my personal role and asked how much I was prepared to risk in these final months.

'Everything,' I told him. 'I came China nothing carrying, leave China nothing carrying. All not problem.'

After scolding me for being so dramatic, he continued that he had seen 'Luo Wen' fighting on TV many times. He even let the smallest of smiles appear as he recalled my appearance on a CCTV show to demand unsuccessfully that the state-owned broadcaster give back to football all the profit it made on the World Cup.

'Audience knows you, media trusts you, let you say many, China people not allowed say, things. You have many friends. If you truly want government support you, with (the) people directly exchange. You have your own club from two fish ponds start; you study Chinese football history, football politics, football ethics; you have courage quote Deng Xiaoping words, research international football laws and Chinese state regulations. You are true football person, and Chinese people can respect you, know you speaking with reason. Write political thoughts, write give people see your own Long March.'

His allusion to the Long March referred to the pair of adventurous foreigners, Ed Jocelyn and Andrew McEwen, who became the first people of any nationality to retrace the Chinese Red Army's famous Long March. They wrote an excellent book about their experiences and the Chinese version was popular bedtime reading among senior Party officials. Dr Man leaned in even closer and told me to listen to him very carefully. 'Lord Ye loves dragons, right not right? OK, if Lord Ye runs away, then clever Dragon should what do?' Before I had a chance to admit I didn't know, he continued by whispering, 'First say, later do,' contradicting twenty years of belief that the opposite was the best way to progress. 'Now is secretly concentrate all forces, international and domestic, time,' he persisted, repositioning in his seat to better convey his politician's confidence. 'With modern society technology development, your propaganda tools are TV, radio, print, internet and mobile devices. Your army is loving football small children, all types big people, especially happy big-nose foreigners, black, white, fat, thin, all good. Understand?'

I understood him perfectly and, as his rapid speech had stopped temporarily, I asked him when was the right time to launch this bold offensive. 'I tell you, now must control your own mouth, too early. Spring offensive! 2008 is best time, (Chinese) New Year after. Well well use winter time do preparation, in spring objectively say harsh thoughts but give everybody show happy happy big smiles grassroots football activities. Victory or defeat, Chinese people will Olympics before give you answer.'

24

China Now or Maybe Later

Buzzing with confidence with Dr Man's strategy to concentrate all activities into a single pre-Olympic 'Spring Offensive', I set about coordinating my campaign around a Chinese book which had yet to be written and a celebration of football that had yet to be organized. He had told me to marshal international forces and, almost immediately, I concluded negotiations with a British charity for a project that would encourage thousands of Beijing kids to join after-school courses and create strong football links between Britain and China.

The charity was China Now, a UK-based special-purpose vehicle mounting a celebration of contemporary China in 2008. It was conceived and developed by an elevated group from the British establishment led by HSBC Chairman Stephen Green. His friends all agreed that the proposed China Now ClubFootball Exchange, through which coaches from the UK would enable children in Beijing to bring football into their lives, was an outstanding project. In particular, it aimed to make a social impact in China, unlike many of the UK-based events. Public support from Tony Blair and Gordon Brown would also be useful in my wider hunt for recognition back in China where Premier Wen Jiabao, a confessed football fan, had also publicly given China Now his approval.

Building on the so-called 'Olympic bridge' between China and Britain, Keith and Dave reshaped our coaching resources to handle what would, combined with our existing programmes, be the largest ever public junior football coaching project in China and one of the first to deliberately encourage kids outside elite programmes. As we looked at the logistical implications, I felt that several tons of proverbial cabbages had been lifted from my shoulders. At last, I was being recognized in my own country, and the China Now project would provide an amateur highlight in the final countdown to the Olympics.

Despite Dr Man's instructions to refrain from airing my political views on football until I was ready to publish my collected thoughts about it, I still looked for chances to test the waters and jumped at the opportunity when the CFA's Madame Study asked if she could nominate me to speak at another high-level conference, organized by the prestigious Tsinghua University. The subject was 'Post-Olympics', and the speakers included important foreigners and Chinese from various government, academic, commercial and sporting disciplines. I was not prepared for what I found at the conference and quickly forgot about controlling my voice.

Early in proceedings, a senior academic suggested that the Olympic Games had been responsible for putting back China's sports reforms by at least ten years, and I realized this was a place where people were unusually confident in expressing their alternative views. Other speakers also hinted that serious changes would be required after the Games, and I was hopeful that the two foreign speakers before me would challenge the audience even further. However, both simply read from tired English scripts and left as soon as they had done their speaking duty. If they had stayed they might have learned something about the urgency building around calls for change in the sports system; even the abolition of the Sports Ministry following the Olympics was discussed in the corridors between sessions. The reworked version of my Communist football pyramid address received roars of approval and clapping, starting with the title, 'One World, One Football'. It was just like the bizarre TV quiz show I had done before the England match in 1996. This time I was not making jokes about donkeys on football pitches, but littering my explanations of the challenges China faced with real anecdotes, citing the great Deng Xiaoping and challenging the fundamental structure of government-controlled sport. I totally forgot the time limit until handed a small piece of paper by the organizers.

Also present on that day was the new deputy director at the Beijing Sports Bureau. In his speech, he announced a new annual budget of 500 million *renminbi* to be spent improving Beijing's sports sector in the coming years. When asked how that money would be allocated, I followed up on his answer about community initiatives by asking if non-governmental organizations like Club-Football might qualify. His response was a massive compliment that few beyond China or Canada will fully appreciate. He said that, while I was speaking, it had struck him that I was like a football version of Dr Norman Bethune, and that ClubFootball was the kind of organization that should receive support through this new fund. He promised to instruct the BFA to visit me. For the uninitiated, Norman Bethune was a Canadian doctor who dedicated himself to supporting Mao Zedong's Red Army. In his well-recorded essay on the good doctor's last months alive, Mao told everyone in China that Norman was a good example to follow, writing:

> We must all learn the spirit of absolute selflessness from him.
> With this spirit everyone can be very helpful to each other.
> A man's ability may be great or small, but if he has this spirit,
> he is already noble-minded and pure, a man of moral integrity
> and above vulgar interests, a man who is of value to the people.

Not even my mother would go that far in my case, but the response from this latest public event made me bolder and bolder about arguing my case in Chinese. Serious people were now starting to take notice, but I was still not convinced they could or would act and I was even more frustrated that Dr Man's strategy demanded restraint until the next year. The news that British companies were among those allocating huge budgets to fluffy corporate hospitality around the 2008 Olympics, made it even harder to keep quiet, but I knew he was right: speaking out now would only dissipate the impact next year.

I really didn't care if people thought I was Norman Bethune or his English cousin, Norman Buffoon. I was happy to be labelled anything that would achieve universal football suffrage in China and I relished the opportunity to wash all the dirty socks in public. This sometimes painful process of review wasn't helped by the alarming fact that I was also forty years old and facing the start of my twentieth year in China. How the hell did that happen so fast? Helena said I didn't feel forty, but each week I was forced to deal with this milestone on the pitch. I was still playing up front for Forbidden City but, from my original position tearing apart defences on the left, I had slowly drifted infield. When team captain Jason introduced my new striking partner, a young Belgian who had joined straight from school, our registration forms revealed I had been playing football in China since before he was born.

Four years after being booed for their second-place finish on home soil, the Chinese national team set off for the 2007 Asian Cup in South-east Asia, the last big tournament before the Olympics, with little hope of making its fans happy this time round, victory excepted. After a satisfying 5-1 win over co-hosts Malaysia and a 2-2 draw with Iran, China only needed a draw against Uzbekistan to qualify for the knock-out phase.

It was a close match, but when China hit the bar in the second half it seemed as if a win was possible. Even when the Uzbeks scored from a set piece in the seventy-second minute, neutral observers saw plenty of time for China to get back into the match and hold out for the draw they needed. The first signs that the team would crumble rather than fight came from the CCTV commentators. As soon as the first goal went in, they became depressed and started talking about the crisis in Chinese football, the failure, the humiliation and the shame. It was 1-0 with fifteen minutes to go! By the time the Uzbeks scored a second in the eighty-sixth minute, China had already turned its back on the team, the tournament and even the game of football. Again.

If anyone was still watching, the Uzbeks added a third goal in injury time, and China were well and truly out. It was the worst performance at the Asian Cup since 1980: the first time China had failed to progress from the group stages. Just as I had celebrated when England had beaten China in 1996, I loved China and cared so much about its football that I had no option but to welcome this latest humiliation for the system. If, by luck or design, China had won the tournament, the whole country would have mistakenly believed all was wonderful, and making changes would be harder than ever. As it was, China had failed again, and this must give more momentum to those who shared my belief that there needed to be wholesale change in the administration of sports.

Knowing that the soul-searching would dominate the state media, I prepared to receive calls from journalists analysing this latest disaster. First was the magazine *Global Times* attached to the *People's Daily*, the main Communist Party publishing group. In light of China's failure at the Asian Cup, the topic of the feature and the national debate was 'Should China continue to play football or give up and concentrate on other sports?' The journalist was looking for the foreign view, and so I told her bluntly that the question was unbelievable and revealed a serious problem. In fact, it revealed the whole problem. Just like an obnoxiously spoiled child, China only wanted to play if it could win! If that was the case everywhere, there would only be three or four countries playing football in the whole world. 'From this question,' I said, 'we can see very clearly, your paper towards sports have how deep an understanding? A little even not understand. Nothing.'

Then she asked a follow-up question about the worst piece of football news I had heard recently. That was easy and had nothing to do with the national team. Having announced in 2006 that Beijing schools should open their facilities for all to enjoy as a sporting remit of the Olympics, the government had changed its mind, declaring instead that sports facilities must be closed to outside use under the 'public safety' remit of the Olympics. After twenty years in China, I told her, it was very easy for me to predict that all social sports activities would be cancelled in the final weeks leading to the Olympics, just as sport had its best ever chance to bridge cultural divides.

When the Chinese Olympic team hosted a four-team invitational tournament in Shenyang a couple of weeks later, it lost its final match to North Korea by a single goal to nil, and the national football depression was complete. Again, there seemed to be no effort to reverse the score, and over half the crowd had left before the end. This time the commentators had no more to say and simply prayed the team's problems could be sorted out before the Olympics began.

Time was running out, and a number of foreign clubs wanted to take advantage of the last full summer before the Olympics to make visits to China, including US-owned Manchester United, who played in Macao and Guangzhou as part of their Asian tour. The English club unleashed the wrath of the AFC president in Malaysia for interrupting the Asian Cup but delighted its fans in the region. In Macao, the visit was sponsored as part of the pre-opening of the Venetian casino and resort in a star-studded series of events that also included matches organized by the NBA.

At United's invitation, I travelled down to Macao for the match and saw first hand how the former Portuguese colony is building its position as the centre of gambling in China, a hugely popular, if illegal, activity just across the border. According to conservative government statistics, US$5 billion left China through illegal internet gambling alone in 2004. This is nearly three times what was generated by the Sports Lottery that year and is partially money lost to sport in China. Football represents a significant proportion of this illegal internet trade, and, in 2005, one group was sentenced for running a syndicate that had raked in US$75 million. People in Macao seemed proud that there was now even more money being spent on legal gambling in Macao than in Las Vegas. Given the source of much of that money, I shuddered and hurried away from the gaming tables, leaving thousands of mainlanders to lose their own, and sometimes other people's, pensions. If private enterprise could make so much out of illegal football gaming from China, shouldn't football in China at least see some of that benefit? In the UK, the privately owned Littlewoods pools alone claims to have returned over £400 million to the national game.

Just before the exhibition match, I had a chance to speak with Sir Bobby Charlton, one of the most famous names in world football and a man whose later years have been dedicated to promoting the game all over the world. I had met him briefly once before but, as we chatted, I fulfilled one half of a lifetime ambition and thanked him in person for providing inspiration when I was in trouble in Brasil. He was delighted and told me how proud he was that his name was quoted so often as a form of welcome and friendship. In a fine performance from Ronaldo, Rooney, Giggs and teammates, the latest generation of Manchester United stars politely thrashed the Shenzhen team 6-0 and the club promised to think further about how it might work to support ClubFootball in China.

Soon after, Barcelona once again chose an inauspicious time to arrive for their second tour. Why did it always come just after the depression of China's exit from the Asian Cup? Not only was the Workers Stadium unusable, none of the new Olympic stadiums were ready, so the match was moved to the Fengtai Stadium, which has not undergone an Olympic facelift. I could not attend the match but was very encouraged that, working with one of the official agencies, we had sold over 1,000 tickets to our members and their friends. Unlike most ticket agencies, we reinvest our commission back into grassroots activities, and every contribution makes a difference.

I caught up with some members and asked about the match. The 'one in crutches' said that facilities for disabled access were appalling. Another told me that he could not help but laugh at the beginning. With all the players ready to kick-off, the fourth official motioned for Ronaldhino to come across to his station. When the bemused Brasilian approached, the official invited him to turn and take a photograph for his personal collection. It was a classic move, and Ronaldhino could only smile. I knew exactly why the official did it. The job of match official is a tough one with low pay, and the only perk is getting close to superstars; he would probably never have the chance again. This urge to abandon protocol and nab a celebrity picture was also causing concerns to those responsible for training the hundreds of thousands of young Olympic volunteers in Beijing, many of whom had signed up for exactly the same reason.

The central authorities were so worried about Olympic football humiliation on home soil that, just one day after IOC guests from over 200 countries left after receiving their invitations at the spectacular One Year Countdown in Tiananmen Square, the government demanded that the CFA scrap the China Super League, divide club competitions into North and South Divisions and drastically reduce the number of games. All so the national Olympic team could train more.

Just in case the CFA or the China Super League itself (supposedly a legally registered enterprise) had other ideas, the central edict made it clear that, if they did not dismantle the league and rearrange their businesses in line with the new policy, they would be suspended and another organ appointed to dismantle it anyway. In an effort to keep their jobs, the CFA and CSL officials, and the clubs, quickly agreed a compromise position.

Like the rest of Chinese football, I was also depressed about the One Year Countdown ceremony, as it marked the first time that I was no longer needed to make things look more international. After years of dedicated service providing 'big noses' who actually believed in the Olympic spirit, there was not even a symbolic place at the table. I was not downhearted: it was the default position I had come across time and again and I was mentally prepared. As always, I continued to go through the motions, visiting the CFA with representatives from China Now and calling the BFA to remind it about its promised visit to discuss the Sports Bureau's sports fund. As usual, the absence of a department dealing with amateur football meant there was no systematic way for anyone to take action.

I did receive a call from Madame Zhang, the head of the Beijing International Sports Exchange Centre, a government-controlled quango established to do what its name suggests. I had met her at the Tsinghua University conference, and we found common interest in further developing Beijing–London sporting links. Madame Zhang invited me to join the Organizing Committee of the Beijing International Tennis Festival, and I accepted, figuring I could at least learn how tennis had emerged from the same background as football in modern China, but seemed to be doing much better at all levels.

I did not have to look far to find the answer. There are over 1,000 tennis courts in Beijing and nearly 400 indoor ones. These are very impressive numbers and certainly better than the statistics for football, despite the latter having vastly superior 'player-per-square-metre' ratio and considering the relative popularity of the two sports among ordinary people. The reason is that senior leaders and rich business people prefer to play tennis and golf. It is not so different in many countries, and I remembered twenty years before, when the leaders at my university had built a new tennis court for themselves.

There is no doubt that plenty of leaders like watching football on television and place huge importance on getting good results in international competition, but very few of them actually play it, so there is no need to build football pitches to keep them happy. As even leaders cannot play tennis all day, the facilities are available for others to use, including the kids who are now developing into world-level talents. Far from being traditionally hardy countryside children willing to make huge sacrifices, many of the upcoming Chinese tennis players are coming from the cities. This is proof that, given the right encouragement, untapped football talent in the big cities could also naturally emerge from facilities built purely for social enjoyment. That this football talent is still not being provided with places to express itself is a sporting crime.

Of all the parts of Dr Man's 'Spring Offensive' plan, I was most confident in the field of propaganda, the industry that I knew better than any and in which I could rely on many people to help from TV station presents to famous presenters. One of my strongest supporters and a trusted friend was called Salty Wall, a long-time football journalist and vice-president at Titan Sports. The publisher of China's biggest-selling sports newspaper, Titan is now a landmark joint-venture between South Africa and the Hunan provincial government, proving that the model can work. Salty had written a brief guide to British football culture while based in the UK, and we often appear together at football conferences or on TV shows, including Arrowthinker's show on Phoenix TV.

Salty agreed to become my Chinese editor and appointed his best translator to help turn what he sarcastically called 'my masterpiece' into something useable in Chinese. He warned that some people were bound to react with the 'friendly' criticism always shown when foreigners point out uncomfortable facts, but that he was ready to justify my position to anyone who said a foreigner could never speak with reason and agreed to serialize my thoughts in his newspaper. Confident that I could make calls to CCTV, Beijing TV and other state media at the right time, I just needed a Chinese publisher.

My first call was to my old friend Professor Fruit, an expert in the publishing trade, and he put me in touch with what he said should be my first choice. SEEC is part of the group that publishes *Caijing* (sigh jing). One of the most respected titles in the country, it frequently incurs the wrath of unscrupulous officials for its dogged investigative reporting. Mr Li from SEEC shared Salty Wall's view that my message was an important one, and that individual Chinese people were struggling to find deeper meaning in modern lives where money was increasingly the only thing that was real, and old community values were being eroded by massive changes in work contracts and residential construction projects. Football was one way of addressing these issues, and we all agreed to aim for a spring 2008 release, as Dr Man had proposed. SEEC proposed a six-city promotional tour, but I was a little surprised when they agreed to rewrite Chinese publishing history and add an extra 2 per cent royalty for ClubFootball. Each copy would now contribute to building more football pitches, and it was an excellent principle to set.

In September 2007, there was positive news from China Now in Britain. The football project was an important part of the festival, and its high-level government supporters were still in place. Even with limited funds, we could extend our junior coaching activities and select sixteen lucky children to take the football tour of a lifetime to Britain just before the Olympic Games. Unlike many Olympic exchanges between elite junior athletes, the project was based on bringing the joy of social football and its amateur values to a new generation in China, and the UK tour party would be our very first ambassadors.

It was China Now's responsibility to organize the tour in the UK and introduce clubs that could host our delegation. After visiting several, we focused on Charlton, home to China's captain, Zheng Zhi. Although Charlton had been relegated the previous season, Zheng had proved to English audiences and fans that Chinese players could give 150 per cent towards their club with a series of battling performances. Charlton is also a club with a proud record of community work and has developed popular programmes that even extend into developed football nations such as Spain. When I visited the club with Oliver from China Now, we found a similar welcome from people with not only an understanding of what I was trying to achieve with ClubFootball, but also the vision to embrace China Now as the catalyst to further cooperation. It was clear that bringing our kids to Britain was opening some doors, and when the FA confirmed it would set up a tour of Wembley and invite them to lunch at FA Headquarters, I felt a growing sense of pride in British football.

Soon after arriving back in China, I got two pieces of news that would both contribute towards delivering Dr Man's proposed 'Spring Offensive'. First, Rob James, who runs Manchester United's Asia office in Hong Kong, suggested that the China Now ClubFootball tour also visit Manchester for a guided tour of Old Trafford. Keith then topped it all by updating me on talks with MasterCard. Not only had it agreed to extend our agreement, it was signalling an intention to look very closely at ClubFootball in 2008, when the stakes will be much higher.

The weather has now turned bitterly cold, and it is once again tempting to miss freezing weeknight training sessions with Forbidden City. Starting in the spring, all my combined forces will emerge from hiding to blitz the Chinese government, industry and people with a passionate celebration of everything that is wonderful about the game of football and everything sport should mean in a nation worthy of hosting the Olympic Games.

While officials celebrate the opening of Beijing's fantastic and futuristic elite Olympic stadia, with the support of Mr Demolish, I will be opening a new community-based ClubFootball Play Centre in south Beijing. This new facility will serve hundreds of thousands of players over the coming years, while we all know the stadia will lie empty. As the world's biggest celebrities descend on the city to hog their place in the Olympic spotlight and top athletes start gathering in Beijing to prepare for their greatest day, I will be flying to Britain with a group of unusual Chinese youngsters, kids who will never reach such heights but who still love to play the game. And, just before the curtain rises on the Olympics, we will return to Beijing bearing not only football gifts, but wonderful stories of far-off communities where the spirit of football permeates daily life.

Even now, there is still a chance that some of the 2008 budgets being allocated by non-official sponsors will be directed to non-government organizations, and we may win last-minute funding from guerilla marketers acting just before the Games. Conceivably, the head of the Beijing Sports Bureau might still take a huge gamble and appoint a Norman Bethune-like independent to advise on the spending of football's share of his RMB500 million.

Ahead of all these uncertain outcomes, Chinese editorial deadlines that once seemed distant are now dates ticked off in my calendar. I still have no idea how my experiences will be received in China; I even hear rumours of state-owned publishers acquiring rights in order to stop controversial books being published before the Olympics. But Master Hog has taught me well. With Deng Xiaoping in goal and a strong legal defence in front of him, I am confident we will not leak many goals next season.

For many years, I have wondered how and why I found myself wandering through politics, media and sport in China, but now it all makes sense, or, rather, I have a clearer perspective of how it doesn't make sense. Dr Man is right: the best that I can hope for is that Chinese people listen to my story and act on its simple message by becoming involved in the game. I can do no more, and therein lies my biggest fear in this whole endeavour.

By putting my final cards on the table, I lay myself open to two outcomes that could destroy everything and shatter the highly fragile balance between the alphabetical and Chinese-character-driven parts of my only brain. Dr Man promises me the Chinese people will give me an answer to my big football question by the Olympics, but what if the answer is they don't really care or, even worse, would like some more time to think about it? As a funny man once despaired, it's the hope that kills you, and never has that been truer than for the game of football in China.

Epilogue

Like hundreds of millions around the world, I learned as a boy that joining a local football team or even a park kick-about is a tried and tested way to keep fit, make friends and, occasionally, achieve the sporting impossible. In Brasil, I found that it could mean even more than that. And so it has been for over a hundred years. It doesn't really matter if there is no common language, because some dialect of football is spoken nearly everywhere.

At the heart of this global network is the humble local club, an established community institution from Aldershot to Zagreb. Sprouting out from factories, churches, pubs, schools, universities, cricket clubs and other social organizations wherever the game was introduced, the millions of amateur clubs in the world today are the basic building blocks of the so-called 'football pyramid'.

Despite increasing concern about the top of that pyramid, where talk of 'millions' refers to individual player salaries, rather than the bottom, where it refers to numbers of actual players, it is the success of the local club model in all its changing shapes, colours and sizes that ensures football is still a participation sport with social relevance today. In a world where there is increasing competition from non-active leisure activities, the committed people who run local sports clubs stand out as champions, the grassroots teachers of generations of players and fans (not just the future stars). Indeed, the amateur sports club is often the first place that young minds are exposed to the concepts of loyalty, team spirit, respect and fair play that transcend politics, religion and language, the first symbol of the virtues that sport still truly represents down where there is no money involved.

When I came to China in 1987 looking for a game of football with the locals, I couldn't find an amateur club to join. Having learned Chinese, for years I tried explaining what football really meant on television, but most viewers only saw the glamour of the elite clubs and did not take the game into their own lives. Part in protest, part in solidarity, and always in hope, it was ten years ago that I started using my understanding of what football could and should be and my position inside the Chinese media to kick back and embark on a peaceful mission to reinvent football in the land without boots, something that should have happened naturally hundreds of years ago.

The fundamental questions about the very rules, spirit and culture of the game of football and, by extension, all Olympic team sports, which I have encountered here first as an amateur enthusiast and, more recently, as the chairman of China's first independent football network, are not ones that I had necessarily expected to raise during this life. Looking back over a twenty-year career working as an entrepreneur and amateur broadcaster in a country that I respect and with people who I love, I have been forced far too many times to acknowledge that, if there is an opposite to the football passion of South America, the heritage of Europe or the hope of Africa, in all three cases it is China. For, while everybody knows China is home to one-fifth of everybody in the discovered universe and football is its favourite sport, China is one of the few countries able to brazenly contradict FIFA regulations about government interference without fear of censure. Before ordinary people ever actually played the game and long before European football became a lucrative TV sport, the dream of elite football success had already been hijacked by those with ulterior motives, including foreign powers, Nationalist and Communist governments and, more recently, commercial enterprises.

FIFA has handed the very game itself to the Chinese government, and, under its control, football has become an entertainment show based on a sport the people have forgotten they are meant to play. As a consequence, the poor people of China have never had any stake in what has always been for most of us 'the people's game'; indeed far too few people in China today even realize that football actually belongs to them.

The personal football-infected journey through China described here has caused me to evolve (I have rarely been driving) from being a naive sporting idealist and rebellious young student of the Chinese language into an often lone foreign voice in the state media and one of the slowly radicalized foot soldiers in the world's largest unfulfilled grassroots sports revolution. It is a journey inspired by the selfless pioneers of amateur football who took the beautiful game to the farthest reaches of the world in centuries past, but it is remarkable only for taking place over 2,000 years since the Chinese Emperors first articulated football's values of fair play, over 100 years after most modern football nations got themselves organized and fifteen years after a game that hardly existed was first professionalized and crucified on the joint altars of politics and profit in New China.

Now that China has finally realized its ambition to host the next-best sports event after the World Cup, the reality is that 'popular' sports like football are still a million miles away from being the people's games. Millions of sports enthusiasts with that very spirit in their hearts turned up in Beijing to celebrate one of humanity's few shared ideals in 2008, to be met with a Chinese banquet: an Oriental feast well organized by truly wonderful and sincere hosts, few of whom have a personal concept of what it actually means to win and lose gracefully on the field of play.

The sorry state of its football sector shows just one slice of life in China, but it also betrays some serious challenges facing its society. The lack of space for team games such as football reflects the glaring absence of any kind of unifying social force in China today beyond money and a raw sense of nationalism that can rear its ugly head all too easily. Despite the amazing ability of its people to welcome outsiders from afar, internally China is in danger of rushing headlong towards a particularly selfish mix of capitalist greed imposed and maintained by a Communist-Confucian order that has no concept of such common forms of organic social networking across classes.

And yet, as long as the basic rules of football remain simple and fair, there surely must be some hope of more and more people in China seeing again the light of their own sporting salvation – an outside chance they will stop equating sport with the inevitable Olympic success of their top athletes and the TV drama of international football.

Football has always been among the most accessible of team sports and (with proper planning) can be introduced wherever there is demand, which I know is lying dormant everywhere. Now, a new generation of middle-class families in major cities with the financial resources to start making 'quality of life' decisions is at last coming to its senses. Slowly, more and more parents are demanding a balanced and all-round educational development path for their child, finally questioning the high-stress traditional model in which endless extra hours are found for more individual academic study, but there never seems to be a single hour for physical exercise that combines with social activities to encourage teamwork. At the same time, more and more workers, white-collar not blue, are finally discovering football and other peer-shared sports as among the most healthy and positive modern lifestyle choices. More and more of these Chinese spare-time players are turning out for teams supported by their companies, reflecting football's role in building team spirit and a sense of identity, the same ideals that sparked the modern game's growth a century and more ago. This adds to the momentum.

If China's economic maturity finally cajoles the people into choosing the grassroots football path that most of the world took while they were still dirt poor, then the potential is virtually endless. I have done the numbers. The UK has about 50,000 football clubs and 60 million people. China has 1.3 billion people (give or take a Britain), so you can stop counting the number of clubs it might need at a million. But, long before anything like that happens, the Chinese nation has to make some fundamental decisions about whether it actually wants the game or not. To do that, Chinese people must understand what they have been missing all these years, the ever so simple game of football. If anything, this book is about how it should be so easy and why it is proving so hard.

Because of all the challenges, I am immensely proud that my vision is alive today and on the rise in China. Thanks to Keith and Dave, ClubFootball has kept growing during a period when, all around us, Chinese football has lurched from crisis to crisis. I have watched as the largest sponsors, most famous clubs and biggest sports marketing agencies have come to China promising the world and shaken my head as they have delivered, at best, only passing entertainment and then disappeared again, shaking their own heads.

On the field of play, I count myself lucky to have played against some of the best and worst players in China, many of them in the same game. Like any enterprising left winger, I continue to share great victories and crushing defeats that are later recounted over loud beers and a giant pizza or bowl of noodles. I have scored (and continue to miss) hundreds of incredible goals that nobody else can remember.

Whatever China decides to make of its Olympic victory, this is my personal reflection on the football bits of my life at the end of the regulation ninety minutes. While many of my old partners and teammates have used these years to grow their own families (even Professor Fruit is now the proud father of two little dancers), I metaphorically join hands with bachelor uncles Keith and Dave and look to the thousands of children of all ages (some older than us) who are now playing proper club football in Beijing and who all have good homes to go to at the end of the day.

Since much of the life of the person known to Chinese people as 'Luo Wen' has unravelled in the public eye through the state media, not even the fiercest critic can deny that it happened. However, taking my lead from Anaesthetic and Salty Wall, I have focused in these pages on approaching football from the harsh perspective of a foreigner with clear ideas of what sport means. These beliefs were not instilled by an education in some kind of sporting utopia, but in England's own idiosyncratic, if enduring, system.

I hope it is not too late, but I must at least acknowledge here how much more my time in China has taught me that has only very little to do with football. Despite my belief that China must think deeply about sport's role, Chinese people have always been the funniest, warmest and the most real I have met, in every other way standing alongside my family and closest friends. Without thousands of sincere smiling welcomes from people who are just people, I would never have abandoned academic convention to stay in Beijing.

At any point in this journey, I could have gone back to Brasil, but China is where my heart lies. My incredible roll call of guilty witnesses and supporters may sound strange in my English translation, but behind national celebrities like Crumbly Forever and Yellow Arrowthinker and dedicated public servants like Professor

Good, Old Field and Big Plum, China is filled with millions of individual souls who must now be ready for their love of football to turn to practical action.

When I was first 'learning to forget the rules' that apply only to Chinese people, I set myself a personal goal that I have never told a Chinese soul until now. It was the dream of being known first as a person and second as a foreigner. As hilarious as my big nose will always make that sound, football never fails to top surveys of positive things Chinese people think about my country and it has already done more to convince people in China to accept that still radical concept than any other popular subject.

I have also learned that, for all the differences in the way the game has been played in China for far too long, football's battle here is really the same battle being fought all the time everywhere – the battle for a world in which we all play by the same rules. Imagine. As Li You wrote 2,000 years ago:

> (If) football is regulated correctly like this,
> How much this must mean for daily life.

Do you think China needs a football revolution?

Have your say at

www.clubfootball.com.cn

Visit **www.panmacmillan.com** to read more about all our books and to buy them. You will also find features, author interviews and news of any author events, and you can sign up for e-newsletters so that you're always first to hear about our new releases.

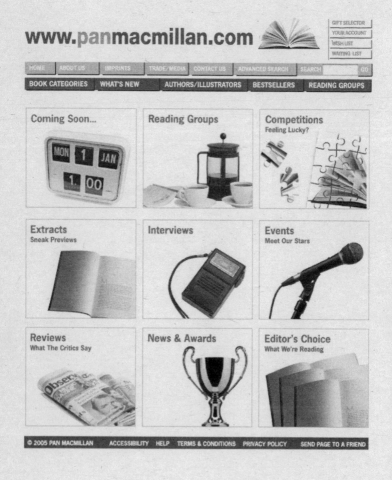